LET'S GO BUDGET

MADRID

Y0-BQS-245

Research Manager
Dorothy McLeod

Managing Editor
Sarah Berlow

Editor
Dorothy McLeod

Contents

Discover Madrid

Welcome to Madrid, where the day starts later, the night ends later, and the locals look like Javier Bardem. Sound good? Well there's more. Much more. Madrid is home to some of the biggest and baddest sights in the world, from museums filled with iconic art to discotheques packed with Spain's most beautiful. From Goya's *The Naked Maya* by day to the (almost) naked *madrileños* at night, Madrid insists that you stay on the move—in only the most laid-back style, of course. When it's time to recuperate, slow down, savor some of the best in Spanish cuisine, and lounge at one of the city's immaculate parks or gardens under the warm Spanish sun. Life is good.

Madrid's plazas, gardens, and monuments tell of the city's rich history. After Philip II made the city the capital of his empire in 1561, Madrid enjoyed centuries of being on top. (Sorry, we couldn't resist.) It served as Spain's artistic hub during the Golden Age, becoming a seat of wealth, culture, and imperial glory, whose legacy can still be felt in literary neighborhoods like Huertas, in the sumptuous interiors of royal estates like the Palacio Real, and in the bad-ass collections of the museums along the Avenida del Arte. So get some rest on the plane, because from here on out it's all dinners at midnight, parties at three, marathon treks through museums the size of small countries by day, and chasing down Javier Bardem at high noon.

Budget Madrid

CHEAP EATS

Picture menus and premade tapas will tempt you, brave traveler, around every corner. But do not surrender. Follow our recommendations and you'll be sinking your teeth into the freshest, most budget-friendly *calamares, gambas* (shrimp, prepared grilled or fried), *patatas bravas* (fried potatoes with romesco sauce), *queso* (cheese; usually manchego), and *tortillas española* (Spanish omelette) in no time.

▶ **CERVECERÍA LOS GATOS:** The tapas at this mostly-local joint in Las Huertas can't be beat (p. 69).

▶ **CAFE BAR MELO'S:** The delicious *zapatillas* (€3) have made this cafe a local institution (p. 67).

▶ **ALMENDRO 13:** Feast on gluttonous tapas like the *huevos rotos* in a pleasant setting off the main drag in La Latina (p. 66).

▶ **MERCADO DE SAN ANTÓN:** Madrid's answer to Whole Foods has the prices to match, but has enough free samples to make a meal for hungry backpackers (p. 79).

▶ **SAN WISH:** The main feature at this novelty bar and restaurant is greasy, crispy Chilean sandwiches like the *hamburguesa voladora* that start at just €5.50 (p. 80).

Freebies

▶ **MUSEO NACIONAL DEL PRADO:** Thousands of priceless works of art at your finger tips for free almost any night of the week (p. 51).

▶ **TEMPO CLUB:** This is the place to enjoy live funk, soul, rock, and hip hop without paying a cover charge (p. 110).

▶ **DOS DE MAYO:** Malasaña's biggest party honors the memory of *madrileños* who were killed in the fight to free Spain from Joseph Napoleon. This means free museum entry, live music, and dancing on May 2 (p. 125).

▶ **REAL ACADEMIA DE BELLAS ARTES DE SAN FERNANDO:** The oldest permanent art institute in Madrid, with a massive collection that includes works by Goya, Ribera, and Rubens, is free on Wednesday nights (p. 50).

BUDGET ACCOMMODATIONS

The key to finding cheap accommodations in Madrid is to book in advance. Your best options will likely be hostels, hostales, or pensiónes (more like budget hotels). Start your search in bustling **Las Huertas** (p. 31), which has the biggest variety of accommodations of any neighborhood in Madrid, including plenty of dirt-cheap backpackers' hostels.

▶ **ALBERGUE JUVENIL MUNICIPAL:** This government-run hostel has four-star hotel amenities—pool table, exercise room, computer lab, complimentary breakfast—and spacious rooms at rock-bottom prices (p. 39).

▶ **MAD HOSTEL:** This affordable and social hostel has an excellent rooftop terrace and a bar that often hosts parties and live music (p. 31).

▶ **CAT'S HOSTEL:** This popular backpackers' hostel offers clean, comfortable beds and goes the extra mile with free tapas tours and pub crawls for guests (p. 33).

▶ **ALBERGUE JUVENIL SANTA CRUZ DE MARCENADO (HI):** This HI hostel is bare-bones, but the cheap beds only a 15min. Metro ride to El Centro make it a steal (p. 42).

▶ **LOS AMIGOS HOSTEL:** Los Amigos in El Centro offers an inexpensive stay, with breakfast, lockers, linens, and Wi-Fi all included in the regular rates (p. 30).

SIGHTSEEING ON THE CHEAP

Face time with priceless works of art need not break the bank, as many of Madrid's art museums open their doors for free on certain days of the week.

▶ **CAIXAFORUM:** This contemporary art, design, and architecture museum is 100% free! Be sure to check out the incredible hortisculpture on the exterior wall before you leave (p. 52).

▶ **PARK IT:** Tired of looking at art? Stayed out 'til 8am this morning? Luckily, Madrid's parks offer locals and tourists respite—for free! Check out the **Jardines de Sabatini** (p. 48) in El Centro; **Real Jardín Botánico** (p. 53) on la Avenida del Arte; **Casa de Campo** (p. 57) in Argüelles; or the granddaddy of them all, **Parque del Buen Retiro** (p. 52).

▶ **ATONE FOR YOUR SINS:** When you tire of Madrid's sinful discos, repent—for free—at one of its many religious sites. Check out **Catedral de la Almudena** (p. 47) in El Centro, **Basilica de San Francisco el Grande** (p. 49) in La Latina and Lavapiés, and **Convento de Las Salesas Reales** (p. 55) in Chueca.

▶ **THEY CAN'T CHARGE FOR THE VIEW:** The Don Quixote statues in **Plaza de España** (p. 53), the tapas bars and restaurants of **Plaza Santa Ana** (p. 62), the 18th-century edifices of **Plaza Mayor** (p. 46), and the view from the tower in **Plaza de Cibeles** (p. 54) are all yours for the taking—and they don't cost a thing.

What To Do

FOREVER YOUNG

Madrid caters to the young and the young at heart. The party doesn't get started 'til well after midnight, and the clubs stay open until dawn (or later) when buzzed locals begin the day with *chocolate con churros,* and recover later during siesta. So grab a book, a cigarette, and a *cortado*, and get ready to discuss Buñuel at **Cafe de Ciculo de Bellas Artes** (p. 63), a *madrileño* institution. When night falls, make your way to **Joy Eslava** (p. 94), Madrid's premier sweaty study-abroad nightclub. For another glimpse of youth culture in Madrid, get tickets to **Día de la Musica** (p. 126), a music festival that brings big names like Janelle Monáe every June.

FESTIVALS

If you thought the weekends in Madrid were crazy—try the festivals. Though some are technically religious, there's no shortage of debauchery. Madrid's festivals can be a great opportunity to get a taste of local culture and to meet young *madrileños,* often without paying a euro cent. Check out **Fiestas de San Isidore** (p. 125), which celebrates the city's patron saint; **Orgullo Gay** (p. 126), one of the biggest pride events in Europe; or the granddaddy of all *fiestas,* **Madrid Carnaval** (p. 124).

JUST DANCE

With blocks full of sweaty clubs, thumping music, refreshing mojitos, and beautiful people, there will be ample opportunity to embarrass yourself on the dance floor. While *Let's Go* can't do much for your dougie, we do know that practice makes perfect, so take a dance class or two and then hit as many clubs as you can. First, hit **Dance Classes Madrid** (p. 202) for a salsa, flamenco, or merengue class. Then, head to **Kapital** (p. 97), which has seven stories of house, hip hop, Spanish pop, and reggae. Still can't get enough? From mid-March to late April, Madrid hosts dance troupes from around the world during **Madrid en Danza** (p. 124). Performances range from ballet to modern, and tickets cost as little as €5.

BEYOND TOURISM

Ready to learn more about Madrid and give back to the community? Take classes at a local university in Spanish or English with **IES Abroad Madrid** (p. 201). Or, sign up for classes at **Babylon Idiomas** (p. 202). With just 20-30 hours of class per week, you'll still have plenty of time to explore the city. If you're hungry for more, check out **Beyond Tourism** (p. 199).

Student Superlatives

- ▶ **BEST PUB CRAWL:** Along C. Cava Baja in La Latina (p. 95).

- ▶ **BEST PLACE TO NAP:** Parque del Buen Retiro (p. 52).

- ▶ **BEST FÚTBOL TEAM:** Real Madrid (p. 121), arguably.

- ▶ **BEST PLACE TO BUY BOOKS YOU CAN ACTUALLY READ:** Casa del Libro (p. 133).

- ▶ **MOST DISORIENTED EGYPTIAN TEMPLE:** Templo de Debod (p. 56).

- ▶ **BEST PLACE TO FIND A HIPSTER HUSBAND:** Club Nasti (p. 108).

Planning Your Trip

WHEN TO GO

Madrid's high season (*temporada alta*) is in the summer, when tons of tourists descend to live *la vida loca*. In Madrid, high season begins during Semana Santa (Holy Week; late March through early April) and includes festival days like Fiesta de San Isidro (early May). July and August bring some serious heat to Madrid. *Madrileños* take vacations in other parts of Europe during August, leaving behind closed offices, restaurants, and empty lodgings for travelers. To be safe, make sure to book ahead if you plan to travel in June, July, and August.

Taking advantage of the low season (*temporada baja*) has many advantages, most notably lighter crowds and lower prices. Some lodgings drastically cut their prices, and there's no need for reservations. Madrid still exudes energy during these months (partly thanks to study abroad students), but the winter remains less accommodating with reduced public transportation and lackadaisical hours of operation for private businesses.

Icons

First things first: places and things that we absolutely love, sappily cherish, generally obsess over, and wholeheartedly endorse are denoted by the all-empowering ◼ **Let's Go thumbs-up.** In addition, the icons scattered at the end of a listing can serve as visual cues to help you navigate each listing:

◼	Let's Go recommends	☎	Phone numbers	⇌	Directions
i	Other hard info	Ⓢ	Prices	◷	Hours

NEIGHBORHOODS

El Centro

Bordered by the beautiful Palacio Real in the west and the relaxing Parque del Retiro in the east, El Centro, the heart of Madrid, encompasses the city's most famous historical sites and modern venues. Clubs and countless tapas restaurants are set beside churches, plazas, and winding cobblestone streets. In the middle is **Puerta del Sol,** the "soul of Madrid," where thousands descend to ring in each New Year. By day, the area around Puerta del Sol is a commercial hub with plenty of name brand stores and fast food chains. The eight streets branching off of Puerta del Sol include C. Mayor, which leads west to **Plaza Mayor,** a vibrant square bordered by restaurants and filled with street performers and vendors. On the western side of Pl. Mayor is **Calle Bailen.** Here you will find El Centro's most famous sights, including **El Palacio Real,** and Madrid's most picturesque formal gardens in **Plaza de Oriente.** While El Centro can be a bit chaotic, it is home to the city's most essential landmarks. El Centro is easily walkable and the Metro provides convenient and reliable access to the rest of the city. The main sights are deceptively close to one another. When in doubt, stick to the main streets **Calle de Alcalá, Calle Mayor, Calle de las Huertas,** and **Calle de Atocha** for adequate restaurants, nightlife, hostels, and cafes.

La Latina and Lavapiés

La Latina and Lavapiés lie just across the southern border of El Centro. These areas are young, hip, and distinctively *madrileño*. While accommodations are limited, these areas provide some of the finest dining and nightlife options in the city. Many unadventurous tourists will stick to the obvious food and drink options surrounding Puerta del Sol and Pl. Mayor, but the *tabernas* of **Calle Cava Baja** and **Calle Alemendro** serve some of the city's best traditional Spanish cuisine. These narrow streets are packed with meal options and one rule is universal: quality matters. While Lavapiés is less active at night, it remains one the best neighborhoods for international cuisine, particularly along **Calle Lavapiés** with its many Indian restaurants. If you are sick of tapas, this is a great place to mix things up. La Latina and Lavapiés are great to explore day and night. If you have the time, try to make it to the Sunday flea market **El Rastro.**

Las Huertas

Las Huertas's walls are etched with quotes from writers like Cervantes and Calderón de la Barca, who lived in this literary neighborhood during its Golden Age. This is its claim to fame, meaning that today it is unmistakably a travelers' haunt, with cafes, bars, pubs, and clubs lining the narrow streets. Unlike El Centro, which is largely commercial and geared toward tourists, Las Huertas feels like a playground for 20-somethings, with small independent shops, cafes, *cervecerías,* bars, and clubs in every direction. **Plaza de Santa Ana** and **Plaza del Ángel** are the vital centers of the area, but you will find a greater diversity of food and drink venues as you move outward, especially east down C. de Last Huertas, and to the north up C. de la Cruz. Huertas' northern boundary is C. de Alcalá, the southern is C. de Atocha, and the eastern is Paseo del Prado. Though it is close to the city, Huertas is very much its own world, particularly at night.

Avenida del Arte

Bordering the eastern edge of the city, **Parque del Buen Retiro** is Madrid's Central Park. This is where the fast pace of cosmopolitan life breaks down, where *madrileño* families come to spend time together, where tourists can escape their hostel bunk beds. Retiro is its own world of walkways, gardens, fields, and trees, and it is deceptively close to the city center. The Avenida del Arte just west of Retiro is the city's cultural endowment. While the city center is largely commercial (save the odd cathedral or convent), Avenida del Arte protects Spain's most prized cultural artifacts, from Picasso's *Guernica* to Goya's *Second* and *Third of May*. While the **Museo Nacional del Prado,** the **Reina Sofía,** and the **Museo Thyssen** have become famous individually, it is their totality that makes the Avenida del Arte such a powerful display of Spain's culture. The walk along the tree-lined **Paseo del Prado** has become a cultural phenomenon of its own, a celebration of the beauty and sophistication of this city.

Gran Vía

Calle Gran Vía is filled with all the stuff that tourists don't need to come to Europe to see: fast-food restaurants, chain stores, and traffic jams. While the main avenue tends to be crowded and commercial, the greater Gran Vía area should not be discounted. Spanning east to west from **Plaza de Cibeles** to **Plaza de España,** Gran Vía has a number of great restaurants, bars, clubs, and live music venues—you just have to look hard. On the southeastern boundary with Chueca, you will find the highest concentration of small restaurants, bars, and boutiques, particularly on **Calle de la Reina** and **Calle de las Infantas.** Calle Gran Vía is nothing glamorous, but as you venture outward, you'll discover plenty of standout venues. They're not always obvious, but they're there.

Chueca and Malasaña

Once the center of bohemian life in Madrid, and the birthplace of a counterculture movement (La Movida) in the 1970s and early '80s, Malasaña is today somewhat of a caricature of its former self. Within a few decades, Malasaña has become one of the most expensive and image-driven *barrios* of the city, with high-end cafes and international novelty restaurants like creperies and fresh juice stands. It is rumored that somewhere in this *barrio* there is a place that sells "Russian Tapas," which begs the question, "WTF?" (We couldn't find it.) Art supply stores can be found on every other block, meaning that there are either a lot of artists in this neighborhood or a lot of people who like to spend money on expensive paints. For the traveler, Malasaña is a total playground, with the city's best nightlife, live music, and dining. Chueca is no different. Malasaña's historically gay neighbor to the east (bordered by C. Fuencarral) is today a high-end *barrio* with great food and nightlife in every direction. In Chueca you will find plenty of art galleries, yoga studios, and boutique shops, but you will also run into the more insidious signs of the bourgeoisie, such as a yoga studios that rent movies and movie rental places where you can practice yoga. Oh yeah, and a lot of sex shops.

Argüelles and Moncloa

Argüelles and Moncloa are quiet residential areas spanning the western edge of the city from the north of Pl. de España to the city's northwest corner at Moncloa. While these areas are less geared towards tourists, they are great areas to explore *madrileño* life in its most simple and unpretentious manner. **Plaza de España, Caso de Campo,** and **Parque del Oeste** provide the city's most expansive green spaces on the west side of Madrid, functioning as both sites of recreation and centers of culture. Outside of the major parks, in these neighborhoods, you will find quiet streets with book stores, small shops, and uninspiring cafes. From Argüelles you can explore the odd and beautiful **Templo de Debod** to the west, and the great restaurants and nightlife options neighboring Malasaña just south. Moncloa is dominated by the presence of Franco's **Arco de la Victoria,** and it is the best outpost from which to explore Parque del Oeste or journey by bus to the palace **El Pardo.** While accommodations are limited in this area, some tourists might find refuge staying in a quiet neighborhood a few stops removed from the chaotic city center.

Salamanca

Salamanca is primarily a high-end residential district filled with luxury shopping and fancy restaurants on the side streets of C. del Castellano and C. de Serrano. While this area may seem posh, buried beneath all of the Gucci and Prada is a neighborhood that is very accessible to budget travelers. Salamanca is also deceptively close to city center, just a 5min. walk north up Paseo de la Castellana from el Arco de la Victoria. Here you will find one of Madrid's most beautiful avenues, with a tree-lined promenade running through the center. As you make your way north you will reach the **Biblioteca Nacional,** and, making your way farther north, you will find two of the city's terrific, less visited art museums: the **Museo Sorrola** and the **Museo de Lazaro Galdiano.** A visit to either of these museums will inevitably take you down some of the city's most beautiful residential streets.

SUGGESTED ITINERARIES

Cheap Date

Madrid is crawling with couples making out. Here's how you can be one of them.

1. I THINK WE'RE ALONE NOW. Making out in a park in Madrid is a couples' right of passage (right after moving in together and just before marriage). With an Egyptian pyramid and some of the best views in Madrid, **Templo de Debod** (p. 56) is as good a park as any.

2. DID IT HURT..WHEN YOU FELL FROM HEAVEN? Head to the **Real Academia de Bellas Artes de San Fernando** (p. 50), which is free on Wednesday nights. Nothing says, "let's go back to making out" quite like Peter Paul Rubens.

3. GOT A RAISIN? HOW 'BOUT A DATE? Share a plate of authentic *racciones* at **Cervecería Los Gatos** (p. 69), a Huertas favorite that the tourists have yet to discover.

4. YOU LOOK LIKE MY NEXT GIRLFRIEND. If you hit **Midnight Rose** (p. 100), the upscale club overlooking Pl. Santa Ana, before 10pm, you can grab a drink without the jaw-dropping cover. Don't worry; we'll tell your date that you're good for it.

5. GRAB SOMEBODY SEXY, TELL 'EM 'HEY.' By our calculations, it's been a couple of hours since your last makeout sesh. Time to hit the dance floor. It's hard to go wrong in Las Huertas, but: **Kapital** (p. 97) and **Sol y Sombra** (p. 98) are both solid options.

Walking Tour

Tired of the tourists in El Centro? Lose the fanny pack (actually, if it's from Urban, consider leaving it on) and wander eastward to Las Huertas. Once the playground of heavyweights like Cervantes and Calderón de la Barca during Spanish literature's Golden Age, today, the neighborhood is crawling with hip 20-somethings. The best approach may be simply to wander, but if you're looking for a place to start, follow our lead to discover one-of-a-kind boutiques, tasty tapas joints, literary cafes, and authentic flamenco.

1. CUESTA DE MOYANO: Start at ⓂAtocha. Get your feet wet with *madrileño* culture with a spin through the stalls at this book market (p. 135) at the southern edge of Parque del Buen Retiro. Pick up a musty paperback—you'll need it as a prop in literary Huertas.

2. CAIXAFORUM: This museum (p. 52) is technically on the Avenida del Arte, but stop in along your way toward the heart of Las Huertas to get your fix of contemporary art, architecture, and design. It's always a good idea to know a thing or two about Madrid's contemporary scene when it comes time to chat up that cute artist in square frames sitting at the bar in Las Huertas. Best of all, Caixaforum is completely free.

3. REAL ACADEMIA DE BELLAS ARTES DE SAN FERNANDO: Window shop your way northwest through Las Huertas until you almost hit Gran Vía. The Real Academia de Bellas Artes (p. 50) is your next dose of Huertas culture. The oldest permanent art institution in Madrid contains works by all the big names, including Goya, Rubens, Ribera, and Sorolla.

4. LA BARDEMECILLA DE SANTA ANA: By now you've worked up an appetite. Backtrack to C. Núñez de Arce, where delicious tapas await at the Bardem family restaurant (p. 69). Tuck into some *huevos de oro estrellados* (eggs scrambled with *jamón iberico* and onions) and keep your eyes peeled—you might see Javier or one of his cousins.

5. CARDAMOMO: Just a few blocks from La Bardemecilla on C. de Echegaray, Cardamomo (p. 118) specializes in traditional flamenco where the focus is more on rhythm and movement than kitschy costumes. Skip the tourist joints and enjoy a short, intense set before heading out to explore nearby nightlife.

Three-Day Weekend

Only in Madrid for three days? Pity. But don't worry: there's still enough time to cruise through museums and cruise a few dance floors. Just remember: art, park, club, repeat.

Day One

1. MUSEO NACIONAL DEL PRADO: Dive into this world-famous collection (p. 51), which includes everything from ancient Greek sculpture to Dutch altarpieces. Must-sees include Goya's *La Maja Vestida* and *La Maja Desnuda, Third* and *Second of May,* and *Portrait of Charles IV and His Family;* Velázquez's *Las Meninas, The Triumph of Bacchus,* and *Las Hilanderas;* and Bosch's *The Garden of Earthly Delights.*

2. REAL JARDÍN BOTÁNICO: When your back starts to hurt and the art starts to blur, head next door to the Botanical Gardens (p. 53), pay €2.50, and pick a place in the shade to sit back and reflect.

3. KAPITAL: Recovered from a day of treking through the museum, get ready to hit Kapital, the Prado of Madrid's nightlife scene (p. 97). Choose from seven floors of trashy fun that play everything from house to Spanish pop to hip hop. Wear something nice and arrive a little before 2am to beat the rush.

Day Two

1. MUSEO NACIONAL CENTRO DE REINA SOFÍA: Madrid couldn't settle for just one megahit, could it? The Reina Sofía (p. 50) picks up where the Prado left off with a kick-ass collection of 20th-century art. Take the glass elevators up to the top floor, and make your way through temporary exhibits on the third and fourth floor to the galleries on the second, which place Picasso's *Guernica* in its art historical context. Then take a spin through the rest of the galleries—you really can't go wrong with the Reina Sofía's collection of the Spanish avant-garde.

2. TEMPLO DE DEBOD: In the '60s, the rapid industrialization taking place in Egypt threatened its most precious archaeological remains, which Spain played a critical role in preserving. To say thank you, the Egyptian government shipped the Templo de Debod (p. 56) to Madrid. Take a look at the archaeology exhibit inside, pose for a photo to convince your Facebook friends you went to Egypt on your trip, and then head around back for one of the most beautiful views of western Madrid.

3. LA VÍA LÁCTEA: Experience this temple (p. 107) to rock, grunge, and Malasaña '70s counterculture without paying a cover if you arrive before 1am. Shoot a game of pool with a new *madrileño* friend, or just relax with a cold beer as you listen to tunes that range from Elvis to Prince.

Day Three

1. MUSEO THYSSEN-BORNEMISZA: Hope you're not tired of art! Don't worry—though impressive by any standard, the Museo Thyssen-Bornemisza (p. 52) is much more manageable in size than its Avenida del Arte neighbors. It houses the private collection of the late Baron Henrich Thyssen-Bornemisza, which includes an impressive Neoclassical and Baroque collection as well as a stellar showing of 19th- and 20th-century modernism. Paintings by the German avant-garde are particularly striking.

2. PARQUE DEL BUEN RETIRO: We've saved the granddaddy of Madrid's parks (p. 52) for last. This former royal hunting ground is today home to two palaces, an artificial lake, a running track, a sports complex, and a lively promenade that is packed with musicians and families. Try your hand at rowing, go for a power-walk, or just lie down in the grass (we won't judge).

3. AREIA: Trendy clubs may come and go in Chueca, but Moroccan-themed Areia (p. 105) is a neighborhood standby where you can chill out after a busy weekend. Lounge on the low cushions and embroidered pillows, snack on international tapas, and take in a DJ set.

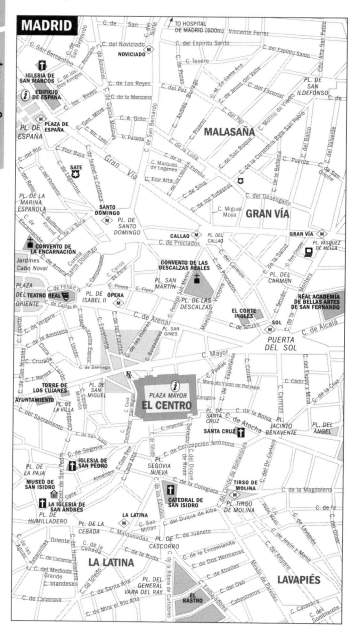

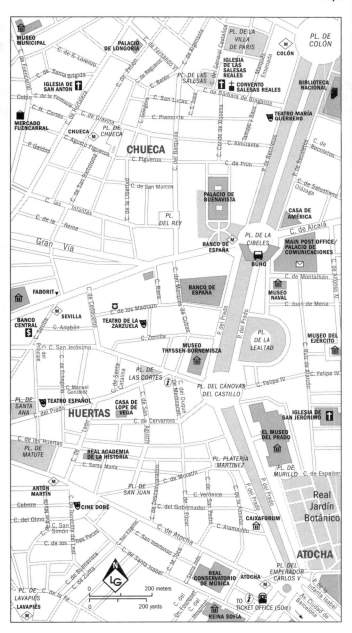

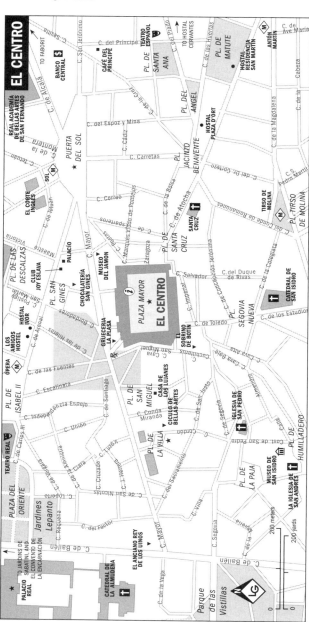

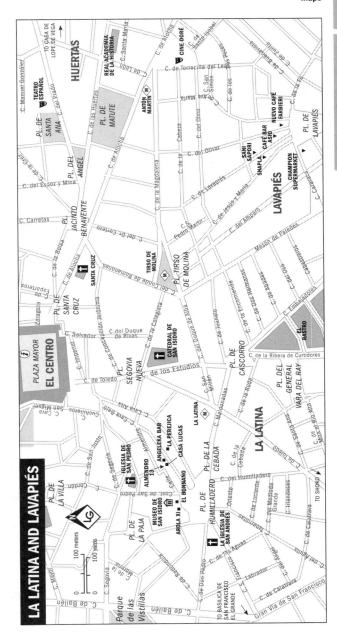

LA LATINA AND LAVAPIÉS

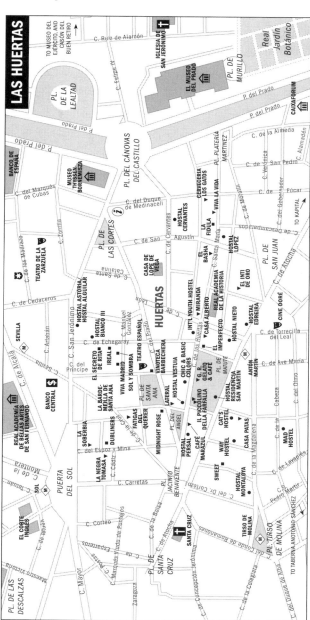

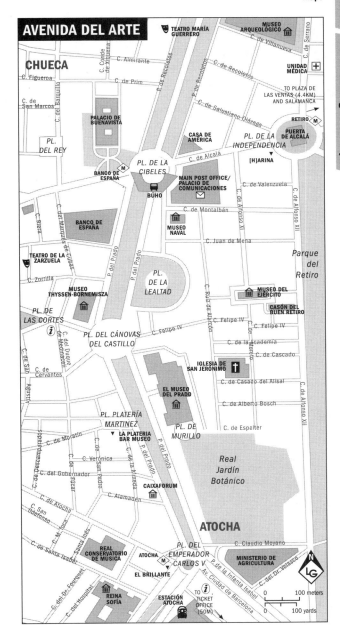

AVENIDA DEL ARTE

CHUECA

TEATRO MARÍA GUERRERO

MUSEO ARQUEOLÓGICO

C. de Villanueva

C. de Serrano

C. Figueroa

C. Conde de Xiquena

C. Almirante

C. de Recoletos

C. de Recoletos

UNIDAD MÉDICA

C. de San Marcos

C. de Prim

P. de Recoletos

C. de Salustiano Olázaga

TO PLAZA DE LAS VENTAS (4.4KM) AND SALAMANCA

C. del Barquillo

PALACIO DE BUENAVISTA

CASA DE AMÉRICA

RETIRO M

PL. DEL REY

BANCO DE ESPAÑA M

PL. DE LA CIBELES

PL. DE LA INDEPENDENCIA

PUERTA DE ALCALÁ

C. de Alcalá

[H]ARINA

BÚHO

MAIN POST OFFICE/ PALACIO DE COMUNICACIONES

C. de Valenzuela

C. de Alfonso XI

C. de Alfonso XII

BANCO DE ESPAÑA

C. de Montalbán

C. del Marqués de Cubas

MUSEO NAVAL

C. Juan de Mena

Parque del Retiro

TEATRO DE LA ZARZUELA

C. Zorrilla

P. del Prado

PL. DE LA LEALTAD

C. Ruiz de Alarcón

MUSEO DEL EJÉRCITO

MUSEO THYSSEN-BORNEMISZA

CASÓN DEL BUEN RETIRO

PL. DE LAS CORTES

C. del Duque de Medinaceli

P. del Prado

C. Felipe IV

C. Felipe IV

C. Felipe IV

PL. DEL CÁNOVAS DEL CASTILLO

C. de la Academia

C. de Cervantes

C. de Cascado

C. San Agustín

IGLESIA DE SAN JERÓNIMO

EL MUSEO DEL PRADO

C. de Casado del Alisal

C. de Alberto Bosch

PL. PLATERÍA MARTINEZ

C. de Alfonso XII

LA PLATERIA BAR MUSEO

PL. DE MURILLO

C. de Espalter

C. de Moratín

C. Verónica

P. del Prado

C. de la Almeda

C. del Gobernador

Real Jardín Botánico

C. de los Desamparados

CAIXAFORUM

C. Alameden

C. de Atocha

C. San Ildefonso

C. M. Fuca

Sta. Inés

ATOCHA

C. de Santa Isabel

REAL CONSERVATORIO DE MÚSICA

ATOCHA M

PL. DEL EMPERADOR CARLOS V

C. Claudio Moyano

MINISTERIO DE AGRICULTURA

EL BRILLANTE

P. de la Infanta Isabel

C. del Dr. Velasco

C. del Dr. Fourquet

REINA SOFÍA

ESTACIÓN ATOCHA

TO TICKET OFFICE (50M)

Av. Ciudad de Barcelona

N

0   100 meters

0   100 yards

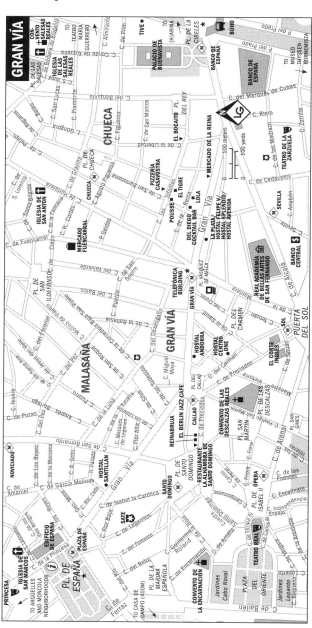

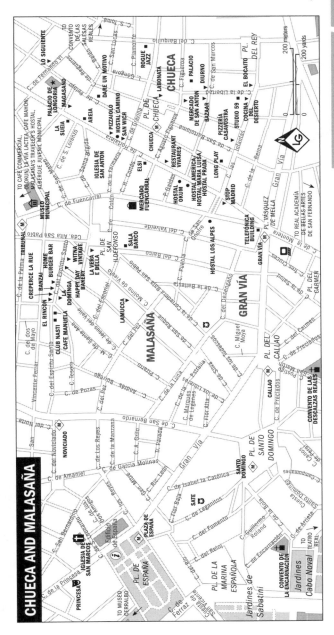

CHUECA AND MALASAÑA

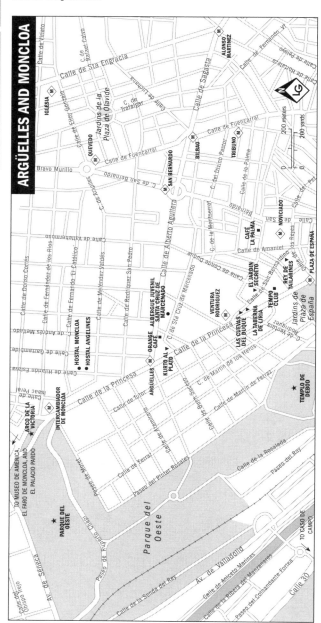

ARGÜELLES AND MONCLOA

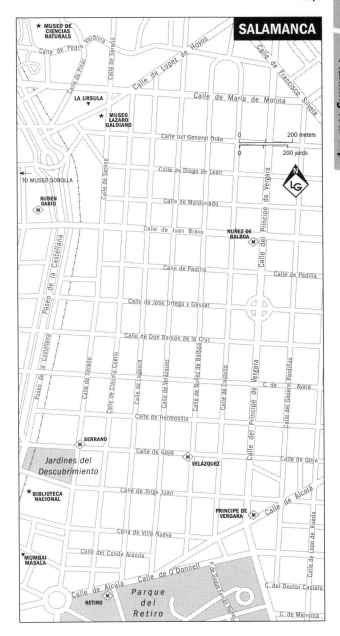

SALAMANCA

★ MUSEO DE CIENCIAS NATURALS
Calle de Pedro Valdivia
Calle de Pinar
Calle de Serrano
Calle de Lopez de Hoyos
Calle de Francisco Silvela
▼ LA URSULA
★ MUSEO LAZARO GALOIANO
Calle de Maria de Molina
Calle del General Oráa
0 ___ 200 meters
0 ___ 200 yards
Calle de Diego de León
N LG
TO MUSEO SOROLLA
Calle de Serrano
RUBEN DARIO M
Calle de Maldonado
Calle de Juan Bravo
NUÑEZ DE BALBOA M
Calle del
Principe de Vergara
Calle de Padilla
Calle de Padilla
Paseo de la Castellana
Calle de Jose Ortega y Gasset
Calle de Don Ramón de la Cruz
Paseo de la Castellana
Calle de Serrano
Calle de Claudio Coello
Calle de Lagasca
Calle de Velázquez
Calle de Nuñez de Balboa
Calle de Castelló
Calle del Principe de Vergara
C. de General Pardiñas
Ayala
Calle de Hermosilla
SERRANO M
Calle de Goya
M VELÁZQUEZ
Jardines del Descubrimiento
Calle de Goya
★ BIBLIOTECA NACIONAL
Calle de Jorge Juan
PRINCIPE DE VERGARA M
Calle de Alcalá
Calle de Villa Nueva
Calle de Lope de Rueda
▼ MUMBAI MASALA
Calle del Conde Aranda
Calle de Alcalá
Calle de O'Donnell
P. de Duque Fernán Núñez
C. del Doctor Castelo
Calle de Alcalá
RETIRO M
Parque del Retiro
C. de Menorca

Accommodations

Madrid has a range of affordable housing options, from cheap hostels to boutique hotels, in almost every neighborhood. In El Centro, most backpackers' hostels are found close to Puerta del Sol; they offer cheap beds and shared bathrooms, and many have kitchens and common spaces. South of Puerta del Sol, a number of hostels offer slightly pricier private accommodations with en-suite bathrooms. Despite noise and pedestrian traffic, Gran Vía is also a deceptively good place to stay and is home to some of the city's best high-end hostels, where doubles offer some of the best value in the city (€50-70). If you're partying in Chueca and Malasaña, staying in the area at one of the fine private-roomed *hostales* (inexpensive hotels that sometimes offer dorm options) will eliminate the late-night odyssey back to your bed. La Latina and Lavapiés do not offer much in the way of accommodations, while Argüelles and Moncloa have a couple of *hostales*.

Budget Accommodations

Staying in Madrid on the cheap is possible, but it takes a little effort. Your best bet for the absolute budget-est are dormitory-style hostels located in slightly out-of-the-way neighborhoods, like **Arguëlles.** If you need some additional privacy (hey, we're not implying anything), inexpensive *hostales* with private rooms are scattered about the city. Bear in mind that **El Centro,** though conveniently located, is not the cheapest bet.

EL CENTRO

Hostal Cervantes   HOSTAL $$$
C. de Cervantes, 34
☎91 429 83 65; www.hostal-cervantes.com

Hostal Cervantes is located in a quiet residential corner of the city center. The rooms are bright, colorful, and somewhat of a relief from the drab accommodations that litter El Centro. The *hostal*'s desirable and affordable rooms have renovated private bathrooms and TVs, but the place is generally booked to capacity. The four rooms with balconies are particularly difficult to reserve in advance.

▶ ⚐ From the Museo Thyssen-Bornemisza, walk toward the Pl. Canovas del Castillo and make a right onto C. de Cervantes. *i* Free Wi-Fi. Check the website for reservation info. Ⓢ Singles €40-45; doubles €50-55; triples €65-70.

Hostal Ivor   HOSTAL $$$
C. del Arenal, 24, 2nd fl.
☎91 547 10 54; www.hostal-ivor.com

Hostal Ivor offers clean, comfortable private rooms with flatscreen TVs and ensuite bathrooms away from the most hectic and noisy parts of El Centro. While Hostal Ivor lacks a kitchen and the common space of neighboring *hostales,* it gives the service and quality of a mid-range hotel at a competitive price. Perhaps most importantly, Hostal Ivor has free Wi-Fi everywhere. Enjoy Skyping your friends and family in the privacy of our own bathroom. What? That isn't socially acceptable?

▶ ⚐ From Puerta del Sol, walk down C. del Arenal a little bit past C. de las Hileras. *i* Free Wi-Fi. Ⓢ Singles €44; doubles €65. Ⓩ Reception 24hr.

Accommodations

Los Amigos Hostel　　　　　　　　　　　HOSTEL $

C. del Arenal, 26, 4th fl.

☎91 559 24 72; www.losamigoshostel.com

Los Amigos is a classic backpackers' hostel. Located on the top floor, Los Amigos is separated from the madness below and the rooms are surprisingly bright and tranquil. This is one of the city's most affordable options. Guests make use of the hostel's great communal spaces, which include a small TV lounge and a well-stocked kitchen that serves complimentary continental breakfast in the morning. Rooms are clean and comfortable, but, like any backpacker haunt, privacy comes at a price.

▶ ⚇ From Puerta del Sol, walk down C. del Arenal until you pass C. de las Hileras; Los Amigos is on the right. *i* Breakfast and linens included. Extra large lockers and towels available for a fee. Free Wi-Fi. Ⓢ Dorms €17, with private bath €19; doubles €45-50. ⚉ Reception 8am-midnight.

Hostal Residencia Martin　　　　　　　HOSTAL $$

C. de Atocha, 43

☎91 429 95 79; www.hostalmartin.com

Hostal Residencia Martin is located between the bars and clubs of Puerta del Sol and the culture and museums of Paseo del Prado. Without any common spaces, it does not provide the social life of a youth hostel, but it does have the comfort and privacy of a small hotel. The rooms are clean, with white tiled floors, geriatric-looking furniture, and floral bedspreads. Though the *hostal*'s location on the major thoroughfare of C. de Atocha may lack glamor, it is within walking distance of all the major attractions in downtown Madrid.

▶ ⚇ Ⓜ Antón Martín. Walk down C. de Atocha. The hostel is on the right, before you hit C. de los Cañizares. *i* Safes and towels included. Free Wi-Fi. Ⓢ Singles €29; doubles €39; triples €49.

Hostal Centro One　　　　　　　　　　HOSTAL $

C. Carmen, 16

☎91 523 31 92

Hostal Centro One is a newly renovated backpackers' hangout in the center of the center (two blocks from the center of the Spanish Kingdom). The communal kitchen, living room, and six internet-access computers keep people around well into the day. The *hostal* has hardwood floors, bright lights, new furniture, and a variety of room styles, all of which have clean, shared bathrooms. While the *hostal* is a four-floor walk up an old and tired building, the silver lining is that you are also four floors removed from the madness of C. Carmen.

▶ ⚶ Ⓜ Sol. Take C. del Carmen northwest 2 blocks. *i* Kitchen and TV lounge. Free Wi-Fi. Ⓢ 8-bed dorms €23; 6-bed €25; 4-bed €28. Doubles €30. Towels €1. Luggage storage €2. Cash only. ⌚ Reception 9am-10pm.

LAS HUERTAS

▨ Hostal Plaza d'Ort   HOSTAL $$

Pl. del Ángel, 13
☎91 429 90 41; www.plazadort.com

Hostal Plaza d'Ort's location on Pl. del Ángel is its biggest attraction. The plaza is a tranquil place to stay, with sophisticated nightlife and none of the chain stores and tasteless bars that swamp so much of El Centro. Hostal d'Ort's private bedrooms are simple and unglamorous. The decor is old-lady-themed. Each room has a flatscreen TV, and some have private bathrooms. The *hostal*'s salon faces the plaza and has a large flatscreen and an espresso bar.

▶ ⚶ Ⓜ Sol. Walk south down C. de la Carretas and take a left onto Pl. del Ángel. *i* Safes included. Free Wi-Fi. A/C. Ⓢ Singles €35; doubles €55-65; triples €80-110. Cash only. ⌚ Reception 9am-10pm.

▨ Mad Hostel   HOSTEL $

C. de la Cabeza, 24
☎91 506 48 40; www.madhostel.com

From the first-floor bar to the rooftop terrace, Mad Hostel is a temple of fun made for student travelers. While it is located in a traditional Madrid apartment complex, everything about Mad Hostel feels new. The dorm-style rooms with bunk beds are simple, as are the shared bathrooms, but the real appeal here is a renovated bar always alive with travelers and a rooftop terrace that is used as a bar during the summer months. The downstairs bar has a pool table and a small stage where they bring in musical acts for evening parties, and there's even a small weight room available on the top floor.

▶ ⚶ Ⓜ Antón Martín. From the Metro, walk down C. de la Magdalena then take the 2nd left onto C. del Olivar. Turn right onto C. de la Cabeza. Look for the Mad Hostel sign on the left. *i* Reservations must be made online ahead of time. Breakfast, safes, and linens included. Towels €5 deposit. Free Wi-Fi. Laundry machines available. €10 key deposit. Ⓢ Rooms €16-23. ⌚ Reception 24hr.

▨ Cat's Hostel   HOSTEL $

C. de los Cañizares, 6
☎91 369 28 07; www.catshostel.com

Cat's Hostel is one of Madrid's most popular backpackers' choices for good reason. Dorms are cheap, clean, and offer the safety of private lockers, but the real appeal here is the hostel's social life. A colorful bar area with beer barrel tables, the "Cat Cave" basement lounge, and a restored Moorish patio, provide guests with plenty of space to mingle. The hostel owners go out of their way to bring guests together through organized events including a complimentary paella dinner for guests each Friday, tapas tours through Las Huertas, and late-night pub crawls. The staff is friendly, but, due to the popularity of the hostel, you might have to wait a bit if checking in during peak hours. While all guests are automatically assigned to the large dorm-style rooms, there are a few double rooms available on request, though these cannot be reserved in advance.

▶ ✚ Ⓜ Antón Martín. Walk 1 block down C. de la Magdalena and make a right onto C. de los Cañizares. Cat's is on the left. *i* Breakfast included. Laundry €5. Ⓢ Dorms €17-22; doubles €38-42. ⏰ Reception 24hr.

▨ Hostal Astoria   HOSTAL $$$

Carrera de San Jeronimo, 32, 5th fl.
☎91 429 11 88; www.hostal-astoria.com

While slightly more expensive than its neighbors, Hostal Astoria has the best quality rooms in the Carrera de San Jeronimo, 32 building. With hardwood floors, extra pillows, and linen changes available, these rooms are an exceptional value, not just for the neighborhood, but for all of Madrid. All rooms come with ensuite bathrooms, flatscreen TVs, and Wi-Fi. The location on Carrera de San Jeronimo is not picturesque but will offer quieter nights than the center of Las Huertas. As an added bonus, Astoria is on the fifth floor of the building, meaning you will be that much more removed from the stammering drunkards below.

▶ ✚ From Puerta del Sol, walk 100m east along Carrera de San Jeronimo toward Paseo del Prado. *i* Reserve in advance online. Ⓢ Singles €40; doubles €60; triples €84. Cash only. ⏰ Reception 24hr.

Way Hostel   HOSTEL $

C. Relatores, 17
☎91 420 05 83; www.wayhostel.com

Way offers the nicest rooms of all the backpacker hostels listed in this section. While all rooms are shared in four- to 10-bed dorms, the hardwood floors and generous layout sets Way apart. The spacious communal kitchen and large TV room feel like upscale college common rooms—perfect for your next beer.

▶ ⚐ Ⓜ Tirso de Molina. Walk toward the museum district and make a left up C. Relatores. The hostel is on the right. *i* Breakfast included. Reserve online. Ⓢ Dorms €18-24. ⏲ Reception 24hr.

Hostal Aguilar   HOSTAL $$$

Carrera de San Jeronimo, 32, 2nd fl.

☎91 429 59 26; www.hostalaguilar.com

With a huge lobby area, swipe access, modern furniture, and private bathrooms, Aguilar is more hotel than *hostal*. Rooms have tiled floors, old TV sets, and light pink bedspreads. The bathrooms are newly renovated. Don't expect the calm of a convent, but, compared to other hostels in the area, you will be paying a good price for a better night of sleep. The availability of four-person rooms is a plus for larger groups.

▶ ⚐ From Puerta del Sol, walk 100m east along Carrera de San Jeronimo toward Paseo del Prado. Ⓢ Singles €40; doubles €50; triples €66, quads €84. ⏲ Reception 24hr.

Hostal Montaloya   HOSTAL $$$

Pl. Tirso de Molina, 20

☎91 360 03 05; www.hostalmontaloya.blogspot.com

Pricier than dorm-style living, with comfortable beds, TVs, ensuite baths, and even desks in all rooms, Montaloya is more of a small hotel than a youth hostel. Though the employees at the front desk speak only Spanish, the *hostal*'s proximity to restaurants, bars, and stores along the Pl. Tirso de Molina make it a convenient choice. For a weekend stay, ask about interior rooms, as rooms facing the plaza are noisy.

▶ ⚐ Ⓜ Tirso de Molina. *i* Call ahead for wheelchair-accessible accommodations. Ⓢ Singles €45; doubles €58; triples €80. ⏲ Reception 24hr.

International Youth Hostel   HOSTEL $

C. de las Huertas, 21

☎91 429 55 26; www.posadadehuertas.com

This is one of the best dorm-style hostels in the city. Located right on the drinking hub of C. de las Huertas, International Youth Hostel is ideal for groups of backpackers looking for other people to join their wolf packs. Guests generally take advantage of the great communal facilities: a TV room, a kitchen that serves complimentary breakfast, and free internet in the computer room. Don't expect much privacy, as all rooms are dorm-style with simple bunk beds and storage lockers. The large shared bathrooms are clean and separated by gender. While rooms are bare-bones, cleanliness, and bargain prices are a major draw.

▶ ⚇ Ⓜ Antón Martín. Walk north up C. de León and make a right onto C. de las Huertas. *i* Single-sex and co-ed rooms available. Luggage storage. Free Wi-Fi. Ⓢ Dorms €16-22. ⚇ Reception 24hr.

Hostal Persal   HOSTAL $$$$
Pl. del Ángel, 12
☎91 369 46 43; www.hostalpersal.com

This location cannot be beat. Situated on Pl. del Ángel between Pl. Santa Ana and C. de las Huertas, Hostal Persal puts you in the perfect place to discover the best of Madrid's tapas bars and nightlife. The rooms here are of a similar size and decor as other hostels in the area with private rooms, but they are in far better condition. A full continental breakfast, which includes fresh fruit and sandwich fixings, is offered in the downstairs restaurant. With a big lobby, swipe keys, and a friendly and professional staff, this hostal is virtually indistinguishable from a medium-sized hotel—and you pay for its identity crisis.

▶ ⚇ Ⓜ Antón Martín. Walk south down C. del Olivar until you see Pl. del Ángel on the right. 2min. from Pl. de Santa Ana. Ⓢ Singles €60; doubles €84; triples €125. ⚇ Reception 24hr.

Chic and Basic Colors   HOTEL $$$$
C. de las Huertas, 14
☎91 429 69 35; www.chicandbasic.com

This chain hotel looks something like the lovechild of the chic boutique hotel and the conventional European hostel. Each room has a bold color scheme, contemporary furniture, and hardwood floors. This is a great place to stay if you like traveling in style and don't mind paying for it. A simple continental breakfast is available in the small common area, and there are snacks in the fridge, fruit, and an espresso machine. Check the website for various discounts and special offers.

▶ ⚇ Ⓜ Antón Martín. From Pl. del Ángel, walk down C. de las Huertas toward the museum district. Chic and Basic Colors is on the right. *i* Ensuite bathrooms. Same company has a high-end hotel called Chic and Basic on C. de Atocha, 113. Ⓢ Singles €60-70; doubles €80-90. ⚇ Reception 24hr.

Hostal Lopez
HOSTAL $$

C. de las Huertas, 54

☎91 429 43 49; www.hostallopez.com

Don't be dismayed by the dreary reception area: Hostal Lopez has some of the best prices for private rooms in Las Huertas. The bedrooms may have cream-colored walls and ugly tiled floors, but they all come with white-tiled ensuite bathrooms. While this isn't much of a backpackers' haunt, the private doubles and triples are relatively affordable, and the location is the biggest draw: Hostal Lopez is close to the nightlife of Las Huertas and just a few minutes walk from Paseo del Prado and Puerta del Sol. Like all hostales in Las Huertas, think twice about getting a streetside room, as they're noisy on weekends.

▶ ⚡ Ⓜ Antón Martín. From the Metro, walk north up C. de León and turn right onto C. de las Huertas. Ⓢ Singles €35; doubles €45; triples €66 . ⏰ Reception 24hr.

Hostal Edreira
HOSTAL $$$

C. de Atocha, 75

☎91 429 01 83; www.hostaledreira.com

Hostal Edreira is located 5min. from the train station between the museum district and the nightlife of Las Huertas. While C. de Atocha is a busy thoroughfare during the daytime, there isn't much heavy pedestrian traffic that will keep you up at night. Rooms are all private, with ensuite bathrooms, hardwood floors, and simple wooden beds, desks, and nightstands. With high ceilings and a generous amount of floor space, the rooms are comfortable and spacious. The *hostal* is often booked, so be sure to check in advance online or by phone.

▶ ⚡ Ⓜ Antón Martín. *i* Flatscreen TVs. Free Wi-Fi. Ⓢ Singles €40; doubles €55; triples €70. ⏰ Reception 24hr.

Hostal Bianco III
HOSTAL $$

C. Echegaray, 5

☎91 369 13 32; www.hostalbianco.com

This *hostal* is situated in the middle of the nightlife of central C. Echegaray, between Puerta del Sol and C. de las Huertas. Rooms are all private with ensuite bathrooms and are as clean and simply decorated as they come. The *hostal* was recently renovated, with plenty of fake marble throughout. The rooms come standard with the same understated furniture and uninspired bedspreads. Keep in mind noise levels—interior rooms are certainly preferable to rooms facing the street, particularly for weekend stays.

▶ ☎ Ⓜ Sol. From the Metro, walk east down Carrera de San Jeronimo and turn right onto C. Echegaray. *i* Free Wi-Fi. Ⓢ Singles €35; doubles €44; triples €60. ⏰ Reception 24hr.

Hostal Nieto

HOSTAL $$

C. de León, 32

☎ 91 369 04 20; www.hostalnieto.com

For better or for worse, Nieto feels more like a homestay than a *hostal,* with a small number of singles, doubles, and triples available. Nieto is located just a block away from the center of C. de las Huertas, but it will likely be less noisy than hostels located directly on the busy street. The rooms are simply decorated with white tiled floors, simple wood-framed beds, and clean private bathrooms. Their special "Salon Room" has pink curved walls and garish gold lamps, if you insist on something more decorative.

▶ ☎ Ⓜ Antón Martín. Walk uphill up C. de Atocha and make a right onto C. de León. Ⓢ Singles €35; doubles €50; triples €66. ⏰ Reception 24hr.

Hostal Vetusta

HOSTAL $$

C. de las Huertas, 3

☎ 91 429 64 04; www.hostalvetusta.com

Hostal Vetusta offers some of the cheapest private rooms in Las Huertas. With just a few rooms, this *hostal* is smaller than most, but if you're pinching pennies and want privacy, it might be a good place to look. The location between the nightlife centers of Pl. Santa Ana and C. de las Huertas is great but will inevitably be noisy, so we suggest ear plugs.

▶ ☎ Ⓜ Antón Martín. Across the street from Pl. del Ángel. Ⓢ Singles €25-30; doubles €35-45; triples €60. ⏰ Reception 24hr.

GRAN VÍA

Hostal Andorra

HOSTAL $$$

C. Gran Vía, 33, 7th fl.

☎ 91 532 31 16; www.hostalandorra.com

Unlike many *hostales* where common spaces are an afterthought, Hostal Andorra does a terrific job with the solarium and breakfast room. High ceilings, hardwood floors, and natural light make for open and inviting common areas. It's actually a pleasant place to catch your breath and read a book. Rooms are spacious, modestly decorated, and come with ensuite bathrooms with clean towels. While €47 is a bit expensive for a single, doubles are a great value.

▶ ✢ Ⓜ Callao. Walk east down C. Gran Vía. Ⓢ Singles €47; doubles €62. 🕐 Reception 24hr.

Hostal Santillan HOSTAL $$

C. Gran Vía, 64

☎91 548 23 28; www.hostalsantillan.com

Hostal Santillan offers a great value with simple and sizable rooms, modern furniture, and crisply painted walls. Rooms come with standard wood furniture, refurbished hardwood floors, and clean ensuite bathrooms. This *hostal* has no illusions of grandeur; it just makes sure to do all the little things that will make your stay comfortable. In a neighborhood that is often noisy, expensive, and uncomfortable, Hostal Santillan offers accommodations that are quiet, affordable, and pleasant.

▶ ✢ Ⓜ Plaza de España. *i* Laundry service. Ensuite bathrooms and daily room cleaning. Ask about scheduled excursions and complimentary luggage storage. Ⓢ Singles €30-35; doubles €50-55; triples €70-75. 🕐 Reception 24hr.

La Plata HOSTAL $$$

C. Gran Vía, 15

☎91 521 17 25; www.hostal-laplata.com

The mismatched antique furniture of La Plata makes the decor tough to decipher, but the rooms are pleasant. This family-run *hostal* works hard to keep the rooms clean. Thanks to the incredibly helpful and friendly staff, *Let's Go* recommends this *hostal* out of all the options at C. Gran Vía, 15.

▶ ✢ Ⓜ Gran Vía. Walk east; the building is on the right. Ⓢ Singles €45; doubles €60; triples €85. 🕐 Reception 24hr.

Hostal Felipe V HOSTAL $$$

C. Gran Vía, 15, 4th fl.

☎91 522 61 43; www.hostalfelipev.com

This *hostal* gets it—you don't book a budget *hostal* to sit in your room and look at the "antiques," you leave that for the Palacio Real. These accommodations are contemporary: rooms all come spacious and standard, with simple furniture, high ceilings, and private bathrooms. At the end of the day, you need a clean and comfortable place to crash, and that is precisely what this *hostal* offers.

▶ ✠ Ⓜ Gran Vía. Walk east; the building is to the right. *i* Breakfast €4.50. Ⓢ Singles €46; doubles €64; triples €78. 🕐 Reception 24hr.

Hostal Splendid   HOSTAL $$

C. Gran Vía, 15, 5th fl.

☎91 522 47 37; www.hostalsplendid.com

If you're pinching euro pennies, Hostal Splendid offers rooms at €5-10 below the standard rate in the building. While most *hostales* in C. Gran Vía offer only suites with ensuite bathrooms, Hostal Splendid has a few individual rooms with shared bathrooms, and a few twin doubles that run smaller and cheaper than the norm. You won't be missing out on any of the basic amenities: Hostal Splendid boasts TV, Wi-Fi, air-conditioning, and clean towels.

▶ ✠ Ⓜ Gran Vía. Walk east; the building is on the right. Ⓢ Singles €25-35; doubles €45-60; triples €65-80. 🕐 Reception 24hr.

Hostal Avenida   HOSTAL $$$

C. Gran Vía, 15, 4th fl.

☎91 521 27 28; www.hostalavenidamadrid.com

Avenida claims to be within 20min. of over 200 tourist attractions—but, then again, the same can be said for all the hostels within this building complex. With so many options in this neighborhood (and even just in this building), there is nothing special about Avenida, but they do all of the basics: fresh towels, flatscreen TVs, Wi-Fi, and kind employees at the front desk.

▶ ✠ Ⓜ Gran Vía. Walk east; the building is to the right. Ⓢ Singles €40; doubles €60. 🕐 Reception 24hr.

CHUECA AND MALASAÑA

🏛 Albergue Juvenil Municipal   HOSTEL $

C. Meija Lequerica, 21

☎91 593 96 88; www.ajmadrid.es

This is one of only a handful of exciting budget accommodations in the city of Madrid. Albergue Juvenil Municipal is a state-of-the-art youth hostel built by the city government in 2007. The decor is more like that of a four-star city hotel with frosted glass, dark tiled floors, and Ikea-style furniture. Add the pool tables, cafeteria, laundry room, exercise room with stationary bikes, and media room with a computer lab, and you have a true paradise for budget travelers. The layout is spacious enough

Accommodations

for you to jump out of bed and rollerblade around the bedroom for a morning workout. Most importantly, the hostel is situated perfectly between the nightlife of Chueca and Malasaña—close to the action but far enough from the busier streets that you're guaranteed a good night's sleep. With the Metro just 2min. away, access to the major sights is a no-brainer, and the English-speaking staff will be happy to give you a free map and point you in the right direction. You may as well be sleeping in the Prado.

▶ ⚡ Ⓜ Bilbao. Follow C. de Sagasta 3 blocks west to C. Meija Lequerica; the hostel is on the right. *i* Breakfast included. Laundry €3. Towels €3. 4- to 6-bed co-ed dorms. Book at least 5 days in advance. Ⓢ €27, under age 25 €20, 25-year-olds €22. Cash only. ⌚ Reception 24hr. Inform the staff if you need to check in after 3pm.

Hostal Los Alpes   HOSTAL $$

C. de Fuencarral, 17, 3rd and 4th fl.

☎91 531 70 71; www.hostallosalpes.com

Recently renovated, Los Alpes is about as clean, cheap, and comfortable as *hostales* get in Madrid. Rooms in Los Alpes have new hardwood floors, nicely made beds, brightly painted walls, and simple drapes. Unlike many *hostales,* the decor doesn't look like it was selected by dead old people. The look here is refreshingly simple, and all of the rooms come with basic amenities: a tiled bathroom, towels, and TV. While there aren't proper common areas to meet other guests, the reception area is nice and cheery. There's a computer available at no charge and Wi-Fi everywhere. While the *hostal*'s address on C. de Fuencarral, one of Madrid's busiest shopping streets, might be hectic for some, the location just blocks from the centers of Chueca and Malasaña may be too good to pass up.

▶ ⚡ Ⓜ Gran Vía. Walk north on C. de Fuencarral. Ⓢ Singles €34; doubles €50. ⌚ Reception 24hr.

Malasaña Traveler's Hostel   HOSTEL $

C. Manuela Malasaña, 23

☎91 591 15 79

With small dorm-style rooms and great common areas, this is a traveler's hostel through and through. The shared bathrooms and bedrooms aren't glamorous, but the private lockers will keep your valuables safe. The common areas are generally in use, particularly the six new computers in the lobby area. The kitchen in back is usually in use by some pajama-clad back-packer cooking up dinner to keep within budget.

▶ ✚ Ⓜ Bilbao. Cross C. de Fuencarral to C. Manuela Malasaña and follow it west for 2½ blocks. Ⓢ 12-bed dorms €16-21; 4-bed €19-27; 2-bed €24-36. Cash only. ⌚ Reception 24hr.

Hostal America   HOSTAL $$$

C. de Hortaleza, 19, 5th fl.

☎91 522 64 48; www.hostalamerica.net

Located on the top floor, America is the best *hostal* in a building full of accommodation options. Rooms feature big windows, new furniture, spacious bathrooms, and paintings on the wall. Service is friendly, quick, and mostly English-speaking. Be sure to check out the view from the outdoor terrace.

▶ ✚ Ⓜ Chueca. Make a right onto C. de Gravina and a right onto C. de Hortaleza. Ⓢ Singles €40-43; doubles €52-55; triples €67-70. ⌚ Reception 24hr.

Hostal Maria Luisa   HOSTAL $$$

C. de Hortaleza, 19, 2nd fl.

☎91 521 16 30; www.hostalmarialuisa.com

Nightstands, patterned bed coverings, and wooden wardrobes make this *hostal* feel more like Great Aunt Fanny's upstairs gue-stroom than the suite of your dreams. The decor might not be Chueca chic, but it's a totally comfortable place to stay. Rooms have hotel-quality amenities like TV, towels, complimentary Wi-Fi, and minibars, all at the standard *hostal* rates. Who needs Chueca? Just stay in your room and drink small nips of alcohol and eat cocktail peanuts and pretend you went out to that club down the block. All things considered, Hostal Maria Luisa does everything that a *hostal* should—it is clean and reasonably priced, particularly if you can swing a double or a triple.

▶ ✚ Ⓜ Chueca. Make a right onto C. de Gravina and a right onto C. de Hortaleza. Ⓢ Singles €39; doubles €50; triples €69; quads €85. ⌚ Reception 24hr.

Hostal Prada   HOSTAL $$$$

C. de Hortaleza, 19, 3rd fl.

☎91 521 20 04; www.hostalprada.com

Recently renovated, this *hostal* has a simple aesthetic and squeaky clean bathrooms that make for an enjoyable stay. Equidistant from Gran Vía and Chueca, Hostal Prada provides a great location amid some of the city's best dining and nightlife options.

▶ ✚ Ⓜ Chueca. Make a right onto C. de Gravina and a right onto C. de

Accommodations

Hortaleza. **Ⓢ** Singles €38; doubles €48, triples €69. **Ⓩ** Reception 24hr.

Hostal Oxum   HOSTAL $$$$

C. de Hortaleza, 31

☎66 472 32 41; www.hostaloxum.com

Oxum feels more like a boutique hotel than a traditional *madrileño hostal*. While the lobby is pretty bare-bones, the rooms offer all the finest amenities: duvets, extra pillows, fine towels, minibars, and even iPod docks and designer clocks. The prices reflect this. If all you care about is a good night's sleep, you might be just as happy saving your money and checking into a nearby family-run *hostal,* but if the little designer touches make a difference, Oxum will be the perfect place to rest your head, dock your pod, and watch the designer clock as the minutes roll by.

▸ ⚒ Ⓜ Chueca. Make a right onto C. de Gravina and a right onto C. de Hortaleza. **Ⓢ** Doubles €65-95; triples €135; quads €175. **Ⓩ** Reception 24hr.

Hostal Camino   HOSTAL $$

C. de Hortaleza, 78

☎91 308 14 95; www.hostalcamino.es

The basic Hostal Camino is ideally located near the best of Chueca shopping and nightlife, but be prepared to climb many flights of stairs for this convenience. Rooms here are on par with other *hostales* of the neighborhood with simple furnishings and the same basic amenities, but tend to be a few euro cheaper. While the staff members speak only Spanish, they go out of their way to make your stay comfortable.

▸ ⚒ Ⓜ Chueca. Make a right onto C. de Gravina and a right onto C. de Hortaleza. **Ⓢ** Singles €30; doubles €50; triples €60. **Ⓩ** Reception 24hr.

ARGÜELLES AND MONCLOA

Albergue Juvenil Santa Cruz de Marcenado (HI)   HOSTEL $

C. de Santa Cruz de Marcendado, 28

☎91 547 45 32

You'll be hard-pressed to find cheaper accommodations than Santa Cruz de Marcenado's €12 dorms. While rooms are anything but private (guests should be prepared to spend the night on the top bunk), the owners place a premium on cleanliness. The TV lounge and dining areas are simply decorated with modern furniture. Rooms and common areas are also kept relentlessly clean, and secure metal lockers are available for use.

Be sure to reserve well in advance, as rooms at this affordable hostel go quickly.

▶ ⚲ Ⓜ Argüelles. Walk 1 block down C. de Alberto Aguilera away from C. de la Princesa, turn right onto C. de Serrano Jover, and then left onto C. de Santa Cruz de Marcenado. *i* Free Wi-Fi. Ⓢ Dorms €12. Discounts available for HI members. 🕐 Reception 9am-9:45pm. Curfew 1:30am.

Hostal Moncloa   HOSTAL $$$
C. de Hilarión Eslava, 16
☎91 544 91 95; www.hostalmoncloa.com

The comfortable rooms at Hostal Moncloa are a bargain. Guests can count on the rooms being nice and quiet, with large ensuite bathrooms, but the lack of natural sunlight might be a moodkiller. This is certainly not a honeymooners' hotel, but it is well kept and well situated in a quiet part of town. Rooms have flatscreen TVs and Wi-Fi.

▶ ⚲ Ⓜ Moncloa. Walk south down C. de la Princesa and make a left onto C. de Romero Robledo. Turn left onto C. de Hilarión Eslava. Ⓢ Singles €45; doubles €50; triples €80. 🕐 Reception 24hr.

Hostal Angelines   HOSTAL $$$
C. de Hilarión Eslava, 12
☎91 543 21 52

If you want to escape the madness of El Centro, this is a great place to do it. Angelines offers simple singles and doubles with private bathrooms and small TVs. While Moncloa might look far from El Centro on the map, it's only a 15min. journey by Metro, and it's within walking distance of Argüelles, Malasaña, and Pl. de España. If you value comfort, sleep, and a clean, private bathroom, Angelines makes for a good refuge.

▶ ⚲ Ⓜ Moncloa. Walk south down C. de la Princesa and make a left on C. de Romero Robledo. Turn left onto C. de Hilarión Eslava. *i* Free Wi-Fi. Ⓢ Singles €40; doubles €45. 🕐 Reception 24hr.

Sights

The Avenida del Arte is reason enough to come to Madrid. A trip down this historic path takes you along Madrid's most picturesque tree-lined avenue, and through the canon of Western art. Other neighborhoods may not have world-class art on every block, but they still pack a punch. El Centro contains some of the city's most iconic sights, like the 18th-century Plaza Mayor. Chueca and Malasaña, Madrid's former bohemian centers, provide ample people-watching opportunities, with streets lined with high-end cafes and shops. Argüelles and Moncloa, crucial fighting grounds during the Spanish Civil War, are marked by the Arco de la Victoria, erected by General Franco and perhaps the most visible remnant of his haunting legacy. The palace El Pardo, just north of Moncloa, offers a view into the dictator's private bunker. Argüelles and Moncloa are also home to the city's most anomalous historical sight, the Egyptian Templo de Debod.

Budget Sights

Most of Madrid's museum admission prices are negligible; many are **free**. Visit big museums like the **Prado** during free entry hours (usually in the evening). If you can't make it for those, showing a student ID will get you a significant discount (descuento) at most museums. Finally, many—dare we say, most—of Madrid's sights happen to be plazas or churches, which are free all of the time.

EL CENTRO

▨ Palacio Real   PALACE
C. de Bailén
☎91 454 88 00; www.patrimonionacional.es

El Palacio Real is the ultimate symbol of the Spanish Empire's wealth and power. The palace was constructed by King Philip V between 1738 and 1755 on the site of a ninth-century Muslim fortress, and one thing is quite clear: the man had a thing for marble. While the palace is the current residence of the Spanish royal family, it is still totally accessible to the general public, and, for a meager entrance fee, you can view the orgy of artistry and craftsmanship of a palace 275 years in the making. The self-guided palace tour (1hr.) takes you through 15 rooms, each of which was curated by a different Spanish royal. The result is an eclectic mix in which artistry and wealth are the only constants. Flemish tapestries, exotic Oriental frescoes, and Persian carpets are thrown together in a maze of opulence, sometimes to gratuitous effect. If you are unconvinced by the end of the tour that the Spanish royal family is actually rich and powerful, rumor has it that they own a condominium in Florida (and a motor boat!). When Carlos IV purchased a set of instruments to be displayed in the Royal Palace, he traveled to Italy and bought the five violins that are displayed in the palace today. And that violin you are looking at ain't just any violin: it was made by Antonio Stradivari, the finest instrument maker the world has ever known. (When the Spanish royal family wants something, they get it.) If you're in town on the first Wednesday of the month between September and May, check out the changing of the guard ceremony, which takes place at noon.

▶ ✠ ⓜ Opera. Walk west down C. de Arrieta. Palacio Real is at the end of the

The Real "Forbidden Fruit"

It's no surprise that the Madrid coat of arms shows a bear climbing up an orange tree. Spain is famous for its bitter oranges, often used to make marmalade, compotes, and orange-flavored liqueurs. One variety, the Bergamot orange, is grown in Italy to produce bergamot oil, and used in perfume and as a flavoring in Early Grey tea. Another closely related variety is the citrus fruit called the "Adam's Apple," thought to have been the forbidden fruit that caused the expulsion of the biblical duo from the Garden of Eden. These fruits were brought to the Iberian peninsula from Asia and the Middle East by Arabs when they moved into Europe. By the 15th century, the exotic citrus was grown throughout Spain where people like Jan van Eyck would have (famously) seen them. In his famous Ghent Altarpiece, van Eyck depicts Eve holding not an apple but a large bumpy thick-skinned citrus.

road. *i* Come early to avoid long lines. Ⓢ €8, with tour €10; ages 5-16, students, and seniors €5. Ⓩ Open Apr-Sept M-Sa 9am-6pm, Su 9am-3pm; Oct-Mar M-Sa 9:30am-5pm, Su 9am-2pm.

Plaza Mayor

PLAZA

Today Pl. Mayor is something of a vestigial structure in the bustling cosmopolitan center of Madrid. It may be about as useful as your appendix, but your appendix is probably a lot less awesome looking. While the plaza itself has been around since the reign of Philip III, the buildings of today's plaza date to the late 18th century. During the Inquisition, the plaza was the site of public executions, but today the plaza is best known for the week-long **Fiesta de San Isidor** (May 8-15), during which the city celebrates its patron saint. The buildings around the plaza have become entirely residential; 237 apartment balconies over-look one of the single most important sites in the city's history. While the presence of King Philip III is memorialized at the plaza's center, he doesn't seem to be able to keep the scam artists away. Costumed Elvis and Spiderman wander the plaza daily, looking like they may have both had a few too many *cervezas*. The **tourist office** in the plaza is helpful and offers free maps.

▶ ⚇ Ⓜ Sol or Ⓜ Opera. From Puerta del Sol, walk 2min. down C. Mayor to-ward the Palacio Real. Pl. Mayor is on the left.

Puerta del Sol

PLAZA

Spain's Kilometre Zero, the point from which all distances in Spain are measured, is located in Puerta del Sol. You certainly can't get more *"el centro"* than the center of the Spanish kingdom itself, but Puerta del Sol is something of a cultural wasteland. The plaza, memorialized in Goya's paintings *The Third of May* and *The Second of May* (which hang in the **Prado**), is today overrun by newsstands, billboards, scam artists, and street performers dressed like Mickey Mouse and Spongebob. If these are what brought you to Madrid, you may in fact find Puerta del Sol "soulful," but otherwise it is more of a quick stopping point before you venture farther into the dynamic areas of El Centro, Las Huertas, La Latina, and Lavapiés. With the regional government situated on the southern end of the plaza, the Puerta del Sol has also been the site of major protests and political rallies.

▶ ✠ Ⓜ Sol.

Catedral de la Almudena

CATHEDRAL

C. de Bailén, 8-10

☎91 542 22 00

Catedral de la Almudena is in many ways a freak of history. While Madrid became the official capital of the Spanish Kingdom during the reign of Philip II, it took many years for the Spanish Catholic Church to recognize the city as a worthy religious center. Favoring the former capital of Toledo, the Church was resistant to the idea of building a new central cathedral in Spain. While Catedral de la Almudena was conceived in the 16th century, construction did not begin until 1879 and was only completed in 1999. Located across from El Palacio Real, this monumental cathedral is little more than a happy accident: the Catholic church's love child with the city of Madrid. The architectural style reflects this precarious past; the roof is painted in bright, bold patterns that resemble the work of Henri Matisse, while the panes of stained glass recall Picasso and the Cubist tradition. In some ways, Catedral de la Almudena may seem like a run-of-the-mill cathedral: you walk into a cavernous space, it looks cool, it feels impressive, you feel insignificant, and then you leave. But if you pay close attention, you will notice that this church is quite peculiar and filled with red herrings. Don't let the exterior fool you—this is a truly modern cathedral.

▶ ✠ Ⓜ Opera. Adjacent to the Palacio Real. Ⓢ Free. 🕐 Open daily 10am-2pm and 5-8pm.

Plaza de Oriente   PLAZA

Across the way from the Spanish Royal Palace, Pl. de Oriente is a monument to the empire in its own right. Formal gardens, fountains, and manicured hedges accent the 20 marble statues of Spain's kings and queens. If the Pl. de Oriente can teach us anything, it's that to be a Spanish ruler you need an impressive bone structure, a grizzly beard, or both. Plaza de Oriente is a relaxing retreat where lovers, tourists, sunbathers, and sunbathing-tourist-lovers lounge midday to escape the streets of El Centro. What better place to practice the art of PDA than under the marble gaze of King Philip III?

▶ ✈ Ⓜ Opera. Across from the Palacio Real. Ⓢ Free.

Jardines de Sabatini   GARDEN
C. de Bailén, 9
☎91 588 53 42

If El Palacio Real had a buttcrack, Jardines de Sabatini would be nestled right up next to it. This maze of trees, hedges, and fountains stand on what used to be the stable grounds of El Palacio Real, originally designed by the Italian architect Francisco Sabatini. The immaculately kept trees, fountains, and hedges create a relaxing environment in which to take a break, breathe deep, look up at the palace, and feel helplessly poor and intimidated.

▶ ✈ Ⓜ Opera. Adjacent to the Palacio Real. Ⓢ Free. 🕐 Open from dawn to dusk.

Plaza de la Villa   PLAZA

Many of the neighboring plazas in El Centro are bigger, but it isn't size that really matters... right ladies? In any case, Pl. de la Villa is easily overlooked, but very much worth a quick visit. The first major building on the plaza is the Casa de la Villa. (Translation? City Hall.) Plaza de la Villa is also home to El Torre de Los Lujanes, the private family home of the Lujanes that was built in the 15th century. This is not only one of the oldest buildings in the square, but it is also one of city's best remaining examples of Mudéjar, or Islamic-influenced architecture. Unlike Pl. Mayor, Pl. de la Villa is quiet, so you won't find yourself accosted by scam artists.

▶ ✈ From the Palacio Real, walk down C. Mayor toward Puerta del Sol; the plaza is on the right. Ⓢ Free.

Convento de la Encarnación   CONVENT

Pl. de la Encarnación, 1

☎91 454 88 00

Every July 27th, it is said that the blood of St. Panthalon, held in a crystal orb, visibly liquefies. It is not entirely clear that St. Panthalon was in fact a living, breathing (and bleeding) person, but a crystal orb containing his alleged blood is on display at the Convento de la Encarnación. Convents are normally incredibly exclusive: it doesn't matter how hot your friends are, you still aren't getting in. This convent is a little different. While it was founded as an exclusive center of monastic life nearly 400 years ago, today it is accessible to the general public for a small entrance fee. The tour takes you through the formerly secluded chapel filled with artwork by European masters and into the famous reliquary, which contains thousands of Christian relics, most notably the blood-filled crystal orb. Located close to El Palacio Real and Pl. de Oriente, the convent is an easy stop and a great opportunity to get some face time with ancient relics.

▶ ⚕ Ⓜ Opera. Take Pl. de Isabel II northwest to C. de Arietta and turn right onto Pl. de la Encarnación. *i* Tours conducted in Spanish every 30min. Ⓢ €3.60. 🕐 Open Tu-Th 10:30am-12:30pm and 4-5:30pm, F 10:30am-12:30pm, Sa 10:30am-12:30pm and 4-5:30pm, Su 11am-1:30pm.

LA LATINA AND LAVAPIÉS

Basilica de San Francisco el Grande   CHURCH

C. de San Buenaventura

☎91 365 38 00

This Roman Catholic Church is one of the most distinctive structures in La Latina. The basilica, designed in a Neoclassical style in the second half of the 18th century, comes to life when lit up at night. The church has three chapels, including the Chapel of San Bernardino de Siena, where Goya's magnificent painting of the chapel's namesake rests. Pay close attention to the picture and you will see that the figure looking down on the right is Goya himself. Don't forget to check out the adjacent gardens, which have spectacular views of western Madrid.

▶ ⚕ Ⓜ La Latina. Walk west down Carrera de San Francisco. Ⓢ Free. Guided tours €3. 🕐 Open Tu-F 11am-12:30pm and 4-6:30pm, Sa 11am-noon.

La Iglesia de San Andrés   CHURCH
Pl. de San Andrés

One of the oldest parishes in Madrid, La Iglesia de San Andrés used to be *the* go-to church for La Latina local San Isidro Labrador, the patron saint of Madrid. Much of the original interior was destroyed during the Spanish Civil War, but the structure still showcases a Baroque style crafted by designer José de Villarreal. Pay specific attention to the 15th-century cupola stationed above the sanctuary of the San Andrés Chapel.

▶ ⚇ Ⓜ La Latina. Make a left onto C. de la Cava. Ⓢ Free.

LAS HUERTAS

Real Academia de Bellas Artes de San Fernando MUSEUM
C. de Alcalá, 13
☎91 524 08 64; rabasf.insde.es

The oldest permanent art institute in Madrid, the Real Academia de Bellas Artes is a short walk away from bustling Puerta del Sol. This is the only museum dedicated exclusively to Spanish artists, and with a collection 1400 paintings, 15,000 drawings, and 600 sculptures, this should be your first stop if you couldn't get enough at El Prado. Particularly notable are the Goya paintings in Room 13, which include two rare self-portraits. The museum also contains notable works by Rubens, Ribera, and Sorolla. The collection is dwarfed by the Prado down the street, but the museum gives a concise tour of art history in Spain from the 17th century through 20th century.

▶ ⚇ From Puerta del Sol, walk east down C. de Alcalá. Real Academia de Bellas Artes is on the left. Ⓢ €5; groups of 15-25, university students, teachers, under 18, and over 65 free. Free to all W. ⌚ Open Tu-Sa 9am-5pm, Su 9am-2:30pm.

AVENIDA DEL ARTE

🖾 Museo Nacional Centro de Arte Reina Sofía MUSEUM
C. Santa Isabel, 52
☎91 774 10 00; www.museoreinasofia.es

Juan Carlos I named the Reina Sofía for his wife and declared it a national museum in 1988. The building itself is a masterpiece: what was once Madrid's general hospital in the 18th century has been gutted and transformed into a temple of 20th-century art.

Two glass elevators at either end of the museum ferry visitors between the four floors of the collection. The second and fourth floors are mazes of permanent exhibits that chart the Spanish avant-garde and include galleries dedicated to Juanw Gris, Joan Miró, and Salvador Dalí. The museum's main attraction is Picasso's *Guernica* in Gallery 206. To make the most of your visit, consider investing in an audio guide, which gives a full historical and critical account of the work. The basement and first floor exhibits focus on more contemporary artists.

▶ ⚑ Ⓜ Atocha. Ⓢ €6, ages 17 and under and over 65 free Sa afternoon and Su. Temporary exhibits €3. Audio guides €4, students €3. ⏰ Open M 10am-9pm, W-Sa 10am-9pm, Su 10am-2:30pm.

🖾 Museo Nacional del Prado   MUSEUM

C. Ruiz de Alarcón, 23

☎91 330 28 00; www.museodelprado.es

El Prado is one of the greatest art museums in the world. Built from the original collection of the Spanish royal family, El Prado celebrates the entirety of western art from Hellenistic Greek sculpture to Dutch altarpieces to Spanish and Italian Renaissance paintings. The museum requires at least a day-long visit, but if you really can't stay, be sure to put in some face time with the following masterpieces.

Diego Velázquez's 🖾**Las Meninas,** one of the most studied pieces of art in the world, captures a studio scene centered on the Infanta Margarita. Velázquez himself stares out from behind his easel on the left side of the painting. It may look like just another picture of wealthy Spaniards and their dwarves, but this piece has been praised as the culmination of Velázquez's career—a meditation on reality, art, illusion, and the power of easel painting. Goya's side-by-side portraits *La Maja Vestida* and *La Maja Desnuda* portray a woman believed to be the Duchess of Alba in different states of undress. (The museum has yet to recover the long-lost third portrait, *La Maja Spread Eagla*.)

The free museum maps offered at the information kiosk will help guide you to the most historically important pieces, while the English audio tour (€3.50) is an invaluable resource for learning about the history of the 1500+ works on display. Evenings are free at the museum, but crowds do gather.

▶ ⚑ Ⓜ Banco de España and Ⓜ Atocha. From Ⓜ Atocha, walk north up Paseo del Prado; the museum will be on your right, just past the gardens. *i* Free entry Tu-Sa 6-8pm, Su 5-8pm. Check the website for an up-to-date schedule. Ⓢ €8, students €4, under 18 and over 65 free. ⏰ Open Tu-Su 9am-8pm.

Sights

▨ Museo Thyssen-Bornemisza   MUSEUM

Paseo del Prado, 8

☎91 369 01 51; www.museothyssen.org

The Thyssen-Bornemisza has a bit more of an international emphasis than either the Reina Sofía or the Prado. The museum is housed in the 19th-century Palacio de Villahermosa and contains the collection of the late Baron Henrich Thyssen-Bornemisza. Today, the museum is the world's most extensive private showcase. Exhibits range from 14th-century Flemish altarpieces to an impressive collection of German avant-garde canvases from the early 20th century. Take advantage of the spread by checking out its Baroque and Neoclassical collection, which includes pieces by Caravaggio, Riber, and Claude Lorraine. Also, be sure to explore the Impressionist, Fauvist, and early avant-garde pieces that paved the way to modern art as we know it today. There are too many famous artists to name-drop—just come here to be wowed by the gigantic collection.

▶ ⚘ From the Prado, walk north up Paseo del Prado. The museum is at the corner of Carrera de San Jeronimo and Paseo del Prado. ⑤ €7, children under 12 free. ⚑ Open Tu-Su 10am-7pm.

▨ Caixaforum   MUSEUM

Paseo del Prado, 36

☎91 389 65 45

The CaixaForum is a visual magnet along Paseo del Prado. The 19th-century factory seems to float on one corner of La Avenida del Arte beside the museum's towering vertical garden. Designed by the same architects as London's Tate Modern, the CaixaForum is an architectural masterpiece and an incredible cultural resource. The interior has two floors of gallery space for art, design, and architecture exhibits, including major retrospectives of internationally renowned architects. The basement auditorium hosts anything and everything cool and relevant, from lectures by architects to dance performances to film screenings. The exterior vertical garden is a marvel of botany and urban design.

▶ ⚘ Ⓜ Atocha. From the Metro, walk north up Paseo del Prado; the Caixa-Forum is on the left. ⑤ Free. Some special events are ticketed. ⚑ Open daily 10am-8pm.

Parque del Buen Retiro   PARK

C. Alfonso XII, 48

☎91 429 82 40; www.parquedelretiro.es

When a run-of-the-mill millionaire needs a break, he goes to a spa. When a Spanish monarch needs some time off, he builds his own retreat. A former hunting ground, the Parque del Buen Retiro was reconstructed by Felipe IV in the 1630s as his personal retreat. Outfitted with an artificial lake (Estanque Grande) and two palaces (Palacio de Velázquez and Palacio de Cristal), this 300-acre park was certainly a royal getaway. More democratic times have rendered El Retiro a favorite escape of all *madrileños,* who use it for both relaxation and recreation thanks to some modern additions, including a running track and a sports complex. On weekends the promenades fill with musicians, families, and young lovers, amateur rowers go out onto the Estanque Grande, and exhibits and performances are showcased at the palaces. Try to avoid the park after dark if you're alone, as shady characters have been known to hang here at night.

▶ ✝ Ⓜ Retiro. Or, from Ⓜ Atocha, pass the roundabout north onto Calle de Alfonso XII. The park is on the right. ⑤ Free. Row boats M-F until 2pm €1.40, Sa-Su and holidays €4.55. ⓓ Open daily in summer 6am-midnight; in winter daily 6am-10pm. Estanque pier open July-Aug 10am-11pm; Sept-June 10am-45min. before sunset.

Real Jardín Botánico   GARDEN

Pl. de Murillo, 2

☎91 420 30 17; www.rjb.csic.es/jardinbotanico/jardin

The Real Jardín Botánico is not just a garden but a self-proclaimed "museum" of plant life. For our purposes, it's a garden. With beautiful trees, fountains, and exotic plant life, the Real Jardín is the perfect place to reflect on the countless pieces of art you've cranially digested.

▶ ✝ Next to the Prado. ⑤ €2.50, students €1.25, groups €0.50. ⓓ Open daily May-Aug 10am-9pm; Sept 10am-8pm; Oct 10am-7pm; Nov-Dec 10am-6pm; Jan-Feb 10am-6pm; Mar 10am-7pm; Apr 10am-8pm.

GRAN VÍA

🖾 Plaza de España   PLAZA

In a city filled with statues of Spanish royalty and Roman deities, Pl. de España is something of an anomaly. Located on the western edge of Gran Vía, Pl. de España is a monument to the father of Spanish literature, **Miguel de Cervantes.** The stone statue of Cervantes at the center of the plaza is surrounded by characters from his most celebrated work, *Don Quixote.* The bronze statues immediately below Cervantes depict the hero

Alonso Quixano and his chubby and slightly less heroic side-kick Sancho Panza. To the right and left are Quixano's two love interests, the peasant lady Aldonza Lorenzo and the woman of his dreams Dulcinea Del Toboso. Like every Spanish plaza, Pl. de España is a prime makeout destination.

▶ ✄ Ⓜ Plaza de España. The western end of C. Gran Vía. Ⓢ Free.

Plaza de Cibeles   PLAZA

When Real Madrid fans want to party before a game they come to Pl. de Cibeles and proudly drape their flags on the central fountain. Commissioned by King Charles III, the fountain depicts the Greek goddess of nature, Cibele, on her morning commute, driving a chariot pulled by two lions. The daringly white **Palacio de Comunicaciones** on the edge of the plaza is the headquarters of Madrid's city government. This building is open to the general public, and it's a worthy stop before or after a day in El Retiro or along La Avenida del Arte. The palace's rooftop tower is open to the public and has one of the best free views of the city.

▶ ✄ Ⓜ Banco de España. From the intersection of C. Gran Vía and C. de Alcalá, walk 1 block east down C. de Alcalá. Ⓢ Free.

Telefónica Building   ARCHITECTURE

C. Gran Vía, 28

If you want skyscrapers, go to Dubai. If that's why you came to Madrid, you're in the wrong place. That said, the Telefónica Building is Madrid's most iconic 20th-century building. Completed in 1920, this was the first skyscraper in Madrid, and arguably the first in all of Europe. During the Spanish Civil War, the Telefónica Building was used as a lookout by the Republicans to scout Franco's advancing Nationalist troops. It became a target of enemy bombings, and reportedly housed Ernest Hemingway on several occasions. Today the building is used as an office headquarters for the telecom giant, but the lobby is open to the general public and has a free museum of communications technology.

▶ ✄Ⓜ Gran Vía.

CHUECA AND MALASAÑA

Palacio Longoria   ARCHITECTURE

C. de Fernando VI, 6

This just might be the ugliest building in the city. Depending on who you are, you will either find Palacio Longoria to be an eyesore or a beautiful relic of *modernista* architecture. Whether you like it or not, you will probably run into it during your time in Chueca, and it is worth noting its peculiarity as the only true example of Catalan *modernisme* (a la Gaudí) in Madrid. Palacio Longoria was built in the early 20th century as a private residence for the banker Javiar González Longoria. In 1950 it was converted into a private office building for the General Society of Spanish Authors and Editors. Unfortunately, the building is rarely open to the public, but its facade is a sight to behold along your way through Chueca.

▶ ⚐ Ⓜ Chueca. Take C. de Gravina 1 block west to C. de Pelayo and follow it 2 blocks north. The building is on the left. *i* The interior is only open to the public during National Architecture Week (2nd week of Oct).

Convento de las Salesas Reales   CHURCH

C. de Bárbara de Braganza, 1

☎91 319 48 11; www.parroquiadesantabarbara.es

Conceived in 1748 by Barbara of Portugal, this monastery continues to function as a church, but for tourists in Chueca it's a great place to slow down, quit eating, and consume some culture instead. Originally designed by Francois Carlier, the church has since suffered a number of fires but still holds King Ferdinand VI and the convent's founder, Barbara of Portugal, in their tombs, which were constructed by Francesco Sabatini and Francisco Gutierrez. The adjacent building of the convent is now the seat of the Supreme Court of Spain, so this would definitely not be the place to go streaking.

▶ ⚐ Ⓜ Colón. From Pl. Colón, go down Paseo de Recoletos and take a right onto C. de Bárbara de Braganza. Ⓢ Free. 🕐 Open M-F 9:30am-1pm and 5:30-8pm, Sa 9:30am-2pm and 5-9pm, Su 9:30am-2pm and 6-9pm. Closed to tourists during mass.

Museo de Historia   MUSEUM

C. Fuencarral, 78

☎91 701 18 63; www.munimadrid.es/museodehistoria

This renovated 18th-century building constructed under Philip V now holds a collection of models, illustrations, and documents that showcase the history of Madrid. The building itself is a historical relic as one of Madrid's few lasting examples of Baroque architecture. While it was saved from destruction in 1919 by the Spanish Society of Friends of Art, only recently has the city decided to make this building a tourist destination. The facade is currently being renovated, and upon completion, the museum will have a totally new state-of-the-art facility to exhibit the history and culture of Madrid.

▶ ✈ Ⓜ Tribunal. Walk north up C. Fuencarral. The large pink building is on the right. Ⓢ Free. ⏰ Open Tu-Sa 10am-9pm, Su 11am-2:30pm.

ARGÜELLES AND MONCLOA

🏛 Templo de Debod   TEMPLE, PARK

Paseo del Pintor Rosales, 2

☎91 366 74 15; www.munimadrid.es/templodebod

On a nice day, this is one of the most beautiful spots in Madrid. In the '60s, the rapid industrialization taking place in Egypt severely threatened its most precious archaeological remains. When the Egyptian government proposed the construction of a hydroelectric dam along the Nile that would have destroyed Egypt's ancient temple complex at Abu Simbel, a team of Spanish archaeologists intervened to rescue the national treasure. In appreciation, the Egyptian government shipped the Templo de Debod to Madrid's Parque de la Montana, where you can now see a small archaeology exhibit inside. The original temple archways are even more impressive at night when lit up and reflected in the adjacent pool. The park surrounding the temple teems with families, runners, tourists, and locals lounging in the afternoon sun. Check out the lookout point behind the temple for one of the most beautiful views of western Madrid.

▶ ✈ Ⓜ Plaza de España. Walk to the far side of Pl. de España, cross the street, and walk a couple of blocks right; Templo de Debod is on the left. Ⓢ Free. ⏰ Open Apr-Sept Tu-F 10am-2pm and 6-8pm, Sa-Su 10am-2pm; Oct-Mar Tu-F 9:45am-1:45pm and 4:15-6:15pm, Sa-Su 10am-2pm. Rose garden open daily 10am-8pm.

🏛 El Pardo   PALACE

C. de Manuel Alonso s/n

☎91 376 15 00

Originally built in the 15th century as a hunting lodge for Henry IV, El Pardo is today most famous having been the private residence of General Franco during his military dictatorship. While much of the palace seems excessively ornate and unremarkable, the tour (45min.) takes you through Franco's private quarters, which have remained untouched since his death in 1975. His wardrobe, prayer room, personal study, and bedroom (where he kept his most treasured personal possession, a relic of St. Teresa's silver-encrusted petrified arm) are all on display. The tour even takes you into Franco's bathroom, and, yes, he had a bidet. In addition to its function as a museum, El Pardo hosts important state galas and (strangely) functions as the official hotel of foreign dignitaries.

▶ ♯ Ⓜ Moncloa. Take bus #601 from the underground bus station adjacent to Moncloa. *i* Mandatory 45min. guided tour in Spanish; last tour leaves 45min. before closing. Ⓢ €4, students and over 65 €2.30. Ⓩ Open Apr-Sept M-Sa 10:30am-5:45pm, Su 9:30am-1:30pm; Oct-Mar M-Sa 10:30am-4:45pm, Su 10am-1:30pm.

Casa de Campo   PARK

Av. de Portugal
Parque de Atracciones
☎91 463 29 00; www.parquedeatracciones.es
Zoo Madrid
☎91 512 37 70; www.zoomadrid.com

Casa de Campo offers many excuses to leave downtown Madrid. While the expansive urban park is a bit removed on the other side of the Mazanares river, Caso de Campo is a totally manageable destination for a morning or afternoon trip out of the city center. Bike trails crisscross the park, and kayaks and canoes are available for rent along the park lagoon. If you are looking for something more than a tranquil afternoon in the park, **Parque de Atracciones** (the amusement park) has rides that will jack your heart rate up without fail. No need to commit yourself to the all-day pass (€24); single and double ride tickets can be purchased on the cheap (single €7; double €12). The park also has Madrid's only **zoo** and **aquarium,** but be prepared to shell out for an entrance pass (€19), and don't expect any particular Castilian flair from the monkeys; they're just regular monkeys. If you plan on visiting these various venues within the park, head to Casa de Campo on quieter weekdays when there aren't long lines.

▶ ♯ Ⓜ Lago, Ⓜ Batan, and Ⓜ Casa de Campo are all within the park. Alternatively, take bus #33 or 65 from the city center. *i* Let's Go does not advise walking here after dark. Ⓢ Entrance to the park is free; venues and rentals are ticketed. Ⓩ Parque de Atracciones open M-Sa 9am-7pm. Zoo Madrid open daily, but check website for hours as schedule changes.

Arco de la Victoria   LANDMARK
Near Parque del Oeste

This Neoclassical arch at the center of Moncloa was built in 1956 by order of General Franco to commemorate the rebel army's victory in the Spanish Civil War. Looking at the concrete Neoclassical arch at the center of Moncloa, you'd think that Franco and his friends came to power stomping through the country Julius-Caesar-style, but that glorious horse and chariot at the top of the arch is actually a few centuries off the mark. The history of Franco's military dictatorship still touches a nerve with many *madrileños,* who prefer to call the arch Moncloa Gate. Surrounded by traffic, the history of Arco de la Victoria has faded somewhat within the fast pace of cosmopolitan life.

▶ ⚡ Ⓜ Moncloa.

Parque del Oeste   PARK
C. de Francisco y Jacinto Alcântara

Less crowded than the popular Retiro Park, Parque del Oeste is a lush break from the concrete jungle of western Madrid. This vast wooded park, with rolling hills, soaring pine trees, and small lagoons, feels more like a nature reserve than a city park. The dirt paths that cross through the park are great for an afternoon walk or jog, but exercise caution at night, as the park is more deserted after sunset. If you're parched, there are plenty of cafes along the nearby Paseo del Pintor Rosales.

▶ ⚡ Ⓜ Moncloa. *i Let's Go* does not advise walking here after dark. Ⓢ Free. Ⓩ Open 24hr.

Museo de América   MUSEUM
Av. de los Reyes Católicos, 6
☎91 549 26 41; www.museodeamerica.mcu.es

In 1771, Carlos III started a collection that brought together ethnographic objects from scientific expeditions and pieces from the first archaeological excavations carried out in America. Today, the modern Museo de América holds a collection that encompasses American cultures from the tip of South America to the tundra of Alaska. Some of the most interesting artifacts are treasures from the pre-Columbian cultures conquered by Spain, including some Mayan hieroglyphic documents.

▶ ⚡ Ⓜ Moncloa. From the Metro, cross the street and make a left. Ⓢ €3; EU citizens €1.50; under 18, over 65, and students free. Ⓩ Open Tu-W 9:30am-3pm, Th 9:30am-3pm and 4-7pm, F-Sa 9:30am-3pm, Su 10am-3pm.

Faro de Moncloa   TOWER

Av. de los Reyes Católicos, 0

☎91 544 81 04; www.elfarodemoncloa.com

> This 100m transmission tower, designed by architect Salvador Pérez Arroyo in 1992, originally had an observation deck and restaurant at the top, but the tower has been closed to the public since 2005 because of safety issues. Plans to re-open are still uncertain, but the futuristic architecture still provides an exciting addition to the Madrid skyline.

SALAMANCA

◪ Museo Sorolla   MUSEUM

Paseo General Martínez Campos, 47

☎91 310 15 84; http://museosorolla.mcu.es/

> This museum will surprise you. While the Valencian painter Joaquim Sorolla (1863-1923) is not quite a household name, he is nonetheless one of Spain's greats. The museum, which resides in Sorolla's former palace and studio, is a living monument to the artist. Sorolla's home has a fantastic bohemian vibe, with his studio preserved with simple wooden bookcases filled with rare books and esoteric objects, canvases framed on easels, and paint brushes tucked into ceramic vases around the room. A trip to this museum gives you a sense of Sorolla's importance in art history, and, more importantly, of his spirit.

▶ ✤ Ⓜ Iglesia. Turn right onto Paseo General Martínez Campos. Ⓢ €3; free on Su. ⌚ Open Tu-Sa 9:30am-8pm, Su 10am-3pm.

Museo Lazaro Galdiano   MUSEUM

C. Serrano, 122

☎91 561 60 84; www.fig.es

> Museo Lazaro Galdiano holds the personal collections of Spain's great patron of art and literature, Jose Lazaro Galdiano. This 13,000 piece collection, housed in Galdiano's former residence, includes a number of significant works, including Goya's *Witch's Sabbath* and El Greco's *Portrait of St. Francis of Assisi*. While these works are certainly worth seeing, the real appeal of this museum is its assemblage of more esoteric works of art, decorative objects, weapons, jewels, and rare books. Galdiano was an influential board member of the Prado and a publisher of art and literary periodicals, and throughout his life he collected everything from rare jewels and Renaissance paintings to

ivory weapons. While the Prado is the obvious stopping point for anyone with even the most fleeting interest in art, Museo Lazaro Galdiano is certainly worthwhile for art lovers interested in visiting one of Madrid's great private collections.

▶ ♣ Ⓜ Gregorio Marañon. Ⓢ €4, students €3, EU citizens free. ⓩ Open M 10am-4:30pm, W-Su 10am-4:30pm.

Museo de Ciencias Naturales   MUSEUM

C. de José Gutiérrez Abascal, 2

☎91 411 13 28; www.mncn.csic.es

You probably went to a natural history museum like this on a fifth-grade field trip, but the great thing about Mother Nature is that she never gets old. This is a particularly great place to go if you enjoy zoos and wild animals but prefer to see them dead. El Museo de Ciencias Naturales, based on the original Cabinet of Curiosities of the Spanish royal family in the 18th century, has today grown into a vast collection of natural specimens, fossils, and minerals. Perhaps the most thrilling room is the public warehouse in the basement, which houses thousands of taxidermied animals in a cramped, dimly lit room. You name it, and you'll likely find it in this room: vultures of every kind, primates, cats, and foxes, all looking at you, ready for the kill. Particularly notable are the preserved 4m African elephant, the giant squid, and the snow leopard (of which there are only 40 living specimens today). This museum is by no means a first stop for tourists, but it is an impressive collection with great historical importance, as it was one of the first state-sponsored collections of natural specimens.

▶ ♣ Ⓜ Gregorio Marañon, walk 2 blocks north on Paseo de la Castellana. Ⓢ €5, students and ages 4-14 €3, under 4 free. ⓩ Open Jan-June Tu-F 10am-6pm, Sa 10am-8pm, Su 10am-2:30pm; July-Aug Tu-F 10am-6pm, Sa 10am-2:30pm, Su 10am-2:30pm; Sept-Dec Tu-F 10am-6pm, Sa 10am-8pm, Su 10am-2:30pm.

Biblioteca Nacional   LIBRARY

Paseo de Recoletos, 20-22

☎91 883 24 02; www.bne.es

This spartan building on Paseo de Recoletos is the flagship of Spain's national library system. While the main corridors of the library are closed to the public, the building hosts a number of temporary exhibits (usually on literary topics) and cultural performances. For many people, this won't be the most thrilling visit because, let's face it, books are a waste of time (especially guidebooks). Nonetheless, the Biblioteca is a major landmark in the Salamanca area. On your way out of the library, check out the adjacent **Jardines del Descubrimiento,** a grassy public plaza smattered with trees and (expensive) outdoor cafes that spans C. Castellano.

▶ ✚ Ⓜ Colón. Ⓢ Free. ⏲ Exhibits open Tu-Sa 10am-9pm, Su 10am-2pm.

Food

Affordable and delicious food is plentiful in Madrid, but you'll have to dodge the many tourist traps in order to find it. For instance, dining options in El Centro are best for a midday refreshment, and drinks are shockingly cheap, but bottled water and mediocre food come with a hefty price tag. Lavapiés is notable for its reasonably priced international fare and La Latina also has some of the city's best *tabernas*. Las Huertas' central plazas (Pl. Santa Ana and Pl. del Ángel) are packed with contemporary tapas bars, iconic 19th-century *tabernas,* and international restaurants. The southern boundary of Argüelles has spectacular bars, cafes, and *tabernas,* particularly on Calle del Duque de Liria, Calle Conde Duque, and Calle San Bernardino. Chueca and Malasaña are packed with gourmet options that will cost you an arm and a leg. For those on a tight budget, your best bet may be to grab a beer and *bocadillo,* which can cost as little as €2.

Budget Food

You may have heard of *el botellón,* the Spanish youths' equivalent to a pregame. But you may be unaware of the newest portable food sensation that's sweeping the nation: *el picnic.* Sometimes the most satisfying—and cheapest—food option is stopping by a market or grocery store before heading to one of Madrid's many parks. You'll find two great markets in Chueca and El Centro, and any shop labeled *alimentaciones* should do the trick for supermarket-style basics.

EL CENTRO

▨ El Sobrino de Botín   TAPAS $$$
C. de los Cuchilleros, 17
☎ 91 366 42 17; www.botin.es

The world's oldest restaurant, El Sobrino de Botín, reeks of roasted pig and illustrious history: Goya was a waiter here; Hemingway ate here and wrote about it. Step inside and you will quickly realize that this is a truly authentic historical landmark and protector of the *madrileño* culinary tradition. From the gilded oil still life paintings to antique revolvers to porcelain-tiled walls, El Sobrino is what so many restaurants in the barren El Centro restaurant scene aspire to be. As you approach the winding wooden staircase, you will notice *"el horno,"* the nearly 300-year-old wood-fire oven that continues to roast the same traditional dishes. Try the infamous roast suckling pig (€22) that Ernest Hemingway memorialized in the final pages of *The Sun Also Rises.* While the food is not cheap at El Sobrino, even their simple dishes like the *sopa de oja* (garlic soup with egg; €7.90) are far better than what you can expect from neighboring El Centro restaurants. Forget sitting outside in Pl. Mayor and getting accosted by street performers; this restaurant is timeless, if a bit touristy.

▶ ⚐ Ⓜ Sol. Walk 6 blocks west down C. Mayor to C. Cava de San Miguel to C. de los Cuchilleros. Ⓢ Food €6-30. ⌚ Open daily 1-4pm and 8pm-midnight.

▨ Café de Círculo de Bellas Artes   CAFE $
C. de Alcalá 42
☎91 521 69 42; www.circulobellasartes.com

This is Madrid's cafe society at its best—a requisite visit for any connoisseur visiting Madrid. Located on the first floor of the Círculo de Bellas Artes, this cafe is part of an institution. The interior is truly grand with crystal chandeliers, columns stamped with Picasso-like figure drawings, and frescoed ceilings. The wicker chairs on the streetside terrace make for a comfortable place to relax and people-watch amidst the bustle of C. de Alcalá. While the cafe has a full menu, simple things like sangria (€5) and *bocadillos* (€5.80) are excellent and a reasonable price of admission into one of Madrid's finest cafes.

▶ ✣ Ⓜ Sevilla, walk 2 blocks west down C. de Alcalá. Ⓢ Coffee drinks €3-6. Wine €3-6. Sandwiches €5-8. ☾ Open M-Th 9:30am-1am, F-Sa 9:30am-3am, Su 9:30am-1am.

Mercado de San Miguel   MARKET $
Pl. de San Miguel, 2
☎91 542 73 64; www.mercadodesanmiguel.es

This almost-open-air market sells fine meats, cheeses, flowers, and wine. It also contains a number of specialty bodegas, bars, and restaurants. Prices here are reasonable, especially compared to the expensive sit-down dining options in nearby Pl. Mayor. The partial air-conditioning makes it the locals' pit stop for a glass of wine (€2-3), a fresh oyster (€1.50-3), or more traditional tapas (€2-4). Just a few years old, this reinvention of the open-market has already become hugely popular with locals and tourists and is reliably packed night and day. While you can still get traditional market goods like fresh produce, fish, and poultry, the market is more popular as a midday and evening hangout.

▶ ✣ At the Pl. de San Miguel, off the northwest corner of Pl. Mayor, adjacent to the cervecería. Ⓢ Prices vary. ☾ Open M-W 10am-midnight, Th-Sa 10am-2am, Su 10am-midnight.

Chocolatería San Ginés   CHOCOLATE $
Pl. de San Ginés, 5
☎91 366 54 31

After spending all day looking at 500-year-old buildings and pretending to care, it's okay to let loose. Sometimes this means treating yourself to a good dinner; sometimes this means ingesting unconscionable amounts of deep fried batter and melted dark chocolate. Since it was founded in 1894, Chocolatería San Ginés has been serving the world's must gluttonous treat: *churros con chocolate* (€4). San Ginés is an institution and an absolute late-night must for clubbers and early risers alike.

▶ ✣ From Puerta del Sol, walk down C. del Arenal until you get to Joy nightclub. Chocolatería San Ginés is tucked in the tiny Pl. de San Ginés. Ⓢ Chocolates from €4. 🕓 Open 24hr.

Museo Del Jamón   TAPAS $$

C. Mayor, 7

☎91 542 26 32; www.museodeljamon.com

There is something very special about your first *bocadillo* in Madrid. Like the birth of your first child, you probably won't forget it, and you will likely be anxiously snapping pictures to capture the magic of it all. The *bocadillo* is the simplest but most satisfying meal you will have in Madrid, and Museo Del Jamón does right by this tradition: crispy Spanish baguettes, freshly sliced *jamón,* rich Manchego cheese, and dirt cheap prices (€1-2). Vegetarians beware: there is meat everywhere—cured pig legs dangle from the ceilings, and the window display brims with sausages. Museo del Jamón is reliably packed with both locals and tourists. Fanny packs and cameras are plentiful, but nothing can take away from the satisfaction of this authentic and criminally cheap meal. The upstairs dining room also offers more substantial entrees like paella (€12) and full *raciones* (€10-15) of *jamón* and *queso.*

▶ ♯ Ⓜ Sol. Walk 2 blocks west down C. Mayor. *i* Several locations throughout El Centro. Ⓢ Sit-down menu €10-20. 🕓 Open daily 9am-midnight.

El Anciano Rey de los Vinos   TAPAS $$

C. de Bailén, 19

☎91 559 53 32; www.elancianoreydelosvinos.es

Right across the street from the Catedral de la Almudena, this is a pit stop for an afternoon drink and snack. Founded in 1909, El Anciano Rey de los Vinos is a granddaddy in the world of tapas bars in El Centro. The cafe has fantastic views, particularly from the terrace tables, but keep in mind the noise and bustle from C. de Bailén. While the menu is not particularly inventive, at a certain point beer is beer and chairs are awesome—especially after a long day of museum-going.

▶ ♯ From the Catedral de la Almudena, walk across the C. de Bailén. Ⓢ Tapas €6-13. Beer €2. Wine €3. 🕓 Open daily 10am-midnight.

Cervecería la Plaza   TAPAS $$

Pl. de San Miguel, 3

☎91 548 41 11

If you are looking to avoid the more expensive restaurants in Pl. Mayor, the nearby Cervecería la Plaza is a solid option. Locals

Alterna-Big Mac

If your siesta lasted a little longer than you expected, you may find yourself with a growling stomach and no place to go, as many restaurants close after lunch and re-open at Madrid's notoriously late dinner hour. Rather than heading to the local McDonald's, pick up a local copy of the global Spanish-language newspaper *El Pais*. The entertainment section, *On Madrid,* will have a listing of restaurants in Madrid open "late" (generally after 5pm) for lunch.

and tourists come here to enjoy the simple tapas menu, cheap beer (€2), and pitchers of sangria (€13). With the canopy of trees above and the large canvas umbrellas, Cervecería la Plaza offers one of the best outdoor drinking and dining options in the area, protected from both the sun and the noise of heavy pedestrian traffic in Pl. Mayor.

▶ 🍴 From the Palacio Real, walk down C. Mayor toward Puerta del Sol. Pl. de San Miguel is on the right. ⑤ Entrees and tapas under €10. Beer €3. 🕐 Open daily 7am-midnight.

Faborit   CAFE, FAST FOOD $
C. de Alcalá, 21
www.faborit.com

The Starbucks of Spain (except with richer coffee), Faborit, with its modern furniture and young, cool vibe, is near almost every major tourist sight in Madrid. Their *shakerettes,* or fresh juice mixes, are delicious. Try the orange and strawberry juice mix or go for an iced coffee frappe. If you can't wait for your next meal, grab a dessert or sandwich (€5).

▶ 🍴 Ⓜ Sol. Walk down C. de Alcalá. Faborit is on the left next to Starbucks. *i* Free Wi-Fi at most locations. ⑤ Juices, coffee drinks, desserts, and sandwiches €3-6. 🕐 Open M-Th 7:30am-10pm, F-Sa 7:30am-midnight, Su 7:30am-10pm.

LA LATINA AND LAVAPIÉS

🔖 Almendro 13   SPANISH $$
C. del Almendro, 13
☎91 365 42 52

While many *madrileño* restaurants serve pre-made tapas at

an uncomfortably lukewarm temperature, everything at Almendro 13 is made hot and fresh to order. Everything comes straight from *la plancha* with enough grease to make your heart murmur "thank you." The restaurant is always packed, with most parties snacking on Almendro's specialty, *huevos rotos* (fried eggs served on top of fries with a variety of toppings; €6-9.50). If this feels gluttonous, just remember that when you split something with a friend, there are no calories. The cold gazpacho (€4) and fresh salads (€7-10) are a welcome vacation from the heavier entrees. While many of the *tabernas* in Latina are cramped and crowded, Almendro 13's setting just off the main drag of C. Cava Baja makes for a quiet and pleasant setting.

▶ ✇ Ⓜ Latina. Walk west on Pl. Cebada 1 block, take a right onto C. del Humilladero, walk 1 block to C. del Almendro, and walk up 1 block. Ⓢ Sandwiches, *tortillas,* and salads €6-8. Entrees €6-9. Beer, wine, and vermouth €3. ⏰ Open daily 1-4pm and 7:30pm-12:30am.

▨ Cafe Bar Melo's   BAR, SANDWICHES $

C. Ave María, 44
☎91 527 50 54

This is an institution in Madrid for good reason. Bread, cheese, and meat, cooked together to perfection. What else do you want in life? A wife? A couple of kids? A home to call your own? Cafe Bar Melo's has mastered the art of the grilled *zapatilla* (grilled pork and cheese sandwich; €3) and subsequently has become a favorite destination for both locals and travelers. Don't expect glamorous decor: Cafe Bar Melo's looks something like a hot dog stand at a major league baseball park after seven innings of play: dirty napkins are littered on the ground, the wraparound wooden bar is covered in half empty beer glasses, and the game blasts on the TV in the corner. This is all part of the magic.

▶ ✇ Ⓜ Lavapiés. Walk up C. Ave María 1 block. Ⓢ Sandwiches €2-5. Beer €1-3. ⏰ Open Tu-Sa 9pm-2am.

▨ Taberna de Antonio Sanchez   TABERNA $$

C. del Mesón de Paredes, 13
☎91 539 78 26

Founded in 1830 by legendary bullfighter Antonio Sanchez, this *taberna* has had plenty of time to perfect its tapas. The menu hasn't changed much, with the standby matador-worthy favorites like the *morcilla a las pasas* (black pudding and raisins;

Food

€9). The interior of this restaurant is every bit as famous as the tapas, with walls covered with original murals by the 19th-century Spanish painter Ignacio Zuloaga and victory trophies from 19th-century bullfights. The dark-wooded interior may not be the most cheery place to spend an afternoon, but it is certainly a chance to step back in time. If all this carnage sounds a little much, they also offer traditional dishes like gazpacho (€4), *sopa de ajo* (garlic soup; €4), and plenty of Manchego cheese and *jamón ibérico* to keep you happy.

▶ ⚔ Ⓜ Tirso de Molina. From the Metro, walk past Pl. de Tirso de Molina and take a left onto C. del Mesón de Paredes. The taberna is on the left. Ⓢ Entrees €3-15. ⚅ Open M-Sa noon-4pm and 8pm-midnight, Su noon-4pm.

Nuevo Cafe Barbieri   CAFE $

C. Ave María, 45
☎91 527 36 58

Nuevo Cafe Barbieri is nothing short of grand. The high molded ceilings and large windows give the cafe an open and breezy quality. While this may be Lavapiés's finest traditional cafe, it is also a buzzing nightlife hub on weekends. With its Cadillac-sized espresso machine and fine selection of alcohols, Barbieri specializes in mixed drinks like The Barbieri (coffee, Bailey's, and vanilla ice cream; €7.50).

▶ ⚔ Ⓜ Lavapiés. Walk up C. Ave María 1 block. Ⓢ Desserts €4-7. Coffee drinks €2-5. Tea €2.50. ⚅ Open M-W 4pm-12:30am, Th 4pm-1:30am, F-Su 4pm-2:30am.

Shapla   INDIAN $$

C. de Lavapiés, 42
☎91 528 15 99

As great as Spanish food is, we get it: it gets fussy. The hearty Indian dishes at Shapla are a welcome relief from picking your way through a bowl of olives and pretending to be full. Shapla serves all of the classics that the world has come to love: *saag paneer* (€7), chicken vindaloo (€7), and freshly baked *naan* (€1.50). In true *madrileño* fashion, Shapla offers a *menú del día* (€7) that lets you sample a few traditional appetizers and entrees at a great value. While the indoor dining is cramped and generally filled to capacity, Shapla has plenty of terrace seating on C. de Lavapiés.

▶ ⚔ Ⓜ Lavapiés. Walk uphill on C. de Lavapiés. Ⓢ Meals €8-20. ⚅ Open daily Oct-Aug 10am-1:30am.

San Sapori
CAFE, BAR $

C. Lavapiés, 31

☎91 530 89 96

While many of the restaurants in Madrid look worn and tired, San Sapori tries its best to keep things bright and upbeat. The cappuccino drinks, tea, pastries, and 10 rotating flavors of gourmet gelato make this a worthy after-dinner stop on C. Lavapiés.

▶ ⚇ Ⓜ Lavapiés. Walk uphill on C. Lavapiés. Ⓢ Coffee €2-5. Gelato €3-6. ⏰ Open daily 11am-midnight.

LAS HUERTAS

🖾 Cervecería Los Gatos
TAPAS $$

C. de Jesús, 2

☎91 429 30 62

If you took one of the grandfather tapas bars of Las Huertas and gave it a healthy dose of Viagra, it would look and feel something like Cervecería Los Gatos. Sandwiched between the madness of Las Huertas and the quieter museum district, Los Gatos is a local hangout for young *madrileños* that most tourists haven't yet discovered. Los Gatos may be old, but it still has a sense of humor: the ceiling sports a version of Leonardo da Vinci's *The Creation of Man,* in which Adam gracefully holds a beer. The decor is eclectic, with a crystal chandelier hanging from the ceiling across from an antique motorcycle. If ever there's a place to snack on traditional *raciones,* this is it. Try the *jamón ibérico* (€18), Manchego (€11), or the house special *boquerones en vinagre* (anchovies soaked in olive oil, garlic, and vinegar; €10).

▶ ⚇ Ⓜ Antón Martín. Take C. de Atocha southeast ½ a block to C. de Moratin. Take C. de Moratin 4 blocks east to C. de Jesús. Turn left (heading north) onto C. de Jesús and walk 2 blocks. Ⓢ *Pinchos* €2-4. *Raciones* €8-18. Cash only. ⏰ Open daily 1:30pm-2am.

🖾 La Bardemecilla de Santa Ana
SPANISH $$

C. Núñez de Arce, 3

☎91 521 42 56; www.labardemcilla.com

C. de Augusto Figueroa, 47

If you're wondering what made Javier Bardem the tall, strapping, dazzling Spanish beauty he is today, look no further than La Bardemecilla. The Bardem family restaurant serves only family recipes like *huevos de oro estrellados* (eggs scrambled with *jamón ibérico* and onions; €8.70). With two Madrid locations, Grandma and Grandpa Bardem are getting some long overdue street cred. The food here is traditional, and each dish has a signature touch, like the *chorizo con los días contados* (Spanish sausage cooked in white wine and clove; €9). Just a few blocks from C. de las Huertas, this is a great spot to grab dinner before a big night out.

▶ ⚲ From Pl. de Santa Ana, take C. de Núñez de Arce on the west side of the plaza north toward Puerta del Sol. Follow C. de Núñez de Arce 1 block. The restaurant is on the right just before C. de la Cruz. ⑤ *Pinchos* €2-4. Entrees €8-10. Cash only. ⏰ Open M-F noon-5:30pm and 8pm-2am, Sa 8pm-2am.

Lateral   TAPAS $$

Pl. Santa Ana

☎91 420 15 82; www.cadenalateral.es

Lateral stands apart form the other *cervecerías* on Pl. Santa Ana. If the curators of the Reina Sofía were to make a tapas restaurant, it would look something like this, with its sparse interior, marble bar, and white leather bar stools. The obvious appeal here is that it's located directly on Pl. Santa Ana, but the restaurant delivers much more, with good service, reasonable prices, and a menu full of freshly prepared tapas. Dishes like the lamb crepe (€4.50) and the salmon sashimi with wasabi (€6.50) are a nice break from the traditional oxtails and sweetbreads. While Lateral's menu racks up major points for variety and quality, it doesn't offer substantial entrees, so either order a lot of tapas or have your mother pack you a PB and J.

▶ ⚲ If you face the ME Madrid Reina Victoria Hotel in Pl. Santa Ana, Lateral is on the left. ⑤ Tapas €3-8. Combination platters €10-20. ⏰ Open daily noon-midnight.

If Your Mother Only Knew

Dirty floors may not be the first thing you look for in a restaurant, but in Madrid you may want to give them another shot. It's customary at tapas bars for patrons to throw their trash on the floor after eating to be cleaned up later, and more trash generally means more people have been passing through. So go ahead and toss your garbage—we won't tell your mom.

Casa Alberto
TABERNA $$

C. de las Huertas, 18

☎91 429 93 56; www.casaalberto.es

Founded in 1827, Casa Alberto is one of Madrid's oldest taverns. Once upon a time, bullfighters came here for a "cup of courage" before they entered the bullring. Today it's a tourist favorite and for good reason. The walls are lined with history, with photographs of famous matadors and celebrities who have visited, and the charm hasn't entirely faded. Enter your own bullring of fear by trying tripe: what could be more carnivorous than putting another animal's stomach inside of your stomach? Maybe eating a pig's ear, another dish proudly served here. More popular, less adventurous dishes include Madrid-style veal meatballs, or the house special, *huevos fritos* (fried eggs; €12), served with garlic lamb sweetbreads and roasted potatoes.

▶ ⚥ From Pl. del Ángel, walk down C. de las Huertas toward the Prado. Casa Alberto will be on your right. ⑤ Entrees €5-20. ⏲ Open daily noon-1:30am.

Fatigas del Querer
SPANISH $$

C. de la Cruz, 17

☎91 523 21 31; www.fatigasdelquerer.es

While it doesn't have the institutional status of some of Las Huertas's other tapas bars, Fatigas del Querer still serves great traditional fare. The large open interior is a nice alternative to the cramped elevator-style dining found throughout Madrid. Expect standard, freshly made tapas. The waitstaff is particularly attentive and they keep the turnaround quick. Dishes like the mixed seafood paella (€7) and calamari (€10) are fantastic and won't break the bank, unless, of course, you develop an addiction.

▶ ⚥ From Pl. del Ángel, go north up C. Espoz y Mina and bear right. The street becomes C. de la Cruz. ⑤ Tapas €4-12. Cash only. ⏲ Open M-F 11am-1:30am, Sa-Su 11am-2:30 or 3am. Kitchen open until 1am.

La Finca de Susana Restaurant
MEDITERRANEAN $$

C. de Arlabán, 4

☎91 429 76 78; www.lafinca-restaurant.com

Madrid is not cheap, but La Finca de Susana does its best to offer a gourmet dining experience (think white tablecloths set with silverware and wine glasses) at a reasonable price. Though the look and feel is formal, don't be dismayed: the menu has plenty to offer the budget-conscious. The Mediterranean-inspired menu offers greater variety than you'll find at the traditional *taberna,* with popular dishes like *arroz negro con sepia* (stewed rice with cuttlefish; €11) and *cordera al horno* (roasted lamb; €12). While the setting may feel a bit corporate, the food is far from that: rich in flavor and affordable in price.

▶ ⚓ Ⓜ Sol. Follow C. de Alcalá east and take a right (south) onto C. de Sevilla. Follow C. de Sevilla to C. de Arlabán and take a left (heading east). Ⓢ Entrees €7-16. 🕐 Open M-W 1-3:45pm and 8:30-11:30pm, F-Sa 1-3:45pm and 8:30pm-midnight, Su 1-3:45pm and 8:30-11:30pm.

Il Piccolino della Farfalla   ITALIAN $

C. de las Huertas, 6
☎91 369 43 91

Forget the frou-frou thin crust: this small Italian restaurant serves cheap pizza loaded with cheese and toppings. The obvious choice here is the *pizza a te gusta* (€7.90) served with any two toppings, but staples like the margherita (€6.90) are perfectly satisfying. Split two ways, these pizzas make for a great budget dinner. While Il Piccolino might not be the most authentic Italian food in the city, it is certainly a step up from the pizza-by-the-slice sold throughout Las Huertas. If dessert is in the cards, the Argentine *alfajore* with *dulce de leche* (€4) is gluttonous in the best way possible.

▶ ⚓ From Pl. del Ángel, take C. de las Huertas east (toward the museum district). Il Piccolino della Farfalla is on the right. Ⓢ Salads €5-7. Pizzas and pastas €6-9. Desserts €3-5. Cash only. 🕐 M-Th 1-4:30pm and 8:30pm-2:30am, F-Su 1pm-2:30am.

Viva la Vida   VEGETARIAN $$

C. de las Huertas, 57
☎91 366 33 49

This mini Whole Foods is a treasure in a city of meat. Everything is vegetarian in this boutique grocery, from the health food products that line the walls to the gourmet buffet in the center. All of the prepared food, including vegan pastries and desserts, are priced by weight. Seating is limited beyond the few stools outside, but the prepared food is great for a picnic in the nearby Parque del Retiro.

▶ ⚓ On C. de la Huertas between C. de San Jose and C. del Fucar. Ⓢ Buffet €21 per kg. 🕐 Open daily 11am-midnight.

Green Ears and Ham

Some international dishes can be difficult for the unfamiliar traveler to stomach. And some dishes actually contain stomach. Or spleen, intestine, or ears. *Gallinejas* is a popular dish in Madrid that usually contains various sheep entrails such as the pancreas, small intestine, and stomach. Fried in their own fat and served with french fries, *gallinejas* are a cheap street food and can be a wonderful introduction to *madrileño* cuisine.

If you're still hungry, *orejas a la plancha* ("ears of the pig"), is another tasty fried specialty. Or perhaps you're craving some *callos a la madrileña,* a centuries-old dish of chorizo, blood sausage, and the hoof and snout of a cow.

When you can no longer stand even to look at another piece of meat, head to the health food store **Viva la Vida** in Huertas and serve yourself a lunch from the vegetarian buffet.

Miranda   INTERNATIONAL $$

C. de las Huertas, 29
☎91 369 10 25

Miranda's burgers, burritos, salads, and other staples make it one of the best budget international menus in the area. While they offer typical bar snacks, items like the Cajun burrito with guacamole (€9.50) or the French burger with chèvre and caramelized onions (€10) are hard to come by in Madrid. While Miranda buzzes through the night, it is particularly popular among travelers for its hearty breakfast menu. The English Breakfast (coffee or juice, eggs, bacon, and toast; €5) is a good alternative to the meager complimentary breakfast at your hostel, and the full brunch (€12 per person) is a major quality-of-life enhancement: fresh orange juice, coffee, eggs, *raciones* of *jamón* and *queso,* and pastries. The walls, covered with portraits of international figures like Jimi Hendrix, Martin Luther King, Jr., and a silver-encrusted statue of the Buddha hammer home the international theme.

▶ ⚥ From Pl. de Santa Ana walk down C. de las Huertas toward the museum district. Miranda is on the left. ⑤ Breakfast €4-12. Entrees €8-12. ⌚ Open daily 8am-2am.

La Soberbia   TAPAS $$

C. Espoz y Mina, 1
☎91 531 05 76; www.lasoberbia.es

La Soberbia has struck the happy medium between cramped

Food

hole in the wall and expansive contemporary tapas bar. It isn't known for a chic interior or an ironic theme, just for well-priced traditional dishes like paella (€7) and better-than-average *tostados* served on warm baguette (€3-4).

▶ ⚒ From Pl. de Santa Ana head North on C. Espoz y Mina toward Puerta del Sol. ⑤ Entrees €4-12. Cash only. ⏰ Open M-W 9am-1:30am, Th-Sa 9am-2:30am, Su 10am-1:30am.

Giuseppe Ricci Gelato and Caffé   GELATO $

C. de las Huertas, 9

☎91 429 33 45; www.heladeriaricci.com

This is the best gelato in the area. What better way to enjoy a walk through Las Huertas than with a fistful of calories? Giuseppe Ricci has dozens of flavors. Seasonal fruit flavors like melon and fig are the specialty, but staples like chocolate and hazelnut are hard to beat. They pack plenty of gelato into the small (€2.20) and are very supportive of flavor pairings.

▶ ⚒ Walk down C. de las Huertas from Pl. del Ángel. Giuseppe Ricci will be immediately on the left. ⑤ Small €2.20; medium €2.70; large €3.20. Cash only. ⏰ Open daily 12:30pm-1:30am.

Cafeteria Marazul   SPANISH $

Pl. del Ángel, 11

☎91 369 19 43

Las Huertas is loaded with places that try really hard; Cafeteria Marazul doesn't seem to give a damn and it's all the better for it. This is a typical *madrileño* cafeteria filled with typical *madrileños* in one of the city's most tourist-heavy plazas. Staples like *patatas bravas* (€6) and *bocadillos* (€4-5) are of standard quality and are served on banged-up steel plates. This is also a great place to pick up a quick-and-dirty breakfast. The Marazul breakfast (€2.40) includes coffee and a plateful of *churros*.

Free Tapas

Don't pull out your wallet just yet. Many bars in Madrid will serve you a tapas plate with each drink order at no extra charge. Whether it's olives and cheese or scrambled eggs and sausage, these appetizer-sized portions are a Spanish tradition. Order enough beers and you may even be able to skip dinner and save a few euro for tomorrow night!

Food

Sometimes you need to take off your fancy pants, tame that bougie beast inside of you, and go to a no-nonsense joint like Cafeteria Marazul.

▶ � ⓜ Antón Martín. From the Metro, walk right down C. de Atocha, and make a right onto C. del Olivar. Walk until you see Pl. del Ángel on your left, just before Pl. de Santa Ana. *i* Expect to be charged extra for terrace seating. Ⓢ Meals €4-10. ⏰ Open daily 6:30am-3am.

El Inti de Oro   PERUVIAN $$

C. Amour de Dios, 9

☎91 429 19 58; www.intideoro.com

While plenty of people have tried ceviche in swank gourmet restaurants, few have had authentic Peruvian cuisine. El Inti de Oro is a good place to start, with a menu that is faithful to traditional recipes, using plenty of cilantro, fresh onion, lime, and pepper. Most stick to what they know on the menu, choosing from the selection of ceviches (seafood cooked in lime juice; €11-13), but the waitstaff is very helpful in suggesting other traditional dishes like *arroz con pato norteno* (duck garnished with cilantro, served with rice; €11), or the *seco de corder* (lamb stew; €13). More daring visitors might consider Peruvian cocktails (€4-6), which use the traditional sweet brandy *pisco* mixed with lemon, sugar, and cream. If you're up for dessert, try the homemade fresh fruit gelato (€4.50).

▶ � ⓜ Antón Martín. Steps from the Metro, down C. del Amor de Dios. Ⓢ Entrees €5-15. ⏰ Open daily 1pm-midnight.

El Basha   MIDDLE EASTERN $

C. de las Huertas, 59

☎91 429 96 10; www.restauranteelbasha.com

El Basha is a tea room, hookah lounge, and Middle Eastern restaurant packed into a single room along C. de las Huertas. Like most Middle Eastern restaurants across town, El Basha sticks to the basics, like kebabs (€4) and falafel (€5), but they also offer full platters of hummus (€5) and *baba ghanoush* (€5). While the interior might seem a bit gloomy for lunch on a bright sunny day, this is a great hangout in the later hours of the evening.

▶ ✤ Between C. de San José and C. del Fúcar. *i* Belly dancing Sa. Ⓢ Loose leaf tea €2.50. Hookah €8. ⏰ Open M-Th 3pm-1:30am, F-Sa 3pm-2:30am, Su 3pm-1:30am.

Food

La Negra Tomasa

CUBAN $$

C. de Cádiz, 9

☎91 523 58 30; www.lanegratomasa.es

La Negra Tomasa is a signature traveler and study-abroad hangout, for better or for worse. Everything at this Cuban restaurant is huge, from the heaping portions of traditional fare to the tall mixed drinks. Live Cuban music dominates the scene as middle-aged couples try to feel young again. Waitresses inside are dressed in colorful traditional garb, and the nighttime bouncer outside is dressed in traditional bouncer attire (head to toe in black). Try one of the main dishes like the *ropa vieja habanera* (shredded flank steak, black beans, and rice; €8-12) or *para picar* (tiny appetizers to share; €3-7).

▶ ⚑ From Puerta del Sol, walk south down C. de Espoz y Mina; the restaurant is on the right. ⑤ Entrees €8-12. Cover €10 after 11:30pm. ② Open M-Th noon-3:30am, F-Sa noon-5:30am, Su noon-3:30am.

AVENIDA DEL ARTE

El Brillante

TAPAS $

Pl. Emperador Carlos V, 8

☎91 539 28 06

El Brillante provides quality budget eating in pricey Avenida del Arte. While its claims to have the best *bocadillo de calamares* (fried calamari sandwich; €6) in Madrid have not been substantiated, patrons don't seem to care, and they order the sandwich in abundance. If nothing else, the sandwich is as cheap and flavorful as anything in the immediate area, with the calamari piping hot from the deep-fryer. The restaurant has indoor bar seating and outdoor terrace seating near the Reina Sofía.

▶ ⚑ Ⓜ Atocha. ⑤ Sandwiches €4-8. Cash only. ② Open daily 9am-1am.

La Plateria del Museo

TAPAS $$

C. de las Huertas, 82

☎91 429 17 22

This upscale tapas bar has some of the best terrace seating along Paseo del Prado. They offer plenty of staples such as *gazpacho andaluz* (€4.50) and *croqueta de jamon* (€3) that are perfect as a post-museum snack. While entrees and daily specials are generally pricey, regular tapas and refreshments come at a standard price. More than anything, La Plateria del Museo stands out for its exceptional terrace and proximity to the three museums of Avenida del Arte. The wine selection changes daily but the sangria (€3.50) and cocktails (€5) stay the same.

▶ ✠ Ⓜ Atocha. From the Metro, follow Paseo del Prado 2 blocks and turn left onto C. de las Huertas. Ⓢ Appetizers €2.50-8; entrees €8-14. Drinks €2-6. ⏰ Open daily 9am-2am.

GRAN VÍA

▩ [H]arina   CAFE $$

Pl. de la Independencia, 10

☎91 522 87 85; www.harinamadrid.com

[H]arina stands out among the many cafes throughout Madrid that feel old and tired. It is one of those places where you will magically feel great after eating a big meal. The menu is made up of all the foods that you likely know and love—fresh salads, sandwiches, and paper-thin-crust pizzas—and the environment is hard to beat. The whitewashed wooden interior makes for a pleasant cafe setting, but the terrace seating overlooking Pl. de la Independencia stands out. Indoor and outdoor seating are both generally packed, particularly on weekends, and many patrons take their food to go from the bakery. The house special lemonade (€3) is made with fresh lemon juice and crushed mint leaves, and keeps people coming back.

▶ ✠ Ⓜ Banco de España. Walk 1 block east to Pl. de la Independencia; the restaurant is on the southwest corner. Ⓢ Salads €8. Sandwiches €6. Pizzas €9-11. *i* Terrace seating extra €1. ⏰ Open daily 9am-9pm.

Pizzería Casavostra   ITALIAN $$

C. de las Infantas, 13

☎91 523 22 07; www.pizzacasavostra.com

Everything on Casavostra's menu is fresh—from the brick-oven pizzas to the traditional appetizers. While many of the restaurants between Gran Vía and Chueca try hard to break out of the tapas mold, Casovostra keeps things simple with a traditional Italian menu. The pizzas (€8.50-14) are fired in the brick oven and topped with ingredients like arugula, fresh mozzarella, and cherry tomatoes. The appetizer salads come in huge portions and are great to share for a first round (€5-10). They also offer a full selection of superb *burrata* (unpasteurized mozzarella) appetizers.

▶ ✠ Ⓜ Gran Vía. Walk east 1 block to C. de Hortaleza and then 2 blocks

I Smell a Rat

The classic Spanish rice dish, paella (the Catalan word for "pan") is traditionally cooked and served in a round shallow pan sometimes also called a *paellera*. In the 18th century, Valencian peasants cooked rice over open-air flames, adding whatever protein they could find. Marsh rat and snail rats were common ingredients, while fishermen added eel, dried cod, and other fish. By the end of the 19th century, living standards had risen and other meats like chicken and rabbit became more common. Today, there are several different styles of paella, including the traditional *paella valenciana* made with chicken or pork, *paella marisco* made with seafood, *paella negra* cooked in squid ink, and even *paella fideus* made with noodles instead of rice. In October 2001, Valencian restaurateur Juan Galbis made what he claims is the world's largest ever paella, feeding approximately 110,000 people.

north to C. de la Infantas. Ⓢ Appetizers €4-12; entrees €7-15. Drinks €2-4. 🕘 Open daily 1:30-4pm and 10pm-midnight.

El Bocaito   TAPAS $$

C. de la Libertad, 6
☎91 521 31 98; www.bocaito.com

Ever since Spain's best-known filmmaker, Pedro Almodóvar, cited El Bocaito as one of his favorites in Madrid, it has been all the rage. El Bocaito is as traditional as tapas bars get, from the matador paraphernalia on the walls to the platters of *pinchos*. El Bocaito sticks to tradition and does it well. Its back-to-back bars and four small dining rooms in back are filled nightly with a mix of locals and tourists. While drinks (€2-4) and tapas (€2-5) won't cost much, a full sit-down dinner with a bottle of wine and entrees (€12-20) makes for a pretty expensive meal.

▶ ✦ Ⓜ Gran Vía. Walk east 1 block to C. de Hortaleza, 2 blocks north to C. de la Infantas, and then follow C. de las Infantas 4 blocks west to C. de la Libertad. Ⓢ Appetizers €2-5; entrees €10-20. 🕘 Open Sept-June M-F 1-4:30pm and 8:30pm-midnight, Sa 8:30pm-midnight.

Mercado de la Reina   TAPAS $$

C. Gran Vía, 12
☎91 521 31 98; www.mercadodelareina.es

Mercado de la Reina is one of the few exciting restaurants amid the dearth of options on C. Gran Vía. While the bar snacks are the standard pre-made *pinchos* (€2.50-5) you find elsewhere, the full dinner menu has some great options, including a winning gourmet burger served with a fried-egg (€12). The tables in the back dining area are a bit more quiet and civil than the swarm up front.

▶ ⚡ Ⓜ Gran Vía. Walk east down C. Gran Vía; the restaurant is on the right. Ⓢ Entrees €10-20. ⏰ Open M-Th 9am-midnight, Sa-Su 10am-1am.

Restaurante la Alhambra de Santo Domingo
MEDITERRANEAN $$

C. de Jacometrezo, 15
☎91 548 43 31

It's hard to mess up your order at this cheap kebab joint. The menu is full of variety and will please vegetarians and carnivores alike. The kebab platters, salads, and sandwiches are as good as you will find at any fast food Mediterranean joint in Madrid. The lunch special (pita wrap, fries, and drink; €6) is budget-friendly and satisfying.

▶ ⚡ Ⓜ Callao. Walk east down C. de Jacometrezo; the restaurant is on the left. Ⓢ Salads €8. Sandwiches €5. Kebab platters €10.

CHUECA

▧ Mercado de San Antón
MARKET $$

C. de Augusto Figueroa, 24
☎91 330 07 30; www.mercadosananton.com

This is Europe's fierce rebuttal to Whole Foods. What was once an open-air market in the middle of Chueca is now a state-of-the-art building filled with fresh produce vendors, *charcuteriás,* bodegas, and a rooftop restaurant. Along with Mercado de San Miguel, this is a terrific place to get a sweeping tour of Spain's culinary landscape, from traditional delicacies to international fare. Prices might be a bit steep, but, much like at Whole Foods, you can easily sample your way through a meal by visiting a few different shops.

▶ ⚡ Ⓜ Chueca. On the southern end of Pl. de Chueca. ℹ For the rooftop terrace, make reservations in advance at ☎91 330 02 94. Visit www.lacocinadesananton.com for more info on the restaurant. Ⓢ Varies greatly, but a full meal at the market costs around €10. Cash only. ⏰ 1st fl. market open M-Sa 10am-10pm. 2nd fl. restaurants and bars open Tu-Su 10am-midnight. Rooftop restaurant open M-Th 10am-midnight, F-Sa 10am-1:30am, Su 10am-midnight.

▨ San Wish
CHILEAN, SANDWICHES $$

C. de Hortaleza, 78

☎91 319 17 76; www.san-wish.com

San Wish is a novelty bar and restaurant that looks like it will actually make it in Chueca. The power of their picture menu is magnetic, displaying a lineup of greasy, crispy traditional Chilean sandwiches like the *hamburguesa voladora* (chicken, tomato, lettuce, grilled cucumbers, melon chutney; €6.50) and the *clásica* (grilled steak, sweet pickle, tomato, and lettuce; €6.50). The list goes on, but, true to their name, they don't offer much that doesn't belong between two pieces of bread. This is as trendy as fast food gets, with all sandwiches made on pressed Chilean bread and served alongside traditional cocktails like the Pisco Sour (grape brandy, lemon juice, egg white, syrup, and bitter herbs; €4.50). The young and wealthy *madrileño* crowd can't seem to get enough of it. Seats are nearly impossible to snag, especially during peak weekend hours.

▶ ✦ Ⓜ Chueca. Take C. de Gravina 2 blocks east and turn right onto C. de Hortaleza. The restaurant is on the right. Ⓢ Sandwiches €5.50-8.90. Beer €1.50-3.50. Wine €2.50. Cash only. Ⓩ Open M 8pm-midnight, Tu-Sa 1-4pm and 8pm-midnight, Su 1:30-4pm.

Bazaar
MEDITERRANEAN $$

C. de la Libertad, 21

☎91 523 39 05; www.restaurantbazaar.com

You would expect this restaurant to be prohibitively expensive, but, somehow, it isn't. The expansive two-story restaurant has the look and feel of a high-end place with white tablecloths and wine glasses waiting on the table, but they offer something completely different than dinky *pinchos* and lukewarm a la carte dishes with a menu of fresh pasta (think fettucine with grilled chicken and sundried tomatoes; €7), salads, and meat dishes, with almost everything falling below the €10 mark. The upstairs and downstairs dining rooms are quite large, but partitioned into smaller, more intimate spaces by shelves filled with artisanal food displays. While the food is not necessarily daring, it is fresh, comes in great portions, and can be enjoyed in a relaxed but formal setting.

▶ ✦ Ⓜ Chueca. Make a left onto C. de Augusto Figueroa and a right onto C. de la Libertad. Ⓢ Entrees €7-10. Ⓩ Open M-W 1:15-4pm and 8:30-11:30pm, Th-Sa 1:15-4pm and 8:30-midnight, Su 1:15-4pm and 8:30-11:30pm.

Lo Siguiente
TAPAS $$

C. de Fernando VI, 11

☎91 319 52 61; www.losiguiente.es

With high bar tables, metal stools, and silver columns, Lo Siguiente has the feel of both a traditional tapas bar and a modern Chueca restaurant. While it may have a cool, polished aesthetic, Lo Siguiente is still an informal restaurant that *madrileños* enjoy for precisely that reason. You can get all of the staples like the classic *huevos rotos* (a fried egg over pan-fried potatoes, garlic, and chorizo; €9.50), but but don't be afraid to try the lighter Mediterranean items like tomato and avocado salad and ceviche served atop grilled vegetables. While the food and decor may be slightly more contemporary, the feel of the restaurant is that of a neighborhood *taberna,* with the standard crowd of smirters (smokers and flirters) out front.

▶ ✦ Ⓜ Chueca. Head 2 blocks northeast on C. de San Gregario and take a left onto C. de Fernando VI. Lo Siguiente is on the right. Ⓢ Meals €10-15. Cash only. ⏲ Open M-Th 8:30am-1:30am, F-Sa 8:30am-2:30am, Su 8:30am-1:30am.

Magasand
CAFE, SMOOTHIES $$

Travesía de San Mateo, 16

☎91 319 68 25; www.magasand.com

True to its motto, this place serves "incredible sandwiches" and "impossible magazines." The long list of gourmet sandwiches makes the traditional *bocadillo* pale in embarrassment and inadequacy, and the upstairs dining area/library has every pretentious magazine you could imagine. All of the sandwiches are served on fresh bread, with greens, fancy condiments, and a wide selection of meat beyond *jamón.* For a bougie afternoon, order the *el rollito de Luisa* (tuna carpaccio, arugula, and bread pressed with tomatoes; €4), and then pick up the latest edition of *Monocle* upstairs. Magasand also serves fresh salads and a spectacular Saturday brunch (a selection of fresh-fruit smoothies, coffee, pastries, fried eggs, sandwiches, and crepes; €16).

▶ ✦ Ⓜ Chueca. Make a right onto C. de Augusto Figueroa, and another right onto C. de Hortaleza. Turn right onto Travesía de San Mateo (a sign on C. de Hortaleza points you in the right direction). Ⓢ Sandwiches €5-8. Salads €4-7. ⏲ Open M-F 9:30am-10pm, Sa noon-5pm.

Il Pizzaiolo
ITALIAN $$

C. de Hortaleza, 84

☎91 319 29 64; www.pizzaiolo.es

The appeal of Il Pizzaiolo is pretty clear: it's the cheap gourmet pizzas, made to order and baked super thin. The menu is full of simple crowd-pleasers, including Italian salads, antipasti, pizza, and pasta. The brightly painted murals of Italian landmarks on the walls are an afterthought. The *diavola* (tomato, mozzarella, spicy chorizo; €9.90) is a favorite on the long list.

▶ ⚶ Ⓜ Chueca. Make a right on C. de Gravina and a right on C. de Hortaleza. The restaurant is on the right. Ⓢ Pizzas €8-10. 🕖 Open M-Th 1:30pm-midnight, F-Sa 1:30pm-12:30am.

Stop Madrid   TABERNA $$
C. de Hortaleza, 11
☎91 521 88 87; www.stopmadrid.es

Founded in 1929, this old-school tapas bar is one of the best in Chueca. *Taberna* fare like *raciones* of *queso, jamón ibérico,* and seafood are of exceptional quality. They serve only *Ibérico de la Belota* (€21), the best quality *jamón* in the world, and the cured Manchego (€10) is richer than most versions in Madrid. But what really sets Stop Madrid apart is its extensive wine list. All of its dozens of wines are available by the glass. For better or worse, this old *taberna* feels a bit out of place in Chueca's clutter of posh cafes and shops selling "XXXleatherXXX."

▶ ⚶ Ⓜ Gran Vía. Walk up C. de Hortaleza. Ⓢ Entrees €5-10. 🕖 Open daily noon-2am.

Restaurant Vivares   SPANISH $$
C. de Hortaleza, 52
☎91 531 58 13; www.restaurantesvivares.com

Restaurant Vivares may be the best meal in Chueca. The interior of the restaurant is unassuming, with a typical bar up front and tables in back, but during peak hours it's packed with locals. While the traditional tapas of stewed and grilled meats are very popular, we also like the burgers: try the classic (with bacon, fried egg and cheddar; €7) or the chicken burger (with cheddar, lettuce, and tomato; €7). They not only offer a *menú del día* (entree, drink, bread, and dessert; €12), but they also offer a *menú de la noche* (burger, drink, bread, and dessert; €9.60). There's no gimmick here, no catchy decor or fancy menu items, but the nightly crowds don't seem to mind. For a more contemporary menu of salads, pasta, and vegetarian options, they have recently opened an annex restaurant, **Vivares 37,** across the street.

▶ ⚶ Ⓜ Chueca. Head 1 block south on C. de Pelayo, make a right onto C. de Augusto Figueroa, and left onto C. de Hortaleza. Ⓢ Entrees €5-12. 🕖 Open daily 12:30-5:30pm and 8:30pm-1:30am.

Diurno

CAFE, VIDEO RENTAL $

C. de San Marcos, 37

☎91 522 00 09; www.diurno.com

This combination cafe, gourmet shop, and DVD store is something of a novelty. At last, Spaniards seem to have figured out that eating a sandwich (try the chicken with pesto and mozzarella; €2.30) is that much better when you get the added pleasure of unwrapping it like a present. Diurno is open through the day for sandwiches and fresh smoothies (€2.50) and serves cocktails (€2-5) in the evening. Browse the DVD rentals on the way out.

▶ ✦ Ⓜ Chueca. Make a left onto C. de Augusto Figueroa and a right onto C. de la Libertad. Diurno is across from Bazaar. Ⓢ Salads €5-7. Sandwiches €2-4. Pasta €5-7. Coffee €1-2. Cocktails €2-5. ⏰ Open M-Th 10am-noon, F-Sa 10am-1am, Su 11am-midnight.

Cocina del Desierto

MIDDLE EASTERN $$

C. Barbieri, 1

☎91 523 11 42

Cocina del Desierto is a cave accessible by a rickety wooden door on C. Barbieri. Like many Middle Eastern restaurants, they use an assemblage of cushions, tapestries, and lanterns to evoke some distant vaguely Middle Eastern land. Are we in Morocco? Israel? Iran? We're not sure exactly sure, but the food is great, and far better than what you'll get in touristy hookah lounges. In addition to staples like hummus, tabouleh, and *baba ghanoush* (€4.20), Cocina Del Desierto offers specialty couscous dishes like lamb and grilled vegetables (€8.50). The *tayin de cordero con circuelas* (lamb stewed with plums; €7.80) is another clear winner. Dishes are served with fresh lemon, parsley, chopped onion, and other Middle Eastern garnishes. If you are looking for wine, the €7.80 bottle of house wine is a pretty great way to start off a long evening.

▶ ✦ Ⓜ Chueca. From the Pl. de Chueca, follow C. Barbieri south 3 blocks. The restaurant is on the right across from the restaurant Empatbelas. Ⓢ Entrees €4-10. Cash only. ⏰ Open daily 1:30-4pm and 9:30pm-midnight.

Labonata

ICE CREAM $

Pl. de Chueca, 8

☎91 523 70 29; www.labonata.eu

If you are going to get ice cream or dessert in Chueca, this is the place to do it. Labonata sells 22 flavors of homemade Italian gelato that will make you feel better about yourself and the world, while padding your hips in preparation for a long winter. The best flavors are the simple ones like vanilla, coffee, and chocolate, or the fresh fruit flavors like strawberry, banana, and coconut. They also make mean smoothies and milkshakes.

▶ ✢ Ⓜ Chueca. On the east side of Pl. de Chueca. Ⓢ Ice cream €2.80-3.90. Smoothies €3.90-4.50. Shakes €3.30-4. Cash only. 🕐 Open daily noon-2am.

MALASAÑA

🔳 La Dominga   TABERNA $$

C. del Espíritu Santo, 15

☎91 523 38 09; www.ladominga.com

Now with two locations (one in Chueca, one in Malasaña), La Dominga is making a name for itself as one of the best family-run *tabernas* in Madrid. Known primarily for traditional dishes like *rabo de toro* (oxtail stew; €14), it also caters to a younger clientele with plenty of contemporary dishes. Dishes like the beef carpaccio (served with parmesan and arugula; €13) are more refined than the heavier stewed and grilled meats that dominate traditional Spanish cuisine. The decor here is equally mixed, with high ceilings that make it feel more like a modern Malasaña restaurant than an old-time *taberna*. Reservations are a must for prime weekend nights (10pm-1am), but many choose to forgo the sit-down menu in favor of the tapas, which include a platter of *croquettas* (fried stuffed bread; €9.70) that critics have called the best in the city.

▶ ✢ Ⓜ Tribunal. Go west on C. de San Vincente Ferrer, make a left onto C. del Barco, and make a right onto C. del Espíritu Santo. Ⓢ Entrees €10-15. 🕐 Open daily 1-4:30pm and 8:30pm-midnight.

🔳 Lamucca   INTERNATIONAL $

Pl. Carlos Carbonero, 4

☎91 521 00 00; www.lamucca.es

Lamucca covers the globe on its menu, and it does it quite well. While appetizers like cheese fondue and "Nachos de le Tek" might raise some eyebrows, these along with many other international dishes at Lamucca are executed with great sophistication. Dishes like Thai curried chicken with jasmine rice (€11) share the menu with Italian pizza and pasta as well as contemporary Spanish dishes like beef carpaccio (€13). Lamucca has certainly stuck to the trends with exposed brick, mismatched furniture,

Food

and chalkboard menus, but, the food here is daring and covers plenty of terrain (from Texas to Switzerland). With a loyal nightly following, Lamucca is well on the way to becoming a neighborhood institution.

▶ ⚡ Ⓜ Tribunal. Head south on C. de Fuencarral a few meters and take a right (west) onto C. de la Palma, then turn left on C. de San Pablo and follow for 2 blocks. Take a right on C. de Don Felipe and a quick left onto C. del Molino de Viento. Follow C. del Molino de Viento until you reach Pl. Carlos Carbonero. The restaurant is on the right. Ⓢ Appetizers €5-12; entrees €12-20. Pizza €10-15. Cash only. 🕐 Open Tu-F 1:30pm-2am, Sa-Su 12:30pm-2:30am.

Home Burger Bar
BURGERS $$

C. del Espíritu Santo, 12
☎91 522 97 28; www.homeburgerbar.com
Other locations: C. San Marcos, 25 and C. Silva, 25

Home Burger Bar is one of many restaurants catching on to the fancy burger craze. This retro diner has dimly lit brown leather booths, plays American doo-wop and soul, and serves American-style burgers with fries. Portions here are large, but the emphasis is on quality, and all the meat is organic. Burgers come either classic (with lettuce and tomato) or dressed up with add-ons like thick-cut bacon, cheddar, avocado, and spinach. They also serve a number of grilled chicken and vegetable club sandwiches, including a hugely popular *hamburguesa caprese* (sun-dried tomatoes, parmesan, and arugula; €14).

▶ ⚡ Ⓜ Tribunal. Go west on C. de San Vincente Ferrer, make a left onto C. del Barco, and make a right onto C. del Espíritu Santo. Ⓢ Burgers €10-13. Sandwiches €8-15. 🕐 Open M-Sa 1:30-4pm and 8:30pm-midnight, Su 1-4pm and 8:30-11pm.

Café Mahón
INTERNATIONAL $$

Pl. del 2 de Mayo, 4
☎91 448 90 02

With a combination of international favorites, Mediterranean-inspired salads, and traditional entrees, Café Mahón is a great budget option on Malasaña's most tranquil plaza. Brightly colored metal chairs and odd tables make for a kooky setup, and the menu of international comfort foods is equally eclectic. Try the nachos with cheese and guacamole (€7), the hummus appetizer (€6), or the moussaka (€8). A menu of specialty teas (€2-3.50) and coffees keeps people coming throughout the day to enjoy the beautiful terrace seating (next to the local jungle gym), and the bar inside gets active post-dinner with locals enjoying cocktails and *chupitos* (shots; €3-4).

▶ ✚ Ⓜ Tribunal. Head west on C. de la Palma 2 blocks west to to C. de San Andrés, take a right and follow until you reach the plaza. Café Mahón is at the northeast corner. Ⓢ Salads €7. Appetizers €6-9; entrees €7-12. ⏰ Open daily July-Aug 3pm-2am; Sept-June noon-2am. Terrace open daily July-Aug 3pm-1am; Sept-June noon-1am.

Suck it Up

With Chupa Chups, Spain's most popular lollipops! The brand was invented in 1958 by Spaniard Eric Bernat and since then the lollipops have been loved by Spaniards—and Spice Girls—the world over. These suckers (*chupar* means "to suck") boast quite the Surrealist logo, designed by artist Salvador Dalí in 1969. So next time you get a boo-boo in Madrid, buy yourself a Chupa Chups and suck it up.

Banzai
JAPANESE $$

C. del Espíritu Santo, 16
☎91 521 70 81

Banzai is clearly a Malasaña take on Japanese food, with 1950s bebop playing in the background and rolls named after great American cities. Really? Albequerque? Whatever—the hip picturebook menu with black etchings of all the dishes reveals great variety beyond standard sushi (€9-11). Dishes like the ground *ibérico* burger (marinated in wasabi; €8.50) are unmistakably of Spanish influence, but they also have a selection of miso soups (€5), *gyoza* (dumplings; €7.50-9.50) and sautees (€6-13). While it's easy to rack up a big bill at Banzai, the generous *menú del día* (sushi, salads, and hot appetizers; €11) is a steal.

▶ ✚ Ⓜ Tribunal. Go west on C. de San Vincente Ferrer, make a left onto C. del Barco, and make a right onto C. del Espíritu Santo. Ⓢ Meals €10-20. ⏰ Open Tu-Su 1-4:30pm and 8:30pm-midnight.

El Rincón
CAFE $$

C. del Espíritu Santo, 26
☎91 522 19 86

El Rincón seems like a perfect caricature of bohemian Malasaña with its mismatched decor, baby-blue walls, and chalkboard menu. In truth, it's a thoughtfully put-together cafe, from the simple five-item menu to the tasteful interior. With basic wooden tables and small Asian prints on the walls, the decor is sparse compared to the kitschy messes throughout the neighborhood. The large awning shades the terrace seating, which is one of the prime people-watching spots in Malasaña, thanks to its location on the edge of the plaza.

▶ ♯ Ⓜ Tribunal. Go west on C. de San Vincente Ferrer, make a left onto C. del Barco, and make a right onto C. del Espíritu Santo. Ⓢ Sandwiches €5. Entrees €10. Cocktails €5-7. Wine €2.50. Coffee €2-3. Ⓧ Open daily 11am-2am.

Lolina Vintage Café   CAFE $

C. del Espíritu Santo, 9

☎66 720 11 69; www.lolinacafe.com

Filled with '50s memorabilia like album covers and movie stills, mismatched armchairs, and vintage lamps, Lolina looks like it was assembled from a shopping spree at a Brooklyn thrift store, but it fits perfectly in trendy Malasaña. The intimate space attracts people at all times of day, whether for morning tea or late-night cocktails. The food offerings are limited, with a selection of salads (€8), bratwurst sandwiches (€5), and open faced *tostas* like the Sobrasada (sausage, brie, and honey; €4). These dishes are simple, satisfying, and good for those who don't want to leave Malasaña with empty wallets.

▶ ♯ Ⓜ Tribunal. Go west on C. de San Vincente Ferrer, make a left onto C. del Barco, then make a right onto C. del Espíritu Santo. Ⓢ Salads €8. Cocktails €6. Coffee and tea €2-5. Ⓧ Open M-Tu 9:30am-1am, W-Th 9:30am-2am, F-Sa 9:30am-2:30am, Su 9:30-1am.

Olokun   CUBAN $$

C. de Fuencarral, 105

☎91 445 69 16

Olokun might not have the quirky decor and garage-sale aesthetic of its Malasaña neighbors, but it has its own appeal with a menu of hearty Cuban dishes. While plenty of restaurants in the neighborhood try to fake different kinds of international cuisine, everything is actually Cuban at Olokun, right down to the dark mojito (made with black rum; €7). Traditional platters like Mi Vieja Havana (pork, fried plantains, black beans; €14) and *soroa* (chili, fried plantains, rice; €15) all come in large portions. With dark walls covered in the etched signatures of customers and a foosball table in the basement, it's pretty clear that Olokun doesn't take itself quite as seriously as many

Malasaña restaurants, bars, and cafes. Sometimes that's a really good thing.

▶ ✇ Ⓜ Tribunal. Walk north up C. de Fuencarral. The restaurant is on the left. Ⓢ Entrees €10-15. ⏰ Open daily noon-5pm and 9pm-2am.

Happy Day   BAKERY $
C. del Espíritu Santo, 11
☎66 720 11 69

Andy Warhol would be proud. With walls of Pepperidge Farm Cookies, Betty Crocker Cake Mix, Aunt Jemima Syrup, and Goober Peanut Butter, this is much more than an American bakery—it's a museum of America's best traditions. (Try not to confuse it with the neighboring store, Sad Day, which sells polluted water, handguns, and junk mortgages). While the cupcakes (€2), muffins (€2), and slices of cake (€3) all look great, what are more intriguing are the overpriced American imports, including bags of marshmallows (€4.50). This is definitely a novelty experience, but they do offer a good selection of American desserts and Spanish gelato.

▶ ✇ Ⓜ Tribunal. Go west on C. de San Vincente Ferrer, then make a left onto C. del Barco and a right on C. del Espíritu Santo. Ⓢ Pastries €2-4. Ice cream €2-3. Packaged goods €2-6. ⏰ Open daily 9am-11:30pm.

Creperie La Rue   CREPERIE $
C. del Espíritu Santo, 18
☎91 189 70 87

Creperie La Rue's small shop is filled with murals of Parisian street scenes, French music, and, most importantly, the aroma of crepes. Sweet and savory offerings here are fairly standard for a small creperie: goat cheese and grilled vegetables, *jamón* and Emmental, and sweet crepes like the *limon cointreau* (lemon, liqueur, and cinnamon) and chocolate and orange. Sweet crepes are large enough to share as a dessert, and savory crepes make a good late-night fix. All crepes are served on paper plates, as there are only a few seats in shop.

▶ ✇ Ⓜ Tribunal. Go west on C. de San Vincente Ferrer, make a left onto C. del Barco, and make a right onto C. del Espíritu Santo. Ⓢ Crepes €4-8. ⏰ Open daily 11:30am-midnight.

La Vita è Bella   ITALIAN $
Pl. de San Ildefonso, 5
☎91 521 41 08; www.lavitaebella.com.es

La Vita è Bella looks and feels like a college-town pizza joint.

With limited seating, most people order cheap and greasy Sicilian-style pizza by the slice (€2.50) or the calzones (ham, mozzarella, and mushroom; €3.50). This joint also bakes personal thin-crust pizzas made to order like the Malasaña (tomato, mozzarella, bacon, egg, and parmesan; €8.50) and the La Vita è Bella (tomato, buffalo mozzarella, and basil; €8.50). While the slices are fine for a quick fix, the personal pizzas are a bit more authentic and still a solid budget option.

▶ ♯ Ⓜ Tribunal. Go west on C. de San Vincente Ferrer, make a left onto C. del Barco, and make a right onto C. del Espíritu Santo. Ⓢ Entrees €2.50-5. ⓩ Open daily noon-2am.

ARGÜELLES AND MONCLOA

📖 La Taberna de Liria   SPANISH $$$
C. del Duque de Liria, 9
☎91 541 45 19; www.latabernadeliria.com

Most of the items on the menu of Taberna de Liria have been staples for years. Head Chef Miguel Lopez Castanier is an authority on traditional Mediterranean cuisine, and has led Taberna de Liria through a very successful 22 years in Madrid and published a cookbook. Dishes are simple and sophisticated, and the house specialty is the menu of foie gras appetizers (€11-14). While this is not a budget restaurant, it offers excellent food and a romantic setting for a special night in Madrid. Call ahead to make reservations, particularly on weekends.

▶ ♯ Ⓜ Ventura Rodríguez. Head left at the fork in the road onto C. de San Bernardino. Ⓢ Appetizers €8-15; entrees €17-25. Tasting menu €50. ⓩ Open M-Sa 2-4pm and 9-11:45pm.

El Jardín Secreto   CAFE $
C. de Conde Duque, 2
☎91 541 80 23

Tucked away in a tiny street close to C. de la Princesa, El Jardín Secreto is, appropriately, Argüelles's best-kept secret. Walk into this eclectic cafe filled with beaded window coverings, wooden ceiling canopies, and crystal-ball table lamps to enjoy one of their dozens of coffees, hot chocolates, and snacks. For a real taste of what Secreto has to offer, try the *chocolate El Jardín,* served with chocolate Teddy Grahams and dark chocolate at the bottom of your cup (€6), or the

Food

George Clooney cocktail with *horchata,* crème de cacao, and Cointreau (€7.25).

► ♯ Ⓜ Ventura Rodríguez. Take the left fork in the road onto C. San Bernardino. Ⓢ Desserts €4.20. Coffee and tea €3-6. Cocktails €7.25. ⓒ Open M-Th 6:30pm-1:30am, F-Sa 6:30pm-2:30am, Su 6:30pm-1:30am.

El Rey de Tallarines   ASIAN $$

C. de San Bernardino, 2

☎91 542 68 97; www.reydetallarines.com

El Rey de Tallarines is a great option for noodles and dumplings in a land of tortillas and *tostados;* it has built a reputation as one of the best options for budget Asian food in Madrid. The specialty here is La Mian, the ancient art of the hand-pulled noodle. Every day at 1 and 9pm the cooks prepare fresh noodles from scratch at the main bar of the restaurant. Dishes like La Mian with chicken and vegetables (€6) do not disappoint. The menu also has a number of meat dishes like the crunchy roast duck (€14), and the assorted dim sum (eight pieces; €9) is particularly popular for sharing with a small group.

► ♯ Ⓜ Ventura Rodríguez. Take the left fork in the road onto C. San Bernardino. Ⓢ Entrees €8-15. ⓒ Open daily 12:30-5pm and 7:30pm-midnight.

Paella Day

Known simply as "Thursday" to the rest of us, in Madrid it's often paella day at many restaurants with *menús del día.* Restaurants in Madrid frequently offer lunch specials in which €10 buys an appetizer, entree, dessert, and—if you're lucky—some *vino.* Legends on the origin of this tradition range from an official order by General Franco to Thursday being the cook's day off.

Las Cuevas del Duque   SPANISH $$$

C. de la Princesa, 16

☎91 559 50 37; www.cuevasdelduque.galeon.com

What distinguishes Las Cuevas del Duque is its selection of big-game dishes like the stewed deer with mixed vegetables (€14). They offer a great selection of steaks and grilled fish; the filet mignon (€20) is a particularly popular choice. The basement location makes the restaurant feel a bit like a cave, but eating meat underground has its own appeal.

Food

▶ ✄ Ⓜ Ventura Rodríguez. Take the left fork in the road onto C. San Bernardino; the restaurant is on a tiny street to the right. Ⓢ Entrees €15-30. 🕐 Open daily 7-11pm.

Kulto al Plato
SPANISH $$

C. de Serrano Jover, 1

☎91 758 59 46; www.kultoalplato.com

Kulto al Plato serves contemporary tapas in an upscale setting. While its location between El Corte Inglés and the neighboring hotel isn't thrilling, it's one of the best dining options near CÁrgüelles. Tapas dishes have a modern take, such as the mushroom ravioli with foie gras sauce (€13). The fish and meat entrees are grilled fresh. The roasted duck with seasoned pear is a house specialty (€16).

▶ ✄ Ⓜ Argüelles Ⓜ. Walk south down C. de la Princesa to C. de Serrano Jover. Ⓢ Meals €12-20. 🕐 Open M-Th 8:30-11:30pm, F-Sa noon-1am, Su 8:30-11:30pm.

Cascaras
SPANISH $

C. de Ventura Rodríguez, 7

☎91 542 83 36; www.restaurantecascaras.com

While the decorations at Cascaras may confuse you, the food is straightforward and convenient for a snack after an afternoon around Pl. de España. Cascaras has a number of good vegetarian options, such as the baked eggplant appetizer (€10). Though it won't change your life, Cascara is perfectly fine for drinks or a casual dinner.

▶ ✄ Ⓜ Ventura Rodríguez. Walk south down C. de la Princesa and make a right onto C. de Ventura Rodríguez. Ⓢ Meals €5-15. 🕐 Open M-F 7:30am-1am, Sa-Su 7:30am-2am.

SALAMANCA

La Úrsula
TAPAS $$

C. López de Hoyos, 17

☎91 564 23 79; www.laursula.com

Across the street from the Museo Lazaro Galdiano, La Úrsula is an upscale tapas bar with terrace seating on a quiet side street off C. Serrano. The setting is fantastic and attracts a steady crowd of wealthy *madrileños*. La Úrsula offers particularly great lunch deals, including one of the city's best hamburger specials (€8)—a large burger with three tasty toppings of your

Food

choice (fried egg, Manchego, sauteed peppers, etc.) and served with fries, a drink, and coffee or dessert.

▶ ♯ ⓜ Gregorio Marañon. Cross Paseo de la Castellana on C. de Maria de Molina. Follow C. de Maria de Molina for 3 blocks until you reach C. de Serrano. ⓢ Menú del día €7-11. Meals €14-20. Cash only. ⓣ Open daily 8am-midnight.

Mumbai Massala   INDIAN $$

C. de Recoletos, 14

☎91 435 71 94; www.mumbaimassala.com

Gourmet Mumbai Massala is not exactly a bargain. Rather than the heaping portions you find at many Indian places, taste and quality are the focus of Mumbai Massala, which garnishes dishes with lemon, fresh parsley, and chopped onion. It has the typical stewed meat and vegetable dishes like tikka masala and *saag gosht,* and the traditional tandoor turns out spectacular charcoal-grilled entrees like Peshwari *gosht tikka* (lamb marinated in yogurt and spices; €14). While the *menú del día* (€15) is a bit expensive for lunch, it's a good deal if you plan on ordering more than one dish.

▶ ♯ ⓜ Colón. Walk 2 blocks south down Paseo de Recoletos. Turn left (east) onto C. de Recoletos and follow for 1 block. ⓢ Appetizers €8-12; entrees €10-16. Menú del día €15. Menú de la noche €25. Cash only. ⓣ Open daily 1:30-4:30pm and 9pm-midnight.

Nightlife

If you came to Europe for the nightlife, you've chosen the right city. Not only does Madrid offer every type of nightlife experience known to man, but thanks to the youth culture of *el botellón,* it offers one experience known only to sleepless teenaged zombies. La Latina and Lavapiés are home to some internationally recognized clubs, a spectrum of bars, *tabernas,* and late-night cafes. Meanwhile, the streets of Las Huertas are packed with *discotecas* that would have the old literati of the neighborhood pondering the great moral dilemma of the dance floor makeout. In Chueca and Malasaña, the nightlife scene is chameleon-like, with clubs and bars opening and closing at a rapid pace. Other neighborhoods, like Argüelles and Moncloa, are more laid-back and offer some great live music venues. So pick your poison, get crazy, and stay hydrated.

Budget Nightlife

The best way to save some dough on clubs is to find someone handing out free admission or drink flyers on the street. These promoters often offer their wares earlyish in the night on the busiest street near their club. Also, be sure to check out club websites (or *Let's Go's* listings, of course) for special deal nights and happy hours.

EL CENTRO

Palacio Gaviria   CLUB

C. del Arenal, 9

☎91 526 60 69; www.palaciogaviria.com

Built in 1850 and inspired by the Italian Renaissance, Palacio Gaviria is a beautiful palace turned nightlife hotspot. Make your royal entrance by heading down the grand marble staircase onto the dance floor, which is powered by techno beats and electric dance moves. Be on the lookout for promoters of Palacio Gaviria in Puerta del Sol, as they will often have vouchers for free entry or drinks.

▶ ⚡ From Puerta del Sol, walk down C. del Arenal. Ⓢ Cover M-Th €10, F-Sa €15, Su €10. Ⓧ Open daily 11pm-late.

Café del Príncipe   BAR

Pl. de Canalejas, 5

☎91 531 81 83

A 2min. walk from Puerta del Sol, this bar and restaurant offers the "best mojitos in Madrid" as well as a variety of entrees and beverages. Come to take a tranquil break from the noisy Sol without venturing too far from all the clubs.

▶ ⚡ At the corner of C. de la Cruz and C. del Príncipe. Ⓢ Mixed drinks €5-15. Ⓧ Open M-Th 9:30am-2am, F-Sa 9:30-2:30am, Su 9:30am-2am. Kitchen open daily 9:30am-4pm and 8pm-2am.

Joy Eslava   CLUB

C. del Arenal, 11

☎91 366 37 33; www.joy-eslava.com

An old standby, this converted theater has stayed strong amid

Late Night Munchies

After a long night of bars and *discotecas,* join the natives for the Spanish munchie of hot chocolate (the thick, pudding-like kind) and *churros,* sticks of fried dough coated in sugar. To make it look like you do this all the time, daintily dip one end of the *churro* in the chocolate before devouring the double sweetness. At 6am, only a few things warrant your consciousness, and a plate of *churros con chocolate* is definitely one of them.

Madrid's rapidly changing nightlife scene. Number one among study-abroad students and travelers, Joy Eslava plays an eclectic mix of music and features scantily clad models (of both genders) dancing on the theater stage. Balloons and confetti periodically fall New-Year's-Eve-style from the ceiling.

▶ > From Puerta del Sol, walk down C. del Arenal. $ Cover M-W €12, Th €15, F-Su €18. 🕐 Open M-Th 11:30pm-5:30am, F-Sa 11:30pm-6am, Su 11:30pm-5:30am.

LA LATINA AND LAVAPIÉS

🏴 Casa Lucas   BAR, TAPAS

C. Cava Baja, 30

☎91 365 08 04; www.casalucas.es

Props to Casa Lucas for making life seem simple and delicious. On a long block of successful restaurants, bars, and *tabernas* that thrive on gimmicks, Casa Lucas stands out by sticking to the basics: freshly prepared tapas and a premium wine list. The interior of the restaurant is bright, comfortable, and packed with locals. The tapas here are a notch above what you will find elsewhere. Dishes like calamari (€14) are cooked fresh, which is something of a rarity in Madrid. The *secreto ibérico* is one the most popular dishes, garnished with fresh greens and mustard vinaigrette (€14). The chalkboard menu of wines changes nightly, and nearly everything is offered by the bottle or the glass.

▶ ⚑ Ⓜ La Latina. Walk west down Pl. de la Cebada. Make a right onto C. de Humilladero and continue right on C. Cava Baja. $ Wine by the glass €2-4, by the bottle €16-25. Raciones €7-15. 🕐 Open M-Th 8pm-midnight, F-Sa 8pm-1am, Su 8pm-midnight.

La Perejila   BAR, TAPAS

C. Cava Baja, 25

☎91 364 28 55

La Perejila feels a bit like the world's most inviting shoebox. The interior is filled with beautiful antiques from the golden age of flamenco, vintage photographs, gold-leafed paintings, and vases of flowers that make this place come alive. Live parakeets greet you at the door. While grabbing a table is tricky, patrons are happy to stick around anyway to enjoy some of C. Cava Baja's freshest *taberna* food. The most popular dish is the namesake La Perejila (veal meatballs served in a clay plot; €9). *Tostados* like the *queso manchego* (€5) are made fresh to order and come piping hot. The wine selection changes daily.

▶ ⚐ Ⓜ La Latina. Walk west down Pl. de la Cebada. Make a right onto C. del Humilladero and continue right on C. Cava Baja. Ⓢ Cocktails €5-10. *Tostados* €5-7. Entrees €9-12. ⚙ Open daily 1-4pm and 8:15pm-12:30am.

Angelika Cocktail Bar   BAR

C. Cava Baja, 24

☎91 364 55 31; www.angelika.es

Vintage DVD posters line the walls, projectors screen international films, and the walls are lined with DVDs for rent. Angelika has over 3000 titles available to borrow from their library, and they also serve a mean mojito. We can't decide if this is the most cinema-friendly bar in Madrid, or the world's bougiest Blockbuster. Sure, it's a gimmick, but sometimes gimmicks are fun. While they certainly try hard to impress with their cool alternative theme, the well-mixed cocktails and hip environment are what make Angelika a worthy stop on a pub crawl down C. Cava Baja.

▶ ⚐ Ⓜ La Latina. Walk west down Pl. de la Cebada. Make a right onto C. de Humilladero and continue right on C. Cava Baja. Ⓢ Cocktails €5-10. ⚙ Open daily 3pm-1am.

El Bonanno   BAR

Pl. del Humilladero, 4

☎91 366 68 86; www.elbonanno.com

Located at the southern end of the bustling C. Cava Baja, El Bonanno makes a great first stop of the evening or last-minute drink before you hit the club. Plaza del Humilladero comes alive late at night, and El Bonanno is close to the action of El botellón. Because space is limited in the bar, people take their drinks to the sidewalk. El Bonanno serves the requisite tapas, but the cramped interior makes it better suited for a quick drink.

▶ ⚐ Ⓜ La Latina. Walk 1 block west down Pl. de la Cabeza. Take a left onto Pl. del Humilladero. Ⓢ Cocktails €3-10. ⚙ Open daily 12:30pm-2:30am.

Aroca XI   BAR, SPANISH

Pl. de los Carros

☎91 366 54 75; www.grupoaroca.com

Aroca XI is painfully posh. And the drinks are objectively great. Fresh fruit makes everything better. The cocktail menu is more like a cocktail bible, with six fresh-fruit mojitos alone. Unlike the many cramped bars that line C. Cava Baja, Aroca XI has plenty of space and the only terrace seating in Pl. del Humilladero; it's the only place to sit among the gathering storm of El botellón in the plaza.

▶ ⚑ Ⓜ La Latina. Walk west down C. del Humilladero until you see Iglesia San Andrés on the right. As you face the church, Aroca XI is on the left. Ⓢ Cocktails €6-8. Entrees €5-15. ⏰ Open daily noon-midnight.

Shoko
DISCOTECA

C. de Toledo, 86

☎91 354 16 91; www.shokomadrid.com

With massive "bamboo" shoots that reach to the ceiling, a huge stage featuring internationally acclaimed acts, and a swanky VIP section that *Let's Go* wishes we could live in, Shoko is an Asian-inspired *discoteca* that violates every last rule of feng shui. Shoko is the big leagues of nightlife in La Latina.

▶ ⚑ Ⓜ La Latina. Head south down C. de Toledo. Ⓢ Cover €10-15. ⏰ Open daily 11:30pm-late.

LAS HUERTAS

Kapital
CLUB

C. de Atocha, 125

☎91 420 29 06; www.grupo-kapital.com/kapital

This is the mothership of Madrid nightlife. Built in a gutted theater, Kapital is a seven-story temple of trashy fun. The first floor, which blasts house music, is where most of the action happens, but it keeps going, with separate dance floors for hip hop, reggae, and Spanish pop on the stories above. There is a little bit for everybody here: the third floor has a karaoke bar; the sixth floor screens movies; the seventh floor terrace has hookahs, pool tables, and killer views; and finally, on the yet-to-be-completed eighth floor, they hold live reenactments of the American Civil War (BYOB: bring your own beard). The good people of Kapital are rumored to be expanding upward at a rapid pace all the way to heaven itself. If you plan on making the pilgrimage, whatever you do, wear nice clothes—no sneakers or shorts. While Kapital doesn't get busy until around 2am, arriving early dressed in something nice will let you avoid the long wait.

▶ ⚑ 2min. walk up C. de Atocha from Ⓜ Atocha. Ⓢ Cover €15; includes 1 drink. Drinks €10-15. ⏰ Open Th-Su 11:30pm-5:30am.

Sol y Sombra
CLUB

C. de Echegaray, 18

☎91 542 81 93; www.solysombra.name

With thousands of LED lights on every last surface, Sol y Sombra might be the most high-tech thing ever to hit Madrid. Unlike the monster warehouse-style *discotecas* around the city, Sol y Sombra is surprisingly intimate. The walls shift in color to accent the bold patterns, while the music shifts between techno, jazz, funk, and hip hop. This is not a sloppy Eurotrash *discoteca;* it's a cool and innovative club. While you should expect a line out the door during prime weekend hours (midnight-3am), you won't be endlessly stranded: people tend to move in and out pretty quickly on their way to bigger *discotecas.*

▶ ♯ Ⓜ Sol. From the Metro, walk toward the museum district on Carrera de San Jeronimo and make a right onto C. de Echegaray. Ⓢ Cover €10. Beer €5. Cocktails €7. 🕐 Open Tu-Sa 10pm-3:30am.

Cafe la Fidula
JAZZ CLUB

C. de las Huertas, 57

☎91 429 29 47; www.myspace.com/lafidula

This jazz bar has been on the Las Huertas strip since long before the tourists started showing up. For more than 30 years, La Fidula has attracted some of the city's best jazz and blues musicians. While it's every bit as famous as Cafe Central and Cafe Populart (see **Arts and Culture: Music**), the setting is more intimate: built inside a 19th-century grocery store, the small stage encircled by tables puts you within spitting distance of the performers. While La Fidula isn't normally packed, this is precisely its appeal—a setting apart from the ebb and flow of Las Huertas where you can enjoy some of the city's most talented musicians. The performance schedule shifts nightly, with a combination of sets in the early evening from 8 to 10pm and jam sessions that carry on until the early hours of the morning.

▶ ♯ Ⓜ Antón Martín. Take C. León north to C. Las Huertas. *i* Visit the MySpace page for an up-to-date schedule, or call to inquire about late night performances. Ⓢ Coffee €3-4. Beer €2-4. Cocktails €5-8. Cash only. 🕐 Open M-Th 7pm-3am, F-Sa 7pm-4am, Su 7pm-3am.

El Imperfecto
BAR

Pl. de Matute, 2

☎91 366 72 11

El Imperfecto is unapologetically kitschy with walls plastered with images from American film, music, and art, and decorations straight from the garage sale (would it be a crime if two stools matched?). This shoebox interior is always fun and upbeat with people sipping cocktails (€6-10) and milkshakes (€4-6). Ice-blended drinks are reasonably priced for Madrid (€7) and much better than anything you'd find at a major club. Expect a crowd, and, on weekend nights, plenty of American study-abroaders, some friendly German accents, and some fanny packs. El Imperfecto is packed during weekend dinner hours (11pm-1am), so expect to stand at the bar.

▶ ⚡ Ⓜ Antón Martín. Walk uphill to Pl. de Matute and make a right toward C. de las Huertas. El Imperfecto is on the right. Ⓢ Drinks €4-10. Sangria €2 per glass; pitchers €11. 🕐 Open daily 3pm-2:30am.

El Secreto de Rita   BAR

C. de Echegaray, 10

El Secreto de Rita is a small bar that holds its own on a long block of *discotecas*. Dim lighting, soul revival music, and cheap cocktails are the major draw. While many bars need a critical mass to keep the energy alive, El Secreto de Rita is still fun even when it isn't packed. If conversation, eye contact, and interpersonal connection are things you value in life, you'll find El Secreto a good alternative to the flashing lights, onerous covers, and mind-numbing sound systems of so many clubs in the area. Bonus points to anyone who can figure out what's up with Rita... why is she always holding back? What's her deal?

▶ ⚡ From Pl. de Santa Ana, walk north up C. de Echegaray toward Puerta del Sol. Rita's on your left. Ⓢ Drinks €3-10. 🕐 Open M-W 6pm-2am, F-Sa 6pm-2:30am.

Viva Madrid   BAR

C. de Manuel Fernández y González, 7

☎91 429 36 40

Viva Madrid has long been a favorite celebrity haunt; it's rumored that Ava Gardner and the bullfighter Manolete got handsy here in the '50s. While this might have once been an artists' hangout, today it's been adopted by young *madrileños* and internationals. The front terrace is in the thick of the pedestrian traffic of Las Huertas nightlife, but the interior feels dramatically removed, with a wood-carved ceiling and velvet drapes straight out of El Palacio Real.

▶ ⚡ Ⓜ Sol. Walk toward the museum district on Carrera de San Jeronimo and turn right onto C. de Manuel Fernández y González. Ⓢ Beer €2.50-4. Cocktails €6-10. 🕐 Open daily noon-2am.

iReal
BAR

C. de Echegaray, 16

Gaga gets old. When you tire of American dance music, iReal is a good place to educate yourself in the latest Spanish discopop. Expect flashing lasers, disco balls, and pulsing Spanish pop brought to you by lyricists that make Rebecca Black sound like T.S. Eliot. Jump on the dance floor and get lost in the fun, or sit on the sidelines in ironic detachment. Drinks run a bit pricey with €5 beers and mixed drinks from €6. iReal doesn't have a cover so at the very least it's a good stop on the way to bigger and badder clubs on Las Huertas.

▶ ⚧ From Pl. de Santa Ana walk up C. de Echegaray toward Puerta del Sol. Ⓢ Drinks €5-8. 🕗 Open daily 11pm-3am.

Midnight Rose
BAR

Pl. de Santa Ana, 14

☎91 701 60 20; www.midnightrose.es

Swanky, bougie, euro-yuppy—these are all words that apply to Pl. de Santa Ana's top-dollar cocktail lounge in the ME Madrid Reina Victoria Hotel. Cocktails are expensive (€12-14), lights are dim, and the young and wealthy European clientele is predictably beautiful. The leather-cushioned penthouse terrace is a total fantasyland, if you can make it up there. It's open to the proletariat but charges a steep cover (€15) on weekend nights when the crowds arrive. The line can be long, so your best bet is to go for an early drink (7-10pm) when there's neither cover nor line.

▶ ⚧ It's the most prominent building on Pl. de Santa Ana (lit purple at night). Ⓢ Cover for penthouse terrace €15 Th-Su. Cocktails €5-15. Cash only.

Words to Know

Go shopping with Spanish girls and you will immediately hear them giddily exclaiming with two words: *"guay"* and *"mono."* You really don't need any other Spanish language skills to enter the world of shopping. *"Guay"* means "cool," and can be used to describe anything or anyone you think is a G. *"Mono"* means cute, and is mostly used to describe adorable children and the latest in fashion. Another word that might stun you is the verb *"coger"* (pronounced co-hehr), which means "to get" or "to take." You might have learned in Spanish class that *"coger"* in other countries means to, well, fornicate, but the Spanish use this word frequently in its more innocent connotation.

🕐 Downstairs lounge open daily 1:30-4pm and 10pm-2:30am. Penthouse terrace open daily 7pm-2:30am.

Dubliners   BAR

C. de Espoz y Mina, 7
☎91 522 75 09

How many *pequeñas cervezas* does it take to get drunk? A lot. This is just one reason why so many come to Dubliners, a traditional Irish pub with traditional Irish pints (€3). It's dark and loud with a fun international vibe, and gets packed and crazy during major sports games. Ever seen grown men from around the world attempt their own drunken rendition of "We Are the Champions"? This is a great place to make friends, taunt enemies, and, when it's all said and done, come back the next morning for the Dubliner's Irish Breakfast (€5.70).

▶ ⚡ From Puerta del Sol, walk south down C. de Espoz y Mina. The bar is on the left. Ⓢ Beers €2-4. Cocktails €6-10. 🕐 Open M-Th 11am-3am, F-Sa 11am-3:30am, Su 11am-3am.

Vinoteca Barbechera   BAR, TAPAS

C. del Príncipe, 27
☎91 420 04 78; www.vinoteca-barbechera.com

Vinoteca Barbechera is a nationally successful chain that delivers premium Spanish and imported wines. Nearly everything on the menu is available by the glass. While Vinoteca Barbechera also offers a range of tapas and *pinchos* (€3-6), the appeal here is clearly the wine list. With over 300 domestic brands, this is a great place to test your palate or your bullshitting skills. The waitstaff can help you find a glass that suits your tastes, and the terrace seating on Pl. de Santa Ana can't be beat.

▶ ⚡ Pl. de Santa Ana. Ⓢ Wine €2-8. Cocktails €5-15. 🕐 Open M-Th noon-1am, F-Su noon-2am.

Sweet Funk Club   CLUB

C. del Doctor Cortezo, 1
☎91 869 40 38; www.myspace.com/sweetfunkclub□

Suspended cages, disco balls, and a daringly clad clientele are staples of this hot club. Sweet is a self-proclaimed funk club that plays American auto-tuned hip hop to a primarily *madrileño* crowd. By 4am on weekends, the dance floor here is usually packed, and women with very little clothing keep things steamy with suggestive dances on the small circular stages throughout the club.

▶ ✇ Ⓜ Antón Martín. From the Metro, walk uphill on C. de Atocha and make a left on C. del Doctor Cortezo. Ⓢ Cover €10-14; includes 1 drink. Beer €5. Cocktails €7. ☾ Open F-Sa 11pm-sunrise.

GRAN VÍA

Reinabruja   CLUB

C. Jacometrezo, 6

☎91 542 81 93; www.reinabruja.com

Reinabruja is not just a club, it's a futuristic fantasyland. Here, the internationally renowned industrial designer Tomas Alia has created a world of endless light and sound. Every surface—including the toilet seats—changes color using cutting-edge LED technology. Reinabruja is Madrid nightlife at its most creative and over-the-top. This subterranean world of phosphorescent lighting and stenciled pillars is hugely popular with tourists but hasn't lost its edge in the *madrileño* scene.

▶ ✇ Ⓜ Callao. Ⓢ Cover €12; includes 1 drink. Wine €7. Mixed drinks €9. ☾ Open Th-Sa 11pm-6am.

El Tigre   BAR

C. de las Infantas, 30

☎91 532 00 72

The motto of El Tigre might as well be "dont f*@% with Spain." On a block with fusion restaurants, contemporary cuisine, and fancy cocktail lounges, El Tigre keeps everything Spanish with beer, mojitos, and sangria in towering glasses and taxidermied bulls on the wall. We can only imagine the interior decorator's philosophy was "put the head on the wall and serve everything else as tapas." Drinks are served with a plate of greasy fries, pork loin, and chorizo. This place is absolutely packed; it can be hard to make your way through the door. While the noise and crowds may be a turn-off for some, this is definitely a place where you can start your night off cheap, drunk, and greasy.

▶ ✇ Ⓜ Gran Vía. Walk north up C. de Hortaleza, then make a right onto C. de las Infantas. Ⓢ Drinks €2-5. ☾ Open daily 10:30am-1:30am.

El Plaza Jazz Club   JAZZ CLUB

C. de Martín de los Heros, 3

☎91 548 84 88; www.elplazacopas.com

The nightly program of live sets at El Plaza is one of the best in the city for jazz, particularly the Wednesday night Dixie Jam.

The typically *madrileño* crowd comes here to drink, socialize, and lounge on comfortable couches, not just to listen to saxophone solos and pretend to understand every last note. El Plaza also screens films and hosts open mic nights and the occasional comedy performance.

▶ ✈ Ⓜ Plaza de España. Walk 1 block west to C. de Martín de los Heros. Ⓢ Most events are free; some ticketed shows €5. Drinks €3-6. Cash only. ⓒ Open daily 7:30pm-2:30am.

El Berlin   MUSIC VENUE

C. de Jacometrezo, 4

☎91 521 57 52; www.nuevocafeberlinmadrid.webgarden.es

This is one of the best-known jazz clubs in all of Madrid. El Berlin attracts the city's most talented artists in jazz, blues, funk, and soul for its nightly sets and is most famous for its Tuesday Jam Sessions (10pm). The crowd is generally more middle-aged and the intimate venue isn't always packed, but El Berlin is a popular alternative to fussy and expensive clubs.

▶ ✈ Next to Ⓜ Callao. Ⓢ Drinks €3-7. ⓒ Opens daily at 9pm. Sets begin at 10pm.

Del Diego Cocktail Bar   BAR

C. de la Reina, 12

☎91 523 31 06

Del Diego is an upscale one-room cocktail lounge that is quiet and spacious and has served the same classic cocktails for 20 years. Drinks are expensive, but Del Diego is one of the nicest cocktail lounges in the area and a better place for conversation than many of the standing-room-only tapas bars.

▶ ✈ Ⓜ Gran Vía. Walk north up C. de Hortaleza and make a right onto C. de la Reina. Ⓢ Cocktails €10. ⓒ Open daily 7pm-3am.

Pousse   BAR

C. de las Infantas, 19

☎91 521 63 01

With refurbished antique furniture and music from every decade, the ambience at Pousse is self-consciously eclectic. The cardboard and fingerpaint art on the walls was made by either avant-garde artists or kindergarteners. The drink menu is every bit as mixed as the decor, with everything from all-natural fresh fruit milkshakes (€6) to gourmet cocktails made with premium liqueurs (€9-13). Each cocktail has its own full-page entry in the lengthy drink menu and specials like Meet Johnny Black (Black

Label whiskey, fresh OJ, sugar, and lemon; €12) are all made with fresh juices and top-dollar booze. Pousse attracts a loyal crowd of locals, but the tourists have caught on.

▶ ♯ Ⓜ Gran Vía. Walk north up C. de Hortaleza and turn right onto C. de las Infantas. Ⓢ Drinks €6-13. Ⓒ Open M-Sa 10pm-2am.

Lola   BAR
C. de la Reina, 25

☎91 522 34 83; www.lola-bar.com

Lola Bar is a cool but unpretentious cocktail bar. Groups of 20-something professional *madrileños* come here for their first drink of the night on a pub crawl through Gran Vía and Chueca. While this bar doesn't pack full, groups arrive as soon as work gets out around 7pm. Lola serves plenty of American favorites such as Coito a la Playa (Sex on the Beach), but they also keep things simple with Spanish wines by the glass (€2-4) and beer on tap (€3).

▶ ♯ Ⓜ Gran Vía. Walk north up C. de Hortaleza and turn right onto C. de la Reina. Ⓢ Cocktails €9-10. Ⓒ Open M-Th noon-2am, F-Sa noon-2:30am.

Museo Chicote   BAR
C. Gran Vía, 12

☎91 532 67 37; www.museo-chicote.com

A longtime favorite of artists and writers, this retro-chic cocktail bar maintains its original 1930s design. During the Spanish Civil War, the foreign press came here to wait out the various battles, and during the late Franco era it became a haven for prostitutes. Today Museo Chicote offers one of the best happy hours on C. Gran Vía (cocktails €5; 5-11pm), but things shift pretty quickly at midnight when the nightly DJ set starts. Well-known DJs play everything from '80s American pop to European house. Located directly on C. Gran Vía, this isn't the most adventurous place, but it's a Madrid institution with a steady crowd.

▶ ♯ Ⓜ Gran Vía. Walk east. Museo Chicote is on the left. Ⓢ Cocktails €7-9. Ⓒ Open daily 8am-3am.

CHUECA

🏴 Bogui Jazz Club   JAZZ CLUB
C. del Barquillo, 29

☎91 521 15 68; www.boguijazz.com

Bogui is one of Madrid's premier jazz venues and most

happening weekend clubs. Nightly sets of live jazz (9 and 11pm) are a fantastic way to get plugged into the local music scene, and during weekend DJ sets (Th-Sa 1am), Bogui brings in some of Madrid's best-known jazz, funk, and soul DJs from Sala Barco. Bogui also caters to a Chueca crowd that likes to dance. The Wednesday midnight set (otherwise known as La Descarga or "The Dump") is when musicians from around the city convene for a late-night jam session after a long night of gigs.

▶ ✦ Ⓜ Chueca. Take C. de Gravina 2 blocks west to C. del Barquillo. The club is on the left. Ⓢ DJ sets Th-Sa free; concerts €10. Beer €4. Cocktails €7. €1 surcharge for all beverages Th-Su. ⏰ Open M-Sa 10pm-5:30am.

Areia   BAR, TAPAS

C. de Hortaleza, 92
☎91 310 03 07; www.areiachillout.com

Areia calls itself a "chillout zone," which must sound cool to native Spanish speakers. While to Americans this slogan seems to fit better in your teen rec center, this is one of the hippest spots in Chueca. The Moroccan-themed bar and lounge has a crimson-draped ceiling, low-lying tables, large cushion seats, and embroidered pillows where people snack on international tapas like pad thai (€6) and tandoori chicken (€6) as well as traditional Moroccan dishes like *tayin de cordero* (stewed lamb). Things stay pretty laid-back, even during the weekend DJ sets (11pm-late). Cocktails are set at standard prices (€6-8) and come served with fresh fruit. Music ranges from house to reggae.

▶ ✦ Ⓜ Chueca. Make a right onto C. de Augusto Figueroa, then a right on C. de Hortaleza; Areia is on the right. Ⓢ Cocktails €6-9. ⏰ Open daily 1pm-3am.

Dame un Motivo   BAR

C. de Pelayo, 58
☎91 319 74 98

Dame un Motivo is a one-room bar with an outlook on nightlife that's refreshing in Chueca: strip it down to its essentials (good music, cheap drinks, and sparse decor). The idea here is to do away with all of the excess of Chueca nightlife—cover charges, overpriced sugary drinks, flashing lights, and loud music—and offer an alternative environment for people to hang out and converse. That Dame un Motivo is busy on the weekends with a primarily local crowd is a testament to its success. During the week, people come to enjoy the film and book library.

▶ ✦ Ⓜ Chueca. Take C. Gravina 1 block west to C. de Pelayo and follow north half a block. The bar is on the right. *i* Check out Dame un Motivo's Facebook page for event listings. Ⓢ Beers €1.30-2.50. Cocktails €5.50. Ⓣ Open W-Th 6pm-2am, F-Sa 4pm-2:30am, Su 4pm-2am.

La Sueca
BAR

C. de Hortaleza, 67

☎91 319 04 87

The drag queen beauties behind the bar are a huge presence in this small cocktail lounge. They joyously shake martinis and mix fruit daquiris for a young and beautiful *madrileño* crowd. Like many bars on the block, La Sueca is small, but it has enough white leather lounge seating to accommodate larger groups. The crystal chandeliers are a nice touch, but nothing out of the ordinary for Madrid's most flamboyant *barrio*.

▶ ⚥ Ⓜ Chueca. Make a right onto C. de Augusto Figueroa and a right onto C. de Hortaleza. Ⓢ Beer €3.50. Cocktails €8. Ⓣ Open daily 8pm-3am.

Studio 54
DISCOTECA

C. de Barbieri, 7

☎61 512 68 07; www.studio54madrid.com

You're going to see a lot of six packs at Studio 54, and we're not talking beer. With pulsing Spanish pop and sculpted bartenders wearing nothing but bow ties, Studio 54 tends to attract a crowd of predominantly gay *madrileños* and American and European tourists. If you haven't spent a night dancing to ridiculous Spanish pop music yet, this is the place to do it, with crystal chandeliers and disco balls hanging above a violet dance floor, surrounded by mirrors and etched silhouettes of curvy women.

▶ ⚥ Ⓜ Chueca. Walk south down C. de Barbieri toward C. Gran Vía. The discoteca is on the right. Ⓢ Cover €10 after 1am. Cocktails €8. Ⓣ Open Th-Sa 11:30pm-3:30am.

EL51
BAR

C. de Hortaleza, 51

☎91 521 25 64

EL51 is a posh single-room cocktail lounge with white leather chairs, crystal chandeliers, and mirrors lit with violet bulbs. Just steps from the center of Chueca's nightlife, it tends to pack people in during prime hours (midnight-2am), but also attracts a steady crowd with a two-for-one happy hour that includes mojitos, caipirinhas, martinis, and cosmopolitans. Spanish pop plays in the background, but, unlike other bars, they keep the volume low enough that you can still hold a conversation (if you're still sober enough, that is).

▶ ✈ Ⓜ Chueca. Make a right on C. de Augusto Figueroa, then a right onto C. de Hortaleza. Ⓢ Cocktails €8-10. ⓩ Open daily 6pm-3am. Happy hour F-Sa 6-11pm, Su 6pm-3am.

Long Play   DISCOTECA

Pl. de Vázquez de Mella, 2

☎91 532 20 66; www.discotecalongplay.net

Clubs in Chueca come and go, but Long Play has been around to see it all. Once a venue of the early 1970s *madrileño* counterculture, today Long Play attracts a crowd of gay *madrileños,* European tourists, and American study abroaders. Things tend to start late at Long Play with the crowds descending en masse around 3am. The downstairs DJ plays a variety of international pop, and things get pretty sweaty on the upstairs dance floor, which plays strictly European house.

▶ ✈ Ⓜ Gran Vía. Head north up C. de Hortaleza, make a right onto C. de las Infantas, and a left to Pl. de Vázquez de Mella. Ⓢ Cover €10 Th-F after 1:30am (includes 1 drink), all night Sa. Drinks €8. ⓩ Open daily midnight-7am.

'Bares Versus 'Tecas

No, it's not Madrid's *West Side Story* rivalry. But it can be an epic struggle for the Madrid nightlife noob to try to go to a famous *discoteca* at 11pm on your first night in the city. Instead, hop around *discobares:* rock, dance, and salsa music bars that are common in Madrid. Even better, take part in *el botellón* and pregame on the cheap. Then, grab your friends and head to a *discoteca.* Just don't go before midnight—*discotecas* usually don't get going until at least 1am.

MALASAÑA

▨ La Vía Láctea   BAR

C. de Velarde, 18

☎91 446 75 81; www.lavialactea.net

La Vía Láctea is a Spanish temple dedicated to rock, grunge, and everything '70s counterculture. It was founded in the early years of Movida Madrileña, the youth-propelled revolution of art, music, fashion, and literature. Today it's more a relic of this past than a continuing force of change, with pop music memorabilia covering the walls from floor to ceiling and a fine perfume of stale beer lingering in the air. The sentimentality of La Vía Láctea is unashamed and seems to draw crowds of loyal *madrileños* and international tourists night after night. Music spans Elvis to Prince and the pool tables are popular.

▶ ✢ Ⓜ Tribunal. Walk north up C. de Fuencarral and make a left onto C. de Velarde. Ⓢ Cover €10 after 1am; includes 1 drink. Beer €3-5. Cocktails €5-7. ☾ Open daily 7:30pm-3:30am.

Club Nasti   DISCOTECA
C. de San Vicente Ferrer, 33
☎91 521 76 05; www.nasti.es

Come to Club Nasti on Saturday nights for a hipster heaven of synth pop, electro beats, and punk jams. For a lighter touch, try Friday nights, when house DJs spin indie rock like The Strokes and The Arctic Monkeys. Now in its 11th year, Nasti is a neighborhood institution that remains hugely popular among locals. The small dance floor gets packed as the night progresses, and you might end up shimmying out of your sweaty plaid shirt to dance in your nevernudes. Don't say we didn't warn you: there's no PBR.

▶ ✢ Ⓜ Tribunal. Walk south down C. de Fuencarral and make a right onto C. de San Vicente Ferrer. Ⓢ Cover €10 after 2am; includes 1 drink. Beer €4-5. Cocktails €8-9. ☾ Open Th 2-5am, F 1-6am, Sa 2-6am.

BarCo   MUSIC, DISCOTECA
C. del Barco, 34
☎91 521 24 47; www.barcobar.com

With a full program of nightly concerts, late-night DJ sessions, and weekly jam sessions, this small venue covers plenty of musical terrain. While many bars and clubs in the area try to attract international bands, BarCo has made its name as a stalwart venue for local acts, with most bands drawing heavily on funk, soul, rock, and jazz. While the concert schedule is continually changing, the nightly DJ sets are given to a handful of veteran European DJs who have been spinning in Madrid for years. For those more interested in live music, the Sunday night jam session brings in some of the city's best contemporary jazz musicians. The cover charge changes with the act, so check online for updates.

► ⚘ Ⓜ Tribunal. Head south on C. de Fuencarral 3 blocks. Take a right onto C. Corredera Baja de San Pablo, walk 2 blocks, and take a left (south) onto C. del Barco. The bar is on the right. Ⓢ Cover €5-10. Beer €4. Cocktails €7. F-Sa €1 drink surcharge. Cash only. 🕐 Open M-Th 10pm-5:30am, F-Sa 10pm-6am, Su 10pm-5:30am.

Café-Botilleria Manuela   CAFE, BAR
C. de San Vicente Ferrer, 29
☎91 531 70 37

Dark wood shelves filled with liquor, a white marble bar, and gilded columns make Café-Botilleria feel like a five-star hotel lobby in miniature. The list of cocktails is standard for the late-night *madrileño* cafe, and so are the prices. Most people choose to imbibe rather than caffeinate, and many take advantage of the cafe's selection of board games. The small tables and red-cushioned booths are nearly always full. Café-Botilleria Manuela is one of the best venues to avoid the here-today-gone-tomorrow side of Malasaña nightlife.
► ⚘ Ⓜ Tribunal. Walk south down C. de Fuencarral and make a right onto C. de San Vicente Ferrer. Ⓢ Wine €2.50-3.50. Beer €1.50-3.50. Cocktails €8-12. 🕐 Open daily June-Aug 6pm-2am; Sept-May 4pm-2am.

Café Comercial   BAR, TAPAS
Glorieta de Bilbao, 7
☎91 521 56 55

Founded in 1887, Cafe Comercial remains a Malasaña institution. Once a meeting point for the anti-Franco Republican army during the Spanish Civil War, today it remains a place for informal gatherings of tourists and locals of all ages. The downstairs dining room, with dark wood pillars, marble tables, and mirrored walls, makes the setting a bit less intimate than smaller tapas bars or *cervecerías* in the area, but that doesn't keep it from being packed. More than anything, it is convenience that keeps people coming to CAFE Comercial: it's a great place to park for a few cheap drinks before pub crawling through the more contemporary bars. There is a surcharge for table service (€0.25-1 per item), but it's small enough that most people don't seem to care.
► ⚘ Ⓜ Bilbao. Ⓢ Beer €1-3. Wine €2-3. Cocktails €5-7. Internet access €1 per hr. Tapas €3-7. 🕐 Open M-W 7:30am-midnight, Th 7:30am-1am, F 7:30am-2am, Sa 8:30am-2am, Su 9am-midnight.

ARGÜELLES AND MONCLOA

▧ Tempo Club   LIVE MUSIC

C. del Duque de Osuna 8

☎91 547 75 18; www.tempoclub.net

International or local, jazz or soul, Tempo Club does not discriminate so long as a rhythm section and horns are involved. Tempo is one of the premier spots in Madrid to catch great live funk, soul, rock, and hip hop, with all of their acts accompanied by a full live band. Even when the DJ takes over for the late night set, the rhythm section often sticks around. While Tempo thrives on rich instrumentals, most of their acts involve talented vocalists. The venue is divided between a street-level cafe and cocktail area and the downstairs concert hall. This is a great alternative to large clubs and *discotecas* where lines are rampant and cover charges are onerous.

▶ ✠ Ⓜ Ventura Rodríguez. From C. Princesa follow C. del Duque de Liria and turn left onto C. del Duque de Osuna. *i* Live performances Th-Sa. Ⓢ No cover. Cocktails €5-8. Cash only. ⏰ Open daily 6pm-late.

Cafe la Palma   LIVE MUSIC

C. de la Palma 62

☎91 522 50 31; www.cafelapalma.com

Cafe la Palma is in many ways a typical Malasaña rock club even though it is just outside of the *barrio*. Like many clubs in the area, La Palma strives for a lot—a cafe that people can enjoy during the day, a cocktail lounge at night, a concert venue in the late night, and a full club with a live DJ set in the early morning. The music acts La Palma attracts are every bit as eclectic as the venue itself. While they try to accomplish a lot within the three small rooms of the cafe, they don't spread themselves too thin. There is a drink minimum (€6) for some live sets, but this is a great alternative to forking over a fat cover charge.

▶ ✠ Ⓜ Plaza de España. Follow C. de los Reyes northeast 2 blocks, take a left onto C. Amaniel, and walk 2 blocks to C. de la Palma. Ⓢ Drink minimum for some events €6; check website for more info. Cocktails €6. Cash only. ⏰ Open M-Th 4pm-3am, F-Su 4pm-4am.

Orange Café   BAR, CLUB

C. de Serrano Jover, 5

☎91 542 28 17; www.soyorangecafe.com

Orange Cafe is a venue for local rock acts in the evening and a packed dance club later at night. If you are more interested in finding a local *madrileño* venue, this club might not be for you, as it normally fills with tourists and travelers looking for American pop music. Women can take advantage of free drinks and free entry Wednesday nights (11:30pm-12:30am). Check the website for a list of concerts and cover charges.

▶ ⚲ Ⓜ Argüelles. Ⓢ Cover €10-15. ⏰ Open F-Sa 11:30pm-6am.

El Chapandaz BAR
C. de Fernando, 77
☎91 549 29 68; www.chapandaz.com

This place is ridiculous. Not only is it designed to look like a cave, but it is a fully functional, lactating cave with stalactites

12 Angry Bulls

For an adrenaline rush like no other, try running away from a dozen angry bulls in a huge crowd of similarly terrified people on a narrow street where you could be trampled or gored at any second. Although it may appear to be just a large group of men running like chickens with their heads cut off as huge beasts charge behind them, the running of the bulls *(encierro)* serves a practical purpose. The bulls must be transported from the corrals where they spend the night to the bullring where they will be killed the next evening. According to Spanish folklore, this tradition began in the early 14th century in northeastern Spain. Men would attempt to get the bulls to market faster by provoking them, and over time this evolved into a competition where young men would try to race in front of the bulls to the pens without being overtaken.

Nowadays, the event starts off with runners gathering in a blockaded street. All hell breaks looses when the police move out of the way and the runners dash pell-mell in front of the oncoming bulls and their pointy horns. The race covers a mere 903 yards in only four minutes, but a surprising amount of chaos can ensue in that time. During the race in San Fermín, 200-300 people are injured each year, mostly minor injuries as a result of falling down and tripping over other people. In late summer every year, the Madrid suburb San Sebastián de los Reyes sponsors a smaller version of the running. Adrenaline junkies in Madrid can have the same experience with a smaller chance of being trampled by other runners, although if you are sane (or slow), the sidelines are a safer option.

hanging from the ceiling that periodically drip milk into glass pitchers. The house drink, Leche de Pantera (panther's milk), is a combination of rum, cinnamon, and that special milk that drips from the ceiling. If you are suspicious (for perfectly good reasons), it also offers standard fare and a full menu of sweet, fruity, and colorful drinks. The bar is generally quiet until 11pm but fills up with a mostly international study-abroad crowd who stop in for the novelty before they head out clubbing.

▶ ✈ Ⓜ Moncloa. Walk down C. de la Princesa and turn left (east) onto C. de Fernando "El Católico." *i* International night Tu. Ⓢ Drinks €10. ⌚ Open daily 10pm-3am.

Arts and Culture

With some of the best art museums, public festivals, and performing arts groups in the world, Madrid's arts and culture scene is thriving. From street performers in Parque del Buen Retiro to Broadway musicals, you can find anything you're looking for in this metropolis.

Budget Arts and Culture

We're gonna be real with you: there's no established way to see flamenco in Madrid for less than the hefty price of an admission ticket. Sure, you can hope that your hostel owner is secretly a virtuoso flamenco guitarist with a lot of dancer-friends and will give you a free show, but we've met a lot of hostel owners, and it doesn't happen often. Sometimes a cultural tradition is worth forking out the dough. Make sure not to get roped into paying for dinner or drinks at the flamenco venue, and perhaps a show can fit within your travel budget.

CORRIDAS DE TOROS

Whether you view it as animal cruelty or national sport, the spectacle of *la corrida* (bullfighting) is a cherished Spanish tradition. Although it has its origins in earlier Roman and Moorish practices, today bullfighting is considered Spain's sport, and some of the top *toreros* (bullfighters) are national celebrities. The sport has been subject to continuing protest in recent years by animal rights activists, and it's common to see demonstrations outside of stadiums, but many tourists observe the tradition nonetheless.

If you choose to go, it is important to know a little bit about the rituals of the sport. The bullfight has three stages. First, the *picadores,* lancers on horseback, pierce the bull's neck muscles. Then, assistants thrust decorated darts called *banderillas* into the bull's back to injure and fatigue it. Finally, the matador kills his large opponent with a sword between the bull's shoulder blades, killing it instantly. Animal rights activists call the rituals savage and cruel, but aficionados call it an art that requires quick thinking, great kill, and an enormous amount of skill.

The best place to see bullfighting in Madrid is at the country's biggest arena, **Plaza de las Ventas,** where you can buy tickets in *sol* (sun) or *sombra* (shade) sections. Get your tickets at the arena the Friday or Saturday leading up to the bullfight. (C. de Alcalá 237 ☎91 356 22 00; www.las-ventas.com ✝ ĊVentas. ☯ Ticket office open 10am-2pm and 5-8pm.) You'll pay more to sit in the shade, but either way you'll have a good view of the feverish crowds, who cheer on the matador and wave white handkerchiefs called *pañuelos* after a particularly good fight. Rent a seat cushion at the stadium or bring your own for the stone seats. Bullfights are held Sundays and holidays throughout most of the year. During the **Fiesta de San Isidro** in May, fights are held almost every day, and the top bullfighters come face to face with the fiercest bulls. People across Spain are bitterly divided about the future of the sport, so visitors should approach the topic with sensitivity.

MUSIC

By 10pm, bars across Madrid are filled with live music. For visitors unfamiliar with local bands and venues, this can seem daunting and difficult to navigate. The best way to tame this beast is to check out the citywide program *Madrid En Vivo* (www.madridenvivo.es; paper copy available at most bars).

The calendar is organized by neighborhood, venue, and musical style. Most events require a cover of €5-10, which usually includes a drink.

El Círculo de Bellas Artes de Madrid EL CENTRO

C. de Alcalá, 42

☎91 360 54 00; www.circulobellasartes.com

El Círculo de Bellas Artes is a factory of culture. This Art Deco tower on the periphery of the city center provides first-rate facilities to support the visual and performing arts and is accessible to the general public. Located on the pulsing C. de Alcalá, this hub of innovation fiercely rejects the idea that art and culture are made in kitschy shops on winding, romantic European roads. The seven floors provide facilities for temporary visual arts exhibits, performing arts exhibitions, and film screenings. The building both celebrates Spain's rich cultural traditions and provides institutional support for emerging artists. Make sure to leave enough time to visit the rooftop terrace, which provides stunning panoramic views of the city. Also check out the streetside cafe—it's one of Madrid's finest. This is where serious art happens in Madrid, and it's not to be missed.

▶ ✠ Ⓜ Sevilla. Walk 1 block northwest to the intersection of C. Gran Vía. *i* Check the website for ticket prices and event schedules. Free Wi-Fi. Ⓢ Rooftop access €2. 🕐 Open M 11am-2pm, Tu-Sa 11am-2pm and 5-8pm, Su 11am-2pm. Cafe open M-Th 9am-midnight, F-Sa 9am-3am.

Cafe Central LAS HUERTAS

Pl. del Ángel, 10

☎91 369 32 26; www.cafecentralmadrid.com

Since 1982, Cafe Central has been a premier venue for live jazz in Madrid. While plenty of cafes and bars of a similar breed have cropped up since then, Cafe Central continues to attract the best groups in the city. With its signature red facade along Pl. del Ángel and cool Art Deco interior, it stands out from the pack. Nightly concerts last from 10pm until midnight and feature primarily instrumental groups and the occasional vocalist. Check online for an up-to-date schedule.

▶ ✠ Ⓜ Antón Martín. From the Metro, take C. de León 1 block north to C. de las Huertas, and follow for 3 blocks until it ends at Pl. del Ángel. The cafe is on the left. Ⓢ Cover €8-12. 🕐 Open M-Th 1:30pm-2:30am, F-Sa 1:30pm-3:30am, Su 1:30pm-2:30am.

Clamores

MALASAÑA

C. de Albuquerque, 14

☎91 445 79 38; www.salaclamores.com

Located just north of Malasaña, Clamores attracts a following of *madrileños* committed to the city's live music scene. While Clamores calls itself a jazz venue, it pushes the envelope with a program of pop, soul, funk, rock, and everything in between. Unlike some of the smaller jazz bars and cafes around Madrid, Clamores has a proper stage and better acoustics, which allows for more dynamic programming across musical genres. Clamores has been around for 25 years, but the program is fresh and new, so be sure to check the website for an up-to-date calendar.

▶ ⚲ Ⓜ Bilbao. Walk north up C. de Fuencarral and make a right on C. de Albuquerque. Ⓢ Cover €5-12. Beer €3-5. Cocktails €6-8. Ⓩ Most shows 9, 9:30, or 10:30pm. Check the schedule online.

Café Jazz Populart

LAS HUERTAS

C. de las Huertas, 22

☎91 429 84 07; www.populart.es

Café Jazz Populart has a mixed program of American jazz, blues, and country for its nightly sets. While many jazz clubs

Juan Belmonte

Known as the "greatest matador of all time," Juan Belmonte revolutionized the art of bullfighting. Although he was born in 1892 with slightly deformed legs and could not run and jump, that did not stop him from becoming a matador. Unlike the other matadors of his time who jumped and twirled around the bull like circus performers, Belmonte stood still and forced the bull to move around him. Within inches of the bull, he stood his ground, while other matadors stayed well out of range. In 1919, he set a record by fighting in 109 *corridas* (bullfights) in a single year, despite being frequently gored as a result of his daredevil style. He sustained one of his most serious injuries in a 1927 bullfight, when he was impaled through the chest and pinned against a wall by a bull. After lifelong injuries and trauma, his doctors informed him in 1962 that he could no longer smoke cigars, ride horses, drink wine, or have sex. In a last act of Tarantino-style defiance, he did all four and then took a pistol to his head, claiming "if I can't live like a man, I might as well die like one."

in Madrid stick to traditional instrumental trios, quartets, and quintets, Café Populart features more vocalists and rowdier groups that get people out of their seats. The small room, styled like an old school *madrileño* cafe with musicians cramped onto a tiny stage, creates the setting for one of the city's most enjoyable live music venues.

▶ ♯ Ⓜ Antón Martín. Walk north up C. de León and make a left onto C. de las Huertas. Ⓢ Cover €5; includes 1 drink. ⏰ Open M-Th 6pm-2:30am, F-Sa 6pm-3:30am, Su 6pm-2:30am. Sets daily 10:15, 11:30pm.

Honky Tonk   SALAMANCA
C. de Covarrubias, 24
☎91 445 68 86; www.clubhonky.com

Honky Tonk is where nostalgic *madrileños* come to hear cover bands play The Rolling Stones, The Beatles, and other classic '60s rock and roll. While Honky Tonk is open throughout the week and has live sets most nights, given its location in the quieter neighborhood of Chamberi (near Salamanca), things can be pretty quiet early in the evening. Honky Tonk is best on weekends, especially when the cover bands take the stage at 12:30pm.

▶ ♯ Ⓜ Alonso Martinez. Go north up C. de Santa Engracia. Make a left onto C. de Nicasio Gallego and a right onto C. de Covarrubias. Ⓢ Cover €10; includes 1 drink. Beer €3-5. Cocktails €9. ⏰ Open M-Th 9:30pm-5am, F-Sa 9:30pm-5:30am. Concerts M-Sa 12:30am.

FLAMENCO

Flamenco is a gypsy art dating back to 18th-century Andalucía that has become a 21st-century business in Madrid. Many flamenco clubs offer overpriced dinners combined with overdone music and dance spectaculars geared toward tourists. There are some clubs in Madrid that offer more traditional and soulful flamenco. You'll still pay a decent amount to see it, but it's a great way to learn about the art form that is often described as Europe's counterpart to the blues.

🪩 Casa Patas   LAS HUERTAS
C. de los Cañizares, 10
☎91 369 04 96; www.casapatas.com

While Casa Patas certainly caters to tourists, it remains one of Madrid's best venues for traditional flamenco. Though it offers dinner, the real attraction is the flamenco stage in back, where some of Madrid's finest dancers perform for packed tourist

Flamenco

Flamenco, an exotic dance involving flowing skirts, castanets, and quick steps, originated with gypsies in southern Spain. Spain first ridiculed the dance, like everything cool done by the gypsies, but gradually accepted and transformed it into a beloved—and lucrative—art. Those gypsies were onto something. In November 2010, UNESCO named flamenco a globally treasured art form. Although Madrid is not the birthplace of flamenco, it does have some great venues. Various restaurants have flamenco performance nights, and you may be able to find clubs offering flamenco lessons.

audiences. Tickets aren't cheap, but they're worth every penny. Shows sell out night after night, particularly in the summer months. The restaurant and tapas bar up front serve the usual suspects: platters of *jamón y queso* (€19), fried squid (€13), and *albondigas de la abuela* (grandma's meatballs; €3). Who could turn down grandma's meatballs?

▶ ✄ Ⓜ Antón Martín. From the Metro, walk up C. de Atocha and turn left onto C. del Olivar. Casa Patas is on the right. Ⓢ Tickets €32; includes 1 drink. Entrees €10-25. ☾ Open M-Th 1-4pm and 8pm-midnight, F-Sa 7:30pm-2am. Flamenco M-Th 8:30pm, F-Sa 9pm and midnight.

Cardamomo   LAS HUERTAS

C. de Echegaray, 15

☎91 369 07 57; www.cardamomo.es

Cardamomo offers traditional flamenco that has a raw improvisational quality to it. The focus is more on rhythm and movement and less on the kitschy costumes that are usually synonymous with flamenco. You can expect to hear syncopated guitars and soulful old men crooning flamenco verse, and to see swift choreography. The nightly sets are short but intense (50min.) and a good way of seeing flamenco without dedicating an entire evening to it.

▶ ✄ Ⓜ Sol. Walk east toward Pl. de las Cortes and make a right onto C. de Echegaray. Ⓢ Tickets €25; includes 1 drink. Check with your hostel for discounts. ☾ Shows daily 10:30pm.

Las Tablas   GRAN VÍA

Pl. de España, 9

☎91 542 05 20; www.lastablasmadrid.com

This newly renovated tapas bar just west of Pl. de España

features a fine ensemble of soulful old guys and fit leading men and women. While the space is more comfortable than the smaller flamenco venues around the city, the intensity of the rhythm and movement doesn't hold up quite as well in the renovated space. Reservations are definitely recommended, as this is one of the more popular tourist venues for flamenco. Arrive early to get a seat up front—it will make a world of difference.

▶ ✣ Ⓜ Plaza de España. Head to the far end of the plaza. Ⓢ Tickets €25; includes 1 drink. ⓘ Shows M-Th 10pm; F-Sa 8, 10pm; Su 10pm.

THEATER

The obvious consideration for those interested in seeing live theater in Madrid is the language barrier. Madrid has a thriving theater scene, but much of it is inaccessible to those who don't speak Spanish. Madrid does host a number of international musicals like *Mamma Mia!* that are written in the universal language of glee. Many theaters also host concerts, dance productions, and flamenco spectacles that don't require any language skills.

Arts and Culture

▨ Teatro Coliseum   GRAN VÍA

C. Gran Vía, 78

☎91 542 30 35

Since C. Gran Vía is often referred to as the Broadway of Madrid, it makes sense that the sprawling Teatro Coliseum, home (at time of research) to the smash hit *Chicago, El Musical,* is located there. One of the largest theaters in the city, Teatro Coliseum has hosted some of Broadway's biggest international hits, like *Beauty and the Beast* and *Mamma Mia!* Tickets can be purchased online at www.arteria.com or at the box office. Teatro Coliseum also hosts concerts featuring Spanish and international pop musicians.

▶ ✣ Ⓜ Pl. de España. From the plaza walk east down C. Gran Vía. The theater is on the left. Ⓢ Tickets €10-40. ⓘ Box office open M-Th noon-8:30pm, F-Sa noon-10pm, Su noon-7pm. Check online for showtimes.

Teatro Español   LAS HUERTAS

C. del Principe, 25

☎91 360 14 84

Funded by Madrid's municipal government, the Teatro Español features a range of classic Spanish plays and performances.

This is Madrid's oldest stage; it dates back to a 16th-century open-air theater. Though the building has since been reconstructed many times, it has consistently played a critical role in the development of dramatic literature in Spain. The present building, which dates to the mid-1800s, has premiered works by Spain's most notable writers, including Benito Galdós and Antonio Vallejo, and played a critical role in the development of the literary culture of Las Huertas. Tickets can be purchased online at www.telentrada.com, by telephone, or at the box office.

▶ ♿ Ⓜ Antón Martín. Walk uphill on C. de Atocha. Make a right at the 1st light and head north until you see Pl. de Santa Ana. The theater is on the east side of the plaza. Ⓢ Tickets €3-20; ½-price on W. ⏰ Box office open Tu-Su 11:30am-1:30pm and 5pm-curtain.

Teatro Häagen-Dazs Calderón   LAS HUERTAS
C. de Atocha, 18

☎90 200 66 17; www.teatrohaagen-dazs.es

Named for its recent takeover by Häagen-Dazs, this theater has a seating capacity of 2000 and features musical, dance, and theaterical performances, with a focus on local Spanish musicals. Tickets can be purchased online at www.arteriaentradas.com, by telephone, or at the box office. Check online for up-to-date box office hours and showtimes.

▶ ♿ Ⓜ Tirso de Molina. From the Metro, walk north up C. del Doctor Cortezo. Ⓢ Tickets €25-60. ⏰ Shows begin most evenings at 8pm.

Teatro Bellas Artes   EL CENTRO
C. del Marqués de Casa Riera, 2

☎91 532 44 37; www.teatrobellasartes.es

Founded in 1961 by Jose Tamayo, the former director of the Teatro Español, this avant-garde theater was originally created to expose audiences to America's great playwrights of the 1950s, such as Arthur Miller and Tennessee Williams. Today Teatro Bellas Artes has a more diverse program with a mix of original Spanish productions and adaptations and translations of famous international works.

▶ ♿ Ⓜ Banco de España. Walk west down C. de Alcalá and make a left onto C. del Marqués de Casa Riera. Ⓢ Tickets €16-25. ⏰ Box office open Tu-Su 11:30am-1:30pm and 5pm-curtain.

FÚTBOL

You might see churches every city you go to in Spain, but the official national religion is fútbol. Matches are a beloved spectacle everywhere in the country, but particularly in Madrid, which is home to **Real Madrid,** arguably the greatest soccer club the world has ever known. On game days, from the end of August through the end of May, locals line the streets and pack bars to watch the match. Celebrations after games are common in public plazas and squares, probably helped by the fact that most matches fall on Saturdays. For Real Madrid, the victory party always takes place in **Plaza Cibeles,** just outside of town hall. The other two major teams in Madrid are **Atlético** and **Getafe.**

Fútbol Fail

After 18 years of disappointing losses, Madrid's soccer team, Real Madrid, finally won back the Copa del Rey trophy in 2011. But within a few hours of defeating archrival Barcelona, Real Madrid lost the trophy again—under the wheels of a bus. In the raucous post-game celebration on the bus back to the city, Sergio Ramos dropped the 33-pound cup on the ground and the team bus ran it over. This generated plenty of smart-assery—"apparently the weight of the win was too much for the team to handle," etc. Needless to say, the cup was a bit squished, and team officials hastened to pick up the broken pieces and get the cup repaired. Sixty thousand fans gathered at Cibeles, the fountain where Real Madrid celebrates its victories, to catch a glimpse of the shiny trophy, but the shattered pieces were hidden from sight. Madrid went wild anyway—even a broken trophy couldn't put a dent in their celebrations.

Seeing a game live with 80,000 other fans can be an incredible experience, but often difficult logistically. Tickets are expensive and hard to come by. All teams sell a number of tickets through their stadium box offices and release a limited number online through their club website. If you are intent on going to a game, research ticket availability at least two weeks in advance. Tickets are also available from vendors outside the stadium, but these are often counterfeited or marked up well above face value. Tickets for Atlético and Getafe tend to be cheaper and more available than tickets for Real Madrid. And if you don't make it to the stadium, it's worth going to a local tapas bar to watch.

🏟 Estadio Santiago Bernabéu   NORTH OF CITY CENTER

Av. de Concha Espina, 1

☎91 464 22 34; www.santiagobernabeu.com, www.realmadrid.com

Site of the 2010 European Final Cup, Estadio Santiago Bernabéu is also home to Real Madrid, named the greatest club of the 20th century by FIFA. Come watch a match and feel the tumultuous energy of the crowd as it cheers on its beloved home team. Tours of the stadium are also available and take you to its most hallowed grounds: from the trophy room to the visitors' dressing room to the pitch itself. Tickets to European club soccer games are notoriously difficult to come by, and Real Madrid is no exception. Most tickets go to season ticket holders, and a limited number of tickets are released at the central stadium box office at Gate 40 located next to tower A. Advance tickets can also be purchased at www.servicaixa.com, and remaining tickets are released on the club website at 11am the Monday before each game.

▶ ✛ Ⓜ Santiago Bernabéu. The stadium is across the street from the Metro. Ⓢ Tickets €30-300. Tours €16, under 14 €10. ⏰ Season runs from the beginning of Sept through the end of May. Check online for game schedules and tour times.

Get Real

You're bound to come across a couple of Real Madrid fans in Madrid. Officially the most popular team in the world with over 228 million supporters, Real Madrid has enjoyed the love of *madrileños* and fans the world over, and the team has the track record to keep it. Real Madrid's biggest rival is Barcelona, against whom they face off twice a year. If you do manage to nab a ticket for a match (whether it's to watch soccer or just ogle attractive men running across a field) during the *fútbol* season, remember to cheer *"Hala Madrid!"*—or else feel the wrath of a stadium full of raucous *madrileños*.

Estadio Vicente Calderón   SOUTH OF CITY CENTER

Paseo de la Virgen del Puerto, 67

☎91 364 22 34; www.clubatleticodemadrid.com

Estadio Vicente Calderón is home to the Atlético *fútbol* club (red and white stripes). With a storied past that includes European Cups and international recognition, this Madrid-based club participates in the esteemed Primera División of La Liga. While they've had some big wins in the past, they are the perennial underdogs in the city rivalry with Real Madrid. While this stadium may not be the city's biggest stage for soccer, it's a good place to take part in the *madrileño* tradition. Tickets can be purchased at www.servicaixa.com or on the club website.

▶ ✈ Ⓜ Pirámides. From the Metro, head west 1 block to C. de Toledo and follow it 1 block south to Paseo de los Melancólicos. The stadium is on the left. Ⓢ Prices vary. Ⓩ Check the website for schedule.

Coliseum Alfonso Pérez   SOUTH OF CITY CENTER

Av. Teresa de Calcuta
☎91 695 97 71; www.getafecf.com

Coliseum Alfonso Pérez is home to the Getafe *fútbol* club. The club was founded in 1946 and merged with another local club in 1983. This club offers spectators some great soccer, but it pales in comparison to local rivals. Tickets can be purchased in person at the stadium box office or online from www.entrada.com.

▶ ✈ Ⓜ Villaverde Alto. Stop is 1hr. from Puerta del Sol on the number 3 Metro. From the Metro, walk 1 block east to Av. Real de Pinto. Take Av. Real de Pinto 4 blocks through the highway underpass and turn left on Av. Teresa de Calcuta. The stadium is on the left. Ⓢ Tickets €40-80. Ⓩ Check the website for a schedule.

FESTIVALS

Three Kings Procession   EL CENTRO

The one day Spaniards don't party too hard is Christmas. So they instead celebrate the Epiphany, the day when the three kings arrived to Bethlehem to view baby Jesus. During the Three Kings Procession, three Santa-like men parade through the downtown with 30 carriages filled with 7000kg of sweets, making a pathway from from Parque del Buen Retiro to Pl. Mayor via Puerta del Sol. The kings and their helpers (not elves) shower sweets on the huge crowd in the streets, and local establishments host events for children.

▶ ✈ Ⓜ Sol. Ⓩ Jan 5.

El Gordo

What better way to get in the Christmas spirit than by gambling away your savings in a huge, country-wide lottery? Each year on December 22nd, tickets are drawn for the largest prize of any lottery in the world, El Gordo. Starting around mid-September, 85,000 different numbers are sold in a complicated system that involves buying a tenth of a ticket, or *decima*. Tickets are €20 apiece, culminating in a €3 billion prize pot. Of course, like any good European government, the Spanish administration takes 30% off the top, leaving a still ridiculously large pot of €2.142 billion. There are thousands of different prizes, but the coveted first prize is a whopping €3 million. Drawing the tickets is an elaborate ritual that begins on the morning of December 22nd. In the Lotería Nacional Hall of Madrid, one ball from a large cage is drawn bearing the winning number and another ball is drawn from a different cage representing the prize. Life in Spain comes to a halt while children from San Ildefonso school sing out the numbers as they are drawn. With 1787 prizes to award, the whole lottery process takes about three hours, but don't worry about the children—they sing in shifts. When the top prize is drawn, you can almost hear Spain's collective sigh of disappointment (minus the winner, of course, who is busy with a heart attack).

Madrid Carnaval   CITYWIDE

http://carnaval.esmadrid.com/

The week before Lent, Madrid celebrates with a citywide festival of theater, dance, and music, culminating in a grand parade on Saturday evening. The parade starts in Parque del Buen Retiro and travels to Pl. de Cibeles before ending at Pl. de Colón. There's also a tradition called "The Burial of the Sardine," in which participants decked out in black cloaks and hats walk through the streets with a coffin containing an effigy of a dead sardine. Don't understand? Neither do we, but it's cool. You can download a full program of events at the festival website.

▶ 🗓 Mar 4-9. Grand Parade Sa 7pm.

Madrid en Danza   CITYWIDE

www.madrid.org/madridendanza

From mid-March to late April, Madrid plays host to a flurry of dance performances from around the world. From ballet to modern, there's something for everyone at this festival that celebrates movement, not Tony Danza.

▶ *i* Consult the festival website for a performance schedule. Ⓢ Tickets €5-20. Most tickets sold online at www.entrada.com. ⏲ Mar-Apr.

Dos de Mayo   MALASAÑA

On May 2, 1808, the people of Madrid rose up against Joseph Bonaparte, Napoleon's brother, to fight for freedom from French rule. Among the mobs was Manuela Malasaña, a 17-year-old seamstress who died a brutal death defending Spain. Today she and the many other victims of the attacks are honored in Malasaña's biggest party. The center of the festivities is the Pl. del Dos de Mayo, a major site of the uprisings. The gathering of young people in the plaza is one of the most infamous festival events of the calendar year, and the party carries on well into the night in the area's bars, cafes, restaurants, and clubs.

▶ ⚧ Ⓜ Tribunal. From the Metro, take C. de la Palma 2 blocks west to C. de San Andrés. Turn right and head north 1 block.

Fiestas de San Isidore   CITYWIDE

www.esmadrid.com/sanisidro

This week-long festival takes over the city's streets and plazas to celebrate Madrid's patron saint Isidore the Laborer. The primary stage is Pl. Mayor, where street performers, parades, and vendors selling *barquillos* (ice cream cones) take over. There are dance, theater, and music performances throughout the city, and fireworks along the banks of the Mazanares near San Isidore's home. The festivities culminate on May 15 with a large procession across the Mazanares and a mass at the Basilica of San Isidore. While the festival is filled with pomp and circumstance, many *madrileños* celebrate more informally with picnics in Parque del Buen Retiro and parties at bars, cafes, and clubs around the city. For bullfighting enthusiasts, this festival marks the beginning of a month of nightly bullfights at La Plaza de las Ventas, which features the world's best fighters and most vicious bulls. Tickets for these bullfights are difficult to get; check the stadium website www.las-ventas.com for schedules and availability.

▶ ⚧ Ⓜ Sol. *i* Consult the festival website for details on concerts and performances around the city. ⏲ May 8-15.

BollyMadrid   LAVAPIÉS

www.bollymadrid.com

During the first week of June, Lavapiés features Bollywood

dance performances, movies, and amazingly cheap Indian food. Get that henna facial tattoo you always wanted, grab a few samosas, and check out the mighty Sharukh Kahn in one of the open-air film screenings. Check online for an updated schedule of performances.

▶ ✠ Ⓜ Lavapiés. Ⓢ Performances free. Food €1-5. ☾ 1st week of June.

Día de la Música   SOUTH OF CITY CENTER

Paseo de la Chopera, 14

☎91 517 95 56; www.diadelamusica.com

What was once the city's largest slaughterhouse is now home to one of Madrid's biggest music festivals. Within a few years, Matadero Madrid, with help from the city government, has been converted from an industrial wasteland into a vast multi-purpose community art center with art installations, exhibition halls, and bandshells. This music festival brings in big name international artists like Janelle Monae and Lykke Li. Día de la Música is one of Matadero Madrid's biggest annual events, with great music and the latest in contemporary art and design.

▶ ✠ Ⓜ Legazpi. From the Metro station, walk 1 block northwest up Paseo de la Chopera. Matadero is on the left. *i* Tickets can be purchased online at www.entradas.com or in person. Ⓢ €15-24. ☾ Mid-June. Concerts M-Tu 8pm-1am, Sa-Su 11am-1am.

Orgullo Gay   CHUECA

www.orgullogay.org

During Orgullo Gay, one of the biggest Pride parades in Europe, Madrid explodes with GLBT celebrations, parades, parties, and more. Chueca, Madrid's gay district, is packed, particularly on the last Saturday of the festival when the parade takes over the neighborhood.

▶ ✠ Ⓜ Chueca. ☾ Last week of June.

PhotoEspaña   EL CENTRO

☎91 298 55 23; www.phe.es/festival

PhotoEspaña is a public photography exhibition that takes over the city center in early summer. From exhibits in the Reina Sofía to sidewalk installations, PhotoEspaña seeks to showcase the latest developments in still photography and video art. Each year the festival exhibits work of a common theme by dozens of artists from around the world. Plans of the exhibition are available at various public info points or online.

▶ *i* Public info points at Real Jardín Botánico; Pl. de Murillo, 2; and Teatro

Fernan Gomez Centro de Arte, Pl. de Colon, 4. $ Free. Exhibits in ticketed museums subject to normal admission fees. 🕐 June-July.

Fiestas de La Latina and Lavapiés   LA LATINA AND LAVAPIÉS

This triumvirate of festivals in La Latina and Lavapiés celebrates the neighborhoods' respective patron saints. These days are typically a hot sweaty mess of tradition, with *madrileños* dressed in unseasonably warm 19th-century clothing and drinking sangria to cool off. The first festival takes place around August 7th, and celebrates San Cayetano in and around Pl. de Cascorro. The second festival (Aug 10), celebrates San Lorenzo near Pl. de Lavapiés. The final festival day (Aug 15) features a parade in which the city firemen carry an image of the Virgin of Paloma between the two neighborhoods as locals sing her praises.

▶ ⚥ Ⓜ Lavapiés or Ⓜ La Latina. 🕐 2nd week of Aug.

Too Many Grapes

On New Year's Eve, thousands gather in Puerta del Sol in the center of Madrid to ring in the New Year. As the clock strikes 12, a strange thing happens—everyone starts eating grapes. For each of the 12 chimes of the clock, each person eats one grape, symbolizing one month of good luck. All the grapes must be finished by the last chime to ensure a year of good fortune, but many people can't eat the grapes fast enough and end up ringing in the New Year looking like chipmunks. This tradition dates back to 1909, when the grape growers of Alicante had a huge grape surplus. One smart fellow decided to invent a new tradition to convince his neighbors to help eat the extras. With everyone in Spain eating grapes on the New Year, the Alicante grape growers will likely be in business for a long time.

Nochevieja   EL CENTRO

To ring in the new year, thousands of *madrileños* gather at the city's version of Times Square, Puerta del Sol, to watch the ball drop from the clock tower. Instead of counting down, the clock chimes 12 times to represent the 12 upcoming months of the year, ending with a fireworks display. According to tradition, you're supposed to eat a grape at every toll and drink at midnight for good fortune.

▶ ⚥ Ⓜ Sol. 🕐 Dec 31.

Shopping

While areas like Puerta del Sol, Pl. Mayor, and Gran Vía are filled with name-brand chains, there are plenty of local boutiques, marketplaces, and flea markets that sell products unique to Madrid. El Rastro is undoubtedly the biggest shopping event in Madrid. This flea market, which takes place on Sundays in La Latina and Lavapiés, was once where thieves went to pawn goods. Today it offers antiques, clothes, books, and more. In the neighborhoods of Chueca and Malasaña you'll find the city's best upscale boutiques, many of which are prohibitively expensive for the budget traveler but always worth it for the window shopping. Salamanca is home to high-end European designers like Gucci and Prada. There, socks cost as much as a suit, and a suit costs more than a single family home.

Generally speaking, buying clothes in Europe isn't easy, it's often expensive, and it's not feasible for the budget traveler. If you're shopping more out of necessity than impulse, department stores like H&M and El Corte Inglés offer the cheapest clothes on the continent. There are also a number of good Spanish chain stores like Zara that offer quality products at reasonable prices.

Budget Shopping

Let's face it: Madrid is no poor man's paradise. Prada and Gucci wait on every corner. Trusty chains like **Zara** are great options with reasonable prices and pieces that will still feel unique (at least to the American traveler). Also be sure to peruse markets like **El Rastro** in La Latina for some vintage duds.

RETAIL STORES

ABC Serrano   SALAMANCA

C. de Serrano, 61

☎91 577 50 31; www.abcserrano.com

Located in the refurbished publishing headquarters of the ABC Newspaper, this complex houses upscale chains that sell everything from jewelry and cosmetics to art, housewares, and electronics. The location in the middle of Salamanca's high-end shopping district tends to attract *madrileños* from nearby. There's a rooftop terrace as well as a few cafes and dining options for when you need a quick break. While ABC Serrano might not be the most glamorous way to spend an afternoon in Madrid, it does conveniently bring all your errand destinations together under one roof.

▶ ⚒ Ⓜ Rubén Dario. From the Metro, walk 2 blocks east down C. de Juan de Bravo (crossing C. de Castelló) and turn right onto C. de Serrano. The complex in on the left. ⓩ Open M-Sa 10am-9pm, Su noon-8pm.

El Corte Inglés   EL CENTRO

C. de Preciados, 3

☎91 379 80 00; www.elcorteingles.es

Many other locations around the city

Steps away from Puerta del Sol, El Corte Inglés is the most conveniently located department store in the city. Located in multiple buildings around the central plaza, El Corte Inglés sells clothing, cosmetics, shoes, books, and electronics. Some staff members speak English.

▶ ⚒ Ⓜ Sol. C. de Preciados is to the left of the fountain as you face north. ⓩ Open M-Sa 10am-10pm.

Shopping

The Royal Family

Like many in the EU, Spain's royal family retains little of the power wielded by their ancestors. Nonetheless, they are still important national symbols. One royal couple that gets particular media attention is heir apparent Prince Felipe and his lovely (OK, hot) wife Letizia. Formerly a journalist, the princess is known for her fashion flare and for dressing up her two gorgeous daughters in Spanish brands like Mango and Zara. Just when you thought she couldn't get more patriotic, she loyally wears Spanish brands as she conducts her royal activities.

Zara   SALAMANCA
C. de la Princesa, 45
☎91 541 09 02; www.zara.es
Other major locations: C. de la Princesa, 58; C. de las Infantas, 5; C. de Preciados, 18.

There is at least one Zara in every major shopping district in Madrid. Much like Banana Republic in the United States, Zara offers professional attire as well as sportswear at reasonable prices. Men's and women's pants cost anywhere from €20 to 60, suits can be purchased for as little as €90, and women's dresses cost €20-60. Zara is a cheaper yet reliable alternative to boutique shopping.

▶ ⚡ Ⓜ Argüelles. ⏰ Open M-Sa 10am-8:30pm.

Camper   GRAN VÍA
C. Gran Vía, 54
☎91 547 52 23; www.camper.es
Other major locations: C. de Serrano, 24; C. de Preciados, 23; C. de Fuencarral, 45.

Camper promises that "Imagination Walks," and delivers with high-fashion leather, suede, and canvas shoes. Over the last 35+ years, Camper has developed into a signature Spanish brand.

▶ ⚡ Ⓜ Santo Domingo. Ⓢ Leather shoes €100-200. Sneakers and sandals €50-100. ⏰ Open M-Sa 9:30am-8:30pm.

EL RASTRO

El Rastro is the biggest thing in Madrid on Sundays. This open-air flea market takes over La Latina beginning at **Plaza de Cascorro** off C. de Toledo and ending at the bottom of **Calle Ribera de Curtidores,** with rows of stalls set in the middle of the road between the city's infamous streetside pawnshops. Modern art, American comics, and Art Deco furniture can all be found throughout the market. Bargains are possible if you keep your eyes peeled and haggle. While El Rastro is hugely popular with tourists, it's still typical for local families to head to the market together and go out to brunch afterward in La Latina or Lavapiés. El Rastro starts at 9am sharp and ends at 3pm, with many of the better shops closing earlier. While El Rastro is generally safe, the large crowds tend to attract pickpockets, so use common sense and be aware of your surroundings.

BOUTIQUES

Yube Madrid   CHUECA
C. de Fernando VI, 23
☎91 319 76 73; www.yubemadrid.com

European boutique shopping is unfortunately expensive and Yube is no exception. The carefully curated store in the middle of Chueca sells beautiful garments from international and local designers that are financial eons beyond reach for budget travelers. Menswear from designers like Paul Smith and women's blouses and dresses from French designer ba&sh are the very pinnacle of European style. While justifying the purchase might be difficult, this is a great place to check out the latest European trends.

▶ ⚕ Ⓜ Alonso Martínez. From the Metro, take Pl. de Santa Bárbara south 2 blocks to C. de Mejía Lequerica. Follow C. de Mejía Lequerica 2 blocks southeast until it becomes C. de Fernando VI. *i* Check the website for info on seasonal sales. Ⓢ Men's shirts €100-200. Women's dresses €100-300. Ⓧ Open M-Sa 9am-6pm.

Poète   SALAMANCA
C. de Castelló, 32
☎91 577 60 62; www.tiendapoete.com

Poète is one of Spain's finest boutique chains specializing in women's apparel. Originally started in Madrid, Poète has now

Shopping

expanded to 14 locations across the country. Poète models itself on the traditional French boutique, offering simple-patterned dresses and blouses. Poète also has more reasonable prices than other *madrileño* boutiques.

▶ ♿ Ⓜ Velázquez. Head east on C. de Goya 1 block and make a left onto C. de Castelló. Ⓢ Dresses and blouses €80-120. Shoes €100. Accessories €10-20.

Mini   ARGÜELLES

C. del Limón, 24

☎91 548 08 35; www.gruposportivo.com

Mini offers a collection of high-end menswear primarily from American upscale brands like Band of Outsiders, Universal Works, and Levi's Vintage, in addition to British brands like Fred Perry and Oliver Spencer. Mini's small boutique shop on C. del Limón is complemented by two sibling shops owned by Group Sportivo: **Duke,** which specializes in high-end shoes, and **Sportivo,** which focuses on American vintage. You can expect fairly standard European boutique prices at all three stores, with jeans and long-sleeved cotton shirts starting at €100.

▶ ♿ Ⓜ Ventura Rodríguez. From the Metro, head southeast on C. del Duque de Liria 2 blocks (just past El Jardin Secreto) and take a left onto C. del Limón. *i* Sportivo located at C. del Conde Duque, 20. Duke located at C. del Conde Duque, 18. Ⓢ Shirts €50-150. Pants €50-150. Shoes €100-200. ⏰ Open daily 10am-9pm.

Madrid in Love   CITYWIDE

☎63 989 15 18; www.madridinloveindustrial.com

Modeled on a concept that has taken Paris by storm, Madrid in Love is bringing the novelty of the "pop-up store" to Spain. Rather than owning a set retail space, Madrid in Love showcases a gallery of vintage decorative objects in various industrial spaces around the city. The company's owners travel through Europe carefully collecting, and every three to four months announce a two-week sale that attracts the city's most style-conscious. Though you may not have the chance to see this pop-up store in action, it's worth checking the website to see if there's an event while you're in town.

▶ *i* Location changes; consult the website for latest events. Exhibitions and sales last 2 weeks and take place every 3-4 months.

OhmyGOd   SALAMANCA

C. de Serrano, 70

☎34 914 354 412; www.ohmygod.com.es

Come to OhmyGOd boutique in upscale Salamanca for funky, chunky, one-of-a-kind jewelry. While you may not be able to take your eyes off these fancy baubles, keep in mind that they're about three times as much as a backpacker's daily budget.

▶ ⚡ Ⓜ Serrano. Walk 4 blocks north up C. de Serrano. Ⓢ Items start at €100. ⏰ Open M-Sa 10am-8:30pm.

BOOKS

Finding English books in Madrid can be very difficult. If you're looking for an English title, the best bet is to head to mega-chain stores like **El Corte Inglés** or **Casa del Libro** that sell whatever is on the bestseller list in addition to a small library of classic literature. If you're just browsing, Madrid has plenty of small bookstores that sell secondhand paperbacks and art books. You'll find many of these types of stores in Malasaña on **Calle de la Palma** and in Las Huertas on **Calle de las Huertas. Cuesta de Mayona** marketplace along the southern end of Parque del Buen Retiro has interesting offerings every Sunday, though be prepared to dig around to find something in English.

Casa del Libro   GRAN VÍA

C. Gran Vía, 29

☎90 202 64 02; www.casadellibro.com

Other locations C. de Fuencarral, 119 and C. de Alcalá, 96

This is the city's best bet for English titles. This Spanish equivalent of Barnes and Noble has three locations in Madrid, and many more across the country, each offering as substantial a foreign literature section as you will find. The location on C. Gran Vía has an entire floor of books in English and French where you can find everything from *Harry Potter* to Proust. They carry most bestsellers in English, and prices are reasonable, with paperbacks starting around €12.

▶ ⚡ Ⓜ Gran Vía. Walk west down C. Gran Vía. Ⓢ Paperbacks €8-15. Hardcovers €20-30. ⏰ Open M-Sa 9:30am-9:30pm, Su 11am-9pm.

Arrebato Libros   MALASAÑA

C. de la Palma, 21

☎91 282 11 11; www.arrebatolibros.com

Arrebato Libros is a typical Malasaña bookshop featuring

esoteric books of poetry, philosophy, art, and graphic novels. This two-room shop has plenty of titles in Spanish and a modest English selection, but they are best known for their collections of rare books salvaged from fairs around the city. Secondhand paperbacks run exceptionally cheap (€3-6), and rare secondhand books and art books tend to be more expensive (€20). The shop is also involved in the local literary community, hosting weekly readings and lectures. Check the website for a schedule of upcoming events.

▶ ✈ Ⓜ Tribunal. From the Metro, head west down C. de la Palma. ⌚ Open M-Sa 10:30am-2pm and 5-8:30pm.

Berkana Librería Gay y Lesbiana   CHUECA

C. de Hortaleza, 64

☎91 522 55 99; www.libreriaberkana.com

This Chueca bookstore features a large selection of books related to GLBT issues, from novels by famous gay writers like Truman Capote, Allen Ginsberg, and Tennessee Williams to comics like *El Kamasutra Gay*. It also has a wide collection of books about adolescence, education, religion, and philosophy. Prices here tend to be a bit higher than at most bookstores. Berkana keeps a table of flyers and pamphlets about the latest GLBT happenings in and around the *barrio*.

▶ ✈ Ⓜ Chueca. From the Metro, turn around, make a right on C. de Augusto Figueroa, and make another right onto C. de Hortaleza. Ⓢ Paperbacks €10-25. DVDs €10-15. ⌚ Open M-F 10am-9pm, Sa 11:30am-9pm, Su noon-2pm and 5-9pm.

Altaïr   ARGÜELLES

C. de Gaztambide, 31

☎91 543 53 00; www.altair.es

Altaïr specializes in all books related to travel. They offer an extensive collection of English-language city and country guides as well as handy books of maps, photography, and travel writing. Altaïr's location in Argüelles won't be accessible by foot for most visitors to Madrid, but if you are need of anything travel-related, this is your best bet, as most bookstores in Madrid have very limited travel sections and mostly carry Spanish titles.

▶ ✈ Ⓜ Argüelles. Walk north up C. de Hilarión Eslava, then make a right onto C. de Meléndez Valdés and a left onto C. de Gaztambide. ⌚ Open M-F 10am-2pm and 4:30-8:30pm, Sa 10:30am-2:30pm.

Cuesta de Moyano

AVENIDA DEL ARTE

If you're looking for Spanish books, head to Cuesta de Moyano, the book marketplace on the southern edge of Parque del Buen Retiro. Around 30 stalls set up shop every Sunday to sell secondhand finds and antique books. Come and browse the stalls to find some Spanish first editions before heading to an afternoon picnic in the park.

▶ ✈ Ⓜ Atocha. Cross Paseo del Prado and walk uphill. The market is on the edge of the park on the right. 🕐 Open Su 10:30am-sunset.

Excursions

When you're ready to detox from a week of partying nonstop, hop the high-speed train for some straight chillin' in **Segovia,** marzipan in **Toledo,** and—er—more partying? in the college town of **Salamanca.** Sleepy Segovia offers travelers a respite from busy city-living as well historic sights like the Roman aqueduct and the 12th-century Alcázar, while the winding cobblestone roads and Gothic architecture of Toledo will transport you back to the middle ages. Salamanca's nearly 800-year-old university still hosts 30,000 students every year, which means plenty of budget-friendly nightlife and food for travelers.

Budget Excursions

The excursions we've listed are so close and so small that they can easily be done as day trips, which means you likely won't need to shell out for a hostel. There are a number of things to do to save some money in each destination. First, bring a bag lunch from home: some of the food in these cute little towns comes with not-so-cute price tags. There are ways to get out of paying for the sights, too: while in Toledo, arguably the best sight, **Museo del Greco,** is free during certain hours on the weekend. In Salamanca, the main attraction is the **University,** which is free to visit on Monday mornings. And in Segovia, most of the sightseeing consists of architecture and landmarks and is therefore altogether free. Don't let budget concerns stop you from venturing to these picturesque towns.

TOLEDO

Known as La Ciudad de las Tres Culturas (the city of three cultures), this small town was the medieval home of Muslims, Jews, and Christians. Toledo was the birthplace of the painter El Greco, and it has remained largely unchanged since the 16th century, when it inspired his famous *View of Toledo,* which hangs in New York's Metropolitan Museum of Art. Today, you can walk through winding cobblestone streets to take in beautiful Gothic buildings and views of the surrounding river. The city center has become rather commercial, with souvenir shops selling knight's armor, Damascene swords (a la *Lord of the Rings*), and marzipan, a sweet almond treat.

Orientation

Toledo is a web of cobblestone streets that fork at every opportunity. A wrong turn is almost inevitable, but you'll find yourself back on the right path in no time; while Toledo is a reasonably large city of 80,000 people, the historic city center with all of the major landmarks is small and very walkable. On the eastern edge of the historic center you'll find the **Alcázar,** a third-century CE Roman palace; on the western edge there's the **Monasterio de San Juan de Los Reyes;** and at the city center is the **Cathedral of Saint Mary of Toledo,** which is one of Spain's largest and most significant Gothic cathedrals. The best way to

Excursions

navigate from east to west through the city center is to follow **Calle del Commercio** from **Plaza de Zocódover.** This street turns into **Calle del Hombre de Palo** and then **Calle de la Trinidad.** This path will take you from Pl. de Zocódover past the Cathedral. To get some of the best views of the countryside, follow **Calle de los Reyes Católicos** from Monasterio de San Juan de los Reyes for two short blocks to **Plaza del Barrio Nuevo** on the southwestern edge of the city.

Accommodations

Almost all budget accommodations in Toledo look and feel like small family-run hotels, with proper reception areas, small restaurants, and clean private rooms with ensuite bathrooms. Prices throughout town are fairly standardized: singles generally cost €30-40, doubles €50-60, and triples €70-80. Those traveling to Toledo in the summer, and particularly on summer weekends, should make reservations in advance.

Hotel Palacio   HOSTAL $$

C. de Navarro Ledesma, 1
☎92 528 00 83; www.hostalpalacios.net

Hostal Palacio delivers hotel-quality rooms with pastel walls, tiled floors, and balconies overlooking the street. The rooms are as clean as the guest room in your OCD family friend's house. The *hostal* is located in a beautiful building, with a restaurant and a nice common room with computer access. The standard continental breakfast is cheap (€2), and the hotel owners offer discounts on lunch and dinner as well.

▶ ⚗ From the cathedral, walk northeast up C. de Nuncio Viejo. *i* Breakfast €2. Free Wi-Fi. ⑤ Singles €30-35; doubles €50. ⛫ Reception 24hr.

Hotel Imperio   HOTEL $$

C. de las Cadenas, 5
☎92 522 76 50; www.hotelimperio.es

Long a budget favorite in Toledo, the Imperio has basic hotel amenities, friendly service, and an excellent location, just one block from Pl. de Zocódover and close to the Alcázar and cathedral. Rooms feature well-made beds with crisp white sheets and large ensuite bathrooms with toiletries and fresh towels. The downstairs restaurant serves continental breakfast (€2-4) and there are plenty of quality restaurants nearby. The only drawback here is the temperamental Wi-Fi, which only works in the lobby. C. de las Cadenas is a reasonably quiet sidestreet, so you can count on a good night of sleep.

▶ ⚑ From the cathedral, head straight north. The hotel is next to the Iglesia de San Nicolás. *i* Free Wi-Fi. Groups of 3 or more check availability and prices online. Ⓢ Singles €30; doubles €45, with extra bed €60. ⓩ Reception 24hr.

La Posada de Manolo   HOTEL $$$
C. de Sixto Ramón Parro, 8
☎92 528 22 50; www.laposadademanolo.com

La Posada de Manolo is as good as budget accommodations get in Spain. The rooms have medieval cottage decor (including old-school wooden tools on the wall), and they actually pull it off, successfully avoiding the saggy, abandoned-nursing-home feel that is so often the result elsewhere. The hotel is a beautiful building, with a central staircase leading to the salon dining room where a full breakfast buffet is served daily. The hotel also has a rooftop terrace where you can enjoy a drink with spectacular views of the town and countryside. Its location next to the cathedral is ideal, and should make for a quiet night of sleep unless Sister Maria falls off the wagon again.

▶ ⚑ C. de Sixto Ramón Parro, a quiet street at the southeast edge of the cathedral. *i* Free Wi-Fi. Ⓢ Singles €42; doubles €66. ⓩ Reception 24hr.

Albergue Juvenil Castillo de San Servando (HI)   HOSTEL $
Subida al Castillo
☎92 522 45 54; albergueclm@jccm.es

This hostel is in a castle. Enough said. One of the dominant features on the Toledo skyline, this fortress gave refuge to the top-ranking Castilian general El Cid Campeador during his exile in 1080. Located 10-15min. uphill from the middle of town, the HI hostel features spacious common rooms, a pool with a panoramic view of the center of Toledo, and the lowest rates in the city. Be sure to join Hosteling International and then reserve far in advance if you wish to stay here.

▶ ⚑ From the city center, cross the river using Puente de Acántara. You'll be able to see it from afar. It's the only castle in the area. *i* Wi-Fi €1 per hr. Ⓢ Dorms €14. HI card required. ⓩ Lockout 11am-2pm.

HOSTAL CENTRO   HOSTAL $$$
C. Nueva, 13
☎92 525 70 91; www.hostalcentrotoledo.com

You've seen these rooms before, and you slept just fine: wood-framed beds with floral bedspreads, balconies overlooking the street, and clean private bathrooms that are larger than usual. Hostal Centro is located right next to Pl. de Zocódover, which is terrific if you are arriving by bus and want to settle quickly without meandering too far into the winding streets in town. While Zocódover is fairly tame throughout the year, if you are staying on a summer weekend, you might want to request an interior-facing room.

▶ ⚗ Pl. de Zocódover. *i* Breakfast €2. Free Wi-Fi. ⑤ Singles €30-35; doubles €50; triples €65. ⟡ Reception 24hr.

Sights

Toledo is packed with sights. If it all seems overwhelming, keep in mind that many of these sights can be visited quickly, cheaply, or simply admired from the exterior. Grab a **free map** of local sights from the tourist office.

🖾 Museo del Greco   MUSEUM

Paseo del Tránsito, s/n

☎92 522 36 65; www.museuodelgreco.mcu.es

After a five-year renovation and much anticipation, El Museo del Greco has finally opened to the public, and it does not disappoint. Directly across from the quarters where El Greco lived and worked, this museum offers a unique perspective on El Greco the Artist and Mr. Greco the Man. While his paintings grace the walls of museums around the world, this is one of the few collections dedicated specifically to his work. In a short tour (45min.) through the museum, you can see the bizarre qualities of his art up close: the supernatural use of light and the elongated figures. The collection contains some absolute masterpieces, including a room of portraits of the 13 apostles.

▶ ⚗ From Monasterio de San Juan de los Reyes, follow C. Reyes de los Católicos southeast to Paseo del Tránsito. ⑤ €3, students and seniors €1.50, Sa 2-8pm and Su 2-3pm free. Cash only. ⟡ Open Apr-Sept Tu-Sa 9:30am-8pm, Su 10am-3pm; Oct-Mar Tu-Sa 9:30am-6:30pm, Su 10am-3pm.

🖾 Monasterio de San Juan de los Reyes   MONASTERY

C. Reyes de los Católicos, 17

☎92 522 38 02; www.sanjuandelosreyes.org

Located on the western edge of the city, the Monasterio de los Reyes was commissioned by Ferdinand and Isabella to commemorate their victory in the Battle of Toro. While the building itself is impressive, with an intricately carved granite facade and stunning vaulted ceilings, what is most striking about the monastery is the tranquility of its cloister, with blooming fruit trees and beautiful gardens. This is another quick visit, but absolutely worth the nominal entry fee.

▶ ⚚ Located along the western edge of the city center. Follow the signs. Ⓢ €2.30, students and seniors €2. Cash only. 🕐 Open daily in summer 10am-6:30pm; in winter 10am-5pm.

Catedral Primada Santa María de Toledo   CATHEDRAL

C. del Cardenal Cisneros, s/n
☎92 522 22 41

Built between 1226 and 1493 on the site of a mosque, the Catedral Primada Santa María de Toledo (Cathedral of Saint Mary of Toledo) is considered by many to be Spain's greatest Gothic cathedral. The grandeur of its naves and transepts—and the intricacy of its chapels and altarpieces—is the product of endless toil and craftsmanship. While €7 is a bit steep, if you're going to visit any of the churches in Toledo, this should be one. If you're still too much of a cheapskate, at least walk around the outside. Particularly notable are the three intricately carved doorways on the front facade facing Pl. de Ayuntamiento: the door of forgiveness (center), the door of the last judgment (right), and the door of hell (left).

▶ ⚚ From Pl. de Zocódover, take C. del Commercio southwest to C. del Hombre de Palo and take a left (south) onto C. de Nuncio Viejo. 𝒊 Purchase tickets and audio tours across the street in Pl. de Ayuntamiento. Ⓢ €7. 🕐 Open M-Sa 10am-6:30pm, Su 2-6:30pm.

Iglesia de San Ildefonso   CHURCH

Pl. del Padre Juan de Mariana, 1
☎92 525 15 07

Advertised as the "view from heaven," the lookout point from the top of Iglesia de San Ildefonso features some truly spectacular panoramic views that include the Cathedral and Alcázar. Fair warning: you'll have to hike up quite a few stairs, so tell grandma to take off those stilettos (and wear a bra). This is probably the best view in Toledo, and the church interior's bright white walls and columns make it stand out from the massive stone-carved Gothic churches throughout Toledo.

▶ ⚚ From the cathedral, go north up C. de Nuncio Viejo. 𝒊 No tours during mass or religious ceremonies. Ⓢ €2.30, students €2. 🕐 Open daily May-Aug 10am-6:45pm; Sept-Apr 10am-5:45pm.

Excursions

Alcázar and Museo del Ejército
MUSEUM, PALACE

C. del General Moscardó, 4

☎92 522 16 73

The Alcázar of Toledo has long been equated with the might of the Spanish Empire. Built atop a third-century CE Roman fortress, the Alcázar is best known today as one of the most important battlegrounds of the Spanish Civil War. Because of its symbolic value and historical importance to the Spanish Kingdom, Republican troops believed that a successful capture of the Alcázar would strengthen their image in the public eye. For two months, Republican forces struggled to capture the Alcázar from Nationalist militias, quickly depleting resources of troops and artillery in the Siege of the Alcázar, now considered one of the Republican military's greatest blunders. Evidence of this turbulent history is found in the Alcázar's collection of military equipment, which dates back to the Medieval period. The collection includes firearms, uniforms, flags, and an informative exhibit on the history of the Alcázar going back to the Bronze Age.

▶ ⚔ From Pl. de Zocódover, walk 1 block south on Cuesta de Carlos V. The musem is the contemporary building labeled Museo del Ejército on the left. ⑤ €4, under 9 free. Cash only. ⏰ Open daily Oct-May 10am-7pm; June-Sept 10am-9pm.

Hospital de Tavera
MUSEUM

C. del Cardenal Tavera, 2

☎92 522 04 51

For our time-traveling readers, we would not recommend visiting here 400 years ago: this beautiful Renaissance building was once filled with beds occupied by the deathly ill. Today, the former hospital is hardly recognizable; it's been converted into a museum dedicated to the first Duque de Lerma, the hospital's original benefactor. Deathbeds been replaced by a significant collection of art and decorative objects, including a room of El Greco paintings commissioned by the hospital in the 16th century to give hope to the sick. (El Greco is also rumored to have pooped here once. Great.) Today the museum also includes the original hospital pharmacy and the administrative archives of the hospital. This building is owned by the descendants of the Duque de Lerma, and the basement is still used as the family crypt, just because it wasn't creepy enough otherwise.

▶ ⚔ Directly north of the city wall. From Puerta Nueva de Bisagra, go north up C. del Cardenal Taverna. ⏰ Open M-Sa 10am-1:30pm and 3-5:30pm, Su 10am-1pm.

Sinagoga de Santa Maria la Blanca   SYNAGOGUE

C. de los Reyes Católicos, 4

☎92 522 72 57

Built in 1180, this converted synagogue now owned by the Catholic Church is considered to be one of the oldest Jewish worship centers in Europe. Built by Moorish architects, it is now an art gallery featuring religious art and Toledo landscapes. While the interior is quite nice, the plain white columns and intricate stone details of the synagogue would be just as well appreciated from the exterior gardens without paying for admission.

▶ ⚢ From the monastery, walk east down C. de los Reyes Católicos. The gallery is on the left. Ⓢ €2.30. Cash only. ⏲ Open daily 10am-2pm and 3:30-6pm.

Museo de Santa Cruz   MUSEUM

C. Miguel de Cervantes, 4

☎92 522 10 36; www.jccm.es

Built in 1504 by the Catholic Church, this former church is considered a great work of Spanish Renaissance architecture. Today, the two-story museum holds a sizeable permanent collection of archaeological artifacts dating back to the Roman Empire, Spanish Renaissance paintings and sculpture, and an impressive collection of El Grecos, including his *Immaculate Conception.*

▶ ⚢ From Pl. de Zocódover, take C. de Santa Fe west and make a quick left to the museum entrance. Ⓢ Free. ⏲ Open M-Sa 10am-6:30pm, Su 10am-2pm.

Antiguos Instrumentos de Tortura   MUSEUM

C. de Alfonso XII, 24

☎92 525 38 56

With nooses, wooden cages, and crushing wheels galore, this exhibition of ancient torture devices is an eerie but interesting glimpse into the Spanish Inquisition and medieval justice. Wooden cages seem tame next to the head crusher, thumbscrews, heretic's fork, scold's bridle, and chastity belt. The interrogation chair, a seat made entirely of iron spikes that can be warmed up via fire underneath, is particularly disturbing. All in all, this mini-museum is great for the morbidly curious and S&M enthusiasts.

▶ ⚢ Just south of Iglesia de San Román. Ⓢ €4, children €3. Families €12. ⏲ Open daily 9am-8pm.

Excursions

Puente de Alcántara   BRIDGE, LANDMARK
East of Museo de Santa Cruz

Located on the eastern edge of the city, this footbridge was originally built by the Romans and later rebuilt by the Moors. A short walk to the footbridge offers great views of the River Tagus as well as views of the old city from just below its walls.

▶ ⚕ Located on the eastern edge of the city, near Museo de Santa Cruz. Follow the stairs down. ⑤ Free. ⌚ Open 24hr.

Food

Food in Toledo is not cheap, and it's catered toward tourists. Avoid picture menus and overpriced *prix-fixe* deals. Marzipan, a sweet treat made from almond paste and sugar, is absolutely everywhere. You won't miss it. While traditional hole-in-the-wall tapas bars are few and far between, there are still a number of great restaurants that cater to budget-conscious travelers.

▨ Restaurante Palacios   SPANISH $$
C. de Navarro Ledesma, 1
☎92 522 34 97; www.hostalpalacios.net

Located below the Hostal Palacios, this restaurant is packed throughout the day with locals and budget travelers looking to eat well on the cheap. The most popular dishes here are traditional stewed meat dishes, many of which are unique to Toledo, such as *perdiz a la toldena* (stewed partridge; €9) and *carcamusas* (stewed pork loin; €10). Also popular are grilled meat dishes like *chuleton ternera* (grilled steak; €10) and *venado a la plancha* (grilled venison; €10). While roast suckling pig typically costs €20-25, here they offer a half portion for only €10. Don't be dismayed by the picture menu outside and the English flag stamped on the outside of the restaurant: there's a reason budget travelers keep coming back.

▶ ⚕ From the cathedral, walk northeast up C. de Nuncio Viejo. *i* Discounts for guests of the hostal. ⑤ Breakfast €2-5. Full meals €10-20. Cash only. ⌚ Open daily 8am-1am.

La Flor de la Esquina   SPANISH $$
Pl. Juan de Mariana, 2
☎627 94 50 20; www.laflordelaesquina.com

The quaint decor of white-washed wooden cabinetry and hand-painted ceramic wall tiles at this small cafe belies a fine menu of appetizers, salads, and sandwiches. The obvious choice is the house special burger (with bacon, Manchego, and grilled onions; €7.50). While most places in Spain offer wimpy mixed salads with shredded carrots and tomatoes, here the grilled chicken caesar (€7) is a substantial meal in itself. For something lighter, they offer *bocaditos* (€2.50), miniature sandwiches made with far more love and care than those sloppy mammoths you see sitting behind so many lunch counters. This is one of the few places in town where you can ditch the picture menu and tourist prices and enjoy a quality meal. The terrace seating has some of the best views of the main cathedral.

▶ ⌖ With your back to Iglesia de Los Jesuitas, the restaurant is on the left. ⑤ Entrees €5-12. ⌚ Open daily noon-4pm and 6:30pm-midnight.

Taberna Alfileritos 24 SPANISH $$$

C. de Alfileritos, 24

☎90 210 65 77; www.alfileritos24.com

Taberna Alferitos offers an original menu and atmosphere that doesn't break the bank. While you can certainly eat cheaply with items like the grilled chicken caesar (€9) or the venison burger (€7), the meat and fish entrees are a surprisingly good deal. Rather than serving a la carte like most traditional restaurants, they serve proper entrees with sides, including a *bacalao con espinaca* (cod served with sauteed spinach; €17) and *lomo de cerdo con manzanas asadas* (pork tenderloin with grilled apples; €18). Many restaurants in Toledo struggle to pull off the contemporary aesthetic, but Alfileritos nails it with upstairs tables around the skylit courtyard and tucked into the intimate brick basement downstairs.

▶ ⌖ From Iglesia San Nicolás, make a left onto C. de Alfileritos. The restaurant is on the left. ⑤ Meals €10-25. ⌚ Open M-Sa 10am-1am, Su 10am-midnight.

Dar Al-Chai CAFE $

Pl. del Barrio Nuevo, 6

☎92 522 56 25; www.daralchai.es

Located on the western edge of the city, Dar Al-Chai is a picturesque cafe in a quiet part of town next to one of Spain's oldest synagogues. The interior resembles a dark hookah lounge, and a leafy canopy shades the outdoor terrace. The menu of loose-leaf teas as varied as any in Spain, including specialty teas that will cure all sorts of ailments, including indigestion, insomnia, and menstrual pains, ensures your return with your PMS-ing travel buddy in tow. A great selection of crepes sweetens the deal.

▶ ⚑ From Monasterio de San Juan de los Reyes, walk south down C. de los Reyes Católicos. Pl. del Barrio Nuevo is in a nook on the left. Ⓢ Coffee and tea €2-4. 🕐 Open M-Th 9:30am-10pm, F-Sa 4pm-1am, Su 9:30am-10pm.

Café del Fin

CAFE $$

C. del Taller del Moro, 1

☎92 525 10 52; www.cafedelfin.com

Pop on to one of Café del Fin's comfortable couches and enjoy a coffee and surprisingly high-quality pizza and burgers. While the food might not compare with what you're used to back home, it's a good alternative to blowing your budget on overpriced tapas at an expensive sit-down restaurant. The *hamburguesa de la casa* is the specialty here (half ground beef, half pork, served with sautéed mushrooms, salad, and fries; €7), and they offer a number of classic pizzas like barbecue chicken (€10), margherita (€9), and the Hawaiian (€10). With complimentary Wi-Fi and comfortable lounge seating up front, this is also a great place to bring your computer, even though that is a sacrilege in Spain.

▶ ⚑ From the monastery walk straight east down C. del Ángel and make a right onto C. del Taller del Moro. Ⓢ Entrees €6-14. 🕐 Open M-W 8:30am-6pm, Th 8:30am-1am, F 8:30am-2am, Sa 9am-2am, Su 9am-12:30am.

La Abadia

CERVECERÍA, SPANISH $$$

Pl. de San Nicolás, 3

☎92 525 11 40; www.abadiatoledo.com

While the upstairs bar is fairly standard, the downstairs dining in small brick catacomb rooms offers a unique setting. La Abadia has the standard tapas, but it specializes in larger shared dishes such as the grilled lamb platter (€30), grilled cod (€11), and the sampling platter of grilled beef, pork, and lamb (€17). A tasty selection of European beers on tap (€2) beyond the standard Mahou and San Miguel also help to set this place apart.

▶ ⚑ From Iglesia San Nicolás, walk straight north up C. de Núñez de Arce. The restaurant is on the right. Ⓢ Tapas €2-5. Entrees €10-20. Cocktails €4-9. 🕐 Open daily 1:30-11pm.

La Cure Gourmande

CHOCOLATE $

C. del Comercio, 23

☎92 525 89 90; www.la-cure-gourmande.com

With locations throughout Spain, France, and Belgium, La Cure Gourmande sells traditional European chocolates, candies, cookies, and local specialty marzipan. While they don't have quite the variety of marzipan as smaller local vendors, they make up for it with a huge selection of other European sweets (€3 per 100g) like the *galleta de mantequilla* (butter cookies).

▶ ⚔ Directly north of Mezquita de las Tornerías. Ⓢ Chocolates €1-10. ⏱ Open daily 10am-10pm.

Nightlife

Toledo's nightlife pales in comparison to Madrid's 24hr. party-animal lifestyle, but you can still find some good bars to sit, relax, and enjoy the medieval atmosphere.

🖼 Círculo de Arte Toledo   CAFE, MUSIC HALL

Pl. de San Vicente, 2

☎92 521 43 29; www.circuloartetoledo.org

The Círculo de Arte Toledo is a cafe, art gallery, and concert hall all housed in a renovated church. With modern paintings on the walls, Moorish arches, and white brick, it's a great place to grab an evening cocktail and check out a concert. Live music ranges from house to international pop, country, and folk. It really is a matter of luck here: if you come on the right weekend, you just might get to hear your favorite klezmer band!

▶ ⚔ Adjacent to Convento de Agustinas Descalzas. *i* Consult the monthly program (available at the entrance), as the schedule and cost of admission are subject to change. Ⓢ Wine €1.80-2. Coffee and cocktails €4-8. Tapas €5. ⏱ Hours vary depending on performance times. Concerts tend to start 8-9pm or around midnight.

La Taberna de Livingston   COCKTAIL BAR

C. de Alfileritos, 4

☎92 521 26 75

With zebra-print chairs, black and white pictures of Africa, hunting memorabilia, and British posters, this place screams Colonialism. Despite the decor, the establishment is a good stop for a post-dinner coffee or cocktail. And with portraits of white colonial leaders and pictures of wild animals being slaughtered lining the walls, the place lets all you animal-poaching travelers finally sit back at ease. This is a joke: *Let's Go* does not condone animal poaching, unless it is done with a harpoon gun, in which case coolness outweighs cruelty.

▶ ⚔ From Iglesia San Nicolás, make a left onto C. de Alfileritos. Ⓢ Wine €2-3. Cocktails €6. Tapas and desserts €4-6. ⏱ Open M-Th 9:30am-midnight, F-Sa 9:30am-1am, Su 9:30am-midnight.

Enebro
CAFE, BAR

Pl. de Santiago de los Caballeros, 1
www.barenebro.com
Pl. San Justo, 9

With three locations in tiny Toledo, Enebro is the go-to bar and nightlife stop for students in Toledo. Food here is limited to basic tapas, and the good selection of imported beers (Heineken, Budweiser, Foster's, Guinness; €2.50) is the real draw. While Enebro is primarily a spot for late-night mingling, there are occasional concerts and parties. Check online for an up-to-date schedule.

▶ ✿ Adjacent to Museo de Santa Cruz. ⑤ Drinks €4-6. ✪ Open daily 1pm-2am.

Picaro Cafe Teatro
BAR

C. de las Cadenas, 6
☎62 752 60 76

While Toledo is a fairly sleepy town, this is one of the few venues that keeps things going late. Just around the corner from Pl. de Zocódover, this club and cocktail lounge hosts DJ sets on weekends, playing loud techno beats well into the morning. Sometimes you can find a critical mass of Toledo's university students and tourists partying away, but on an off night during low season, you'll be hard-pressed to find much activity. Picaro's flashing lights and dance floor are a rarity in this town, but if you want them, they are there waiting for you.

▶ ✿ From the cathedral, walk north up C. de Tornerías. Veer right onto C. del Comercio. Make a left onto C. de la Plata and then a right onto C. de las Cadenas. ⑤ Cocktails €6. ✪ Open M-Th 4pm-3am, F-Sa 4pm-6am.

Essentials

Practicalities

- **TOURIST OFFICES:** There is a tourist office located in the **train station** that provides indispensable free maps of Toledo in English and Spanish. Grab one on your way from the station to the city. Another option is the **tourist information office.** (Puerta de Bisagra ☎92 522 08 43 ✪ Open M-F 9am-6pm, Sa 9am-7pm, Su 9am-3pm.) **Casa de Mapa** also provides free city maps. (Pl. de Zocódover ✪ Open daily 11am-7pm.)

- **ATMS: Banco Santander Central Hispano.** (C. del Comercio, 47 ☎92 522 98 00 ✪ Open Apr-Sept M-F 8:30am-2pm; Oct-Mar M-F 8:30am-2pm, Sa 8:30am-1pm.)

- **LUGGAGE STORAGE:** Lockers available at the **bus station.** (⑤ €1.80-3 per day. ✪ Open daily 7am-11pm.)

- **INTERNET ACCESS: Locutorío El Casco.** (C. de la Plata, 2 ☎92 522 61 65 ✦ Across from the post office. ⑤ €1.50 per hr. ✪ Open daily 11am-11pm.)

- **POST OFFICE:** C. de la Plata, 1 ☎92 528 44 37 ✪ Open M-F 8:30am-2pm and 5-8:30pm, Sa 9:30am-2pm.

Emergency

- **LOCAL EMERGENCY NUMBER:** ☎092.

- **NATIONAL EMERGENCY NUMBER:** ☎091.

- **LOCAL POLICE:** Av. de Carlos III, 2 ✦ At the intersection of Av. de la Reconquista and Av. de Carlos III. ☎92 525 04 12.

- **NATIONAL POLICE:** Av. Portugal, s/n ☎92 522 59 00.

- **HOSPITAL: Hospital Virgen de la Salud.** (Av. de Barber ☎92 526 92 00.)

- **PHARMACIES:** Pharmacies are located throughout the city; there's one at Pl. de Zocódover. (☎92 522 17 68 ✪ Open daily 9:30am-2pm and 5-8pm.)

Getting There

By Train

The **RENFE** high-speed train from Atocha is probably the best way to get to Toledo. (⑤ Approximately €11. ✪ 30min., 12 per day.) Student discounts are only available to native residents of the EU. Not all trains run every day. Consult **www.renfe.com** for details or pick up a pamphlet at the train station. If possible, buy your tickets one day prior as lines to buy tickets can be long and unpredictable. From the Toledo RENFE station (Paseo de la Rosa, 2 ☎92 522 30 99), a bus (€0.95) or a taxi (€10) can take you to the center of town. The bus stop is directly outside of the train station, 10m to the right. Take #5, 5D, 6.1, or 6.2 to get to Pl. de Zocódover.

By Bus

Buses run from **Estación Sur** in Madrid. (Ⓢ €5. ⚅ 1hr.; every 30min. M-F 6am-10:30pm, Sa 6:30am-10:30pm, Su 8am-11:30pm.) Buses arrive at **Avenida de Castille-La Mancha.** (☎92 521 58 10 ⚅ 7am-11pm.) To get from the bus station to center of town, take a 5min. bus ride on #8.1 or 8.2. To walk from the bus station, head south on Av. de Castilla-La Mancha, take a soft right (heading west) on C. de la Carrera at the first roundabout, and follow C. de la Carrera (5min.) until you reach the large medieval arch Puerta de Bisagra.

Getting Around

You will need a map to navigate this city. Streets are narrow, poorly marked, and often quite steep. Maps are available at the tourist office in the train station and at each of the locations throughout town. You will be able to access all parts of the historic center of Toledo quite easily by foot. Keep in mind that the city's many steep cobblestone streets may be difficult for visitors in wheelchairs to navigate. The most important **buses** are #8.1 and 8.2, which travel from the bus station to the center of town. Buses #1-7 leave from Pl. de Zocódover on various routes throughout town. (Ⓢ Day ticket €0.95, night €1.25.) For a mixture of transportation and touring, hop on one of the double-decker tour buses. For **taxis,** call Radio Taxi (☎92 522 70 70) or Gruas de Toledo (☎92 525 50 50).

SALAMANCA

Dubbed Spain's "Golden City," Salamanca radiates with beautiful landmarks carved of yellow Villamayor stone. Pretty plazas and cathedrals aside, Salamanca is a college town at heart, famous for the **Universidad de Salamanca,** one of the oldest in Europe. Once a battleground for Arabs and Christians, Salamanca now worries less about rampaging armies and more about its over 30,000 raging students.

Orientation

Salamanca is oriented around three key sights: the **university** at the city center, **Plaza Mayor** just to the north, and the **cathedrals** to the south. The historic Old City is accessible on foot and **Calle de Rua Mayor** is the major thoroughfare.

Accommodations

While Salamanca is certainly doable as a daytrip, many choose to spend the night and do the 3hr. journey back to Madrid in the morning. If you do choose to stay, pick a place in the historic city center, near either Pl. Mayor, the cathedral, or the university. This will put you in easy walking distance of all of major sights, restaurants, and nightlife.

Revolutum Hostel   HOSTEL $

C. de Sanchéz Barbero, 7

☎92 321 76 56; www.revolutumhostel.com

This newly renovated backpackers' hostel is every bit as cool as the made-up word "Revolutum." The social hostel has a range of different commons areas: a "cafe-bar," a "living-cafe," a "chill out," a patio, and a shared kitchen-dining area. It even has its own morgue! (Joke.) Bedrooms are mostly shared with simple bunks, clean white sheets, and a Granny Smith apple waiting for you. Bedrooms are simple enough, but all of the common areas have posh-club-VIP-room decor with low-lying banks of cushions, plastic egg-shaped chairs, and bright pillows. The location is as central as it gets, just a few meters from Pl. Mayor and close to plenty of restaurants. Private rooms are also available, but be sure to book in advance as they go quickly.

▶ ♯ From Pl. Mayor, exit through the south end and take a left onto C. de Sanchéz Barbero, the 1st street that intersects with C. de Rua Mayor. Ⓢ Dorms €20; private rooms €30. 🕐 Reception 24hr.

Hostal Concejo   HOSTAL $$$

Pl. de la Libertad, 1

☎92 321 47 37; www.hconcejo.com

With floral bed coverings, hardwood floors, and full baths, the modern rooms at the Hostal Concejo resemble those of a boutique hotel. Many of the rooms have balconies overlooking the beautiful gardens and cyprus trees of Pl. de la Libertad. The *hostal* is in a peaceful, less tourist-ridden location just a few steps

Excursions

from Pl. Mayor. Hostal Concejo is not the most budget-friendly option out there, but it's a good choice if you're looking for a nice private room and bath. Check online for special discounts.

▶ ⚔ From Pl. Mayor, take C. del Concejo (facing north, it's on the left) 10m to Pl. de la Libertad. Ⓢ Singles €45-49; doubles €56-69; triples €79-83. ⏰ Reception 24hr.

Hostal Sara   HOSTAL $$$

C. de Meléndez, 11

☎92 328 11 40; www.hostalsara.org

Nicely decorated with simple bed coverings and light wooden floors, Hostal Sara is a great option if you want to stay in the center of town. The location between Pl. Mayor and the university is convenient for those staying just one night, and the complimentary Wi-Fi is a rare privilege in Salamanca. Rooms look like hotel rooms and include a mini-fridge and full bath. With a large elevator, the *hostal* is also easily wheelchair-accessible.

▶ ⚔ From the university, walk northeast up C. de Meléndez toward Pl. Mayor. Ⓢ Singles €38; doubles €45-48; triples €78-85. ⏰ Reception 24hr.

Hostal Las Vegas   HOSTAL $

C. de Meléndez, 13

☎92 321 87 49; www.lasvegascentro.net

This ain't the Bellagio. The closest thing you'll find to a million-dollar fountain in this hotel may be a bidet. Despite the name, the accommodations at Hostal Las Vegas are basic with mismatched furniture and particularly small bathrooms. That said, it's cheap. The private rooms and bathrooms are clean and will be a welcome relief to those looking to avoid another night in the dorm. The location on C. de Meléndez puts you in the middle of the major sights, and close to restaurants and nightlife.

▶ ⚔ From the university, walk northeast up C. de Meléndez toward Pl. Mayor. Ⓢ Singles €24; doubles €36-45; triples €60; quads €80. ⏰ Reception 24hr.

Hostal Catedral   HOSTAL $$

C. de Rua Mayor, 46-48

☎92 327 06 14

Located next to the cathedral, this *hostal* has the feel of a small guesthouse. The landlady is very attentive and keeps the rooms tidy, though you can expect the typical odds-and-ends decor of Spanish *hostales*. There are only a few rooms available so reservations are a must. The location across the plaza from the cathedral is quiet, but you can expect plenty of nighttime activity just a block north along C. de Rua Mayor.

▶ ✈ From Pl. de Anaya, facing north, approach C. de Rua Mayor. The hostal is the 1st building on the left. ⑤ Singles €30; doubles €45-48. ⏰ Reception 24hr.

Sights

Salamanca is and always has been a college town. (And we mean always.) The Universidad de Salamanca remains the city's primary attraction, along with Pl. Mayor and the New and Old Cathedrals. In addition to these major sights, there are plenty of small museums with collections dedicated to everything from cars to Art Deco to film.

Universidad de Salamanca   UNIVERSITY

C. de los Libreros

☎92 327 71 00

The heart of Salamanca, this university is one of the most important buildings in the city and a jewel of the Spanish Renaissance. It was founded by Alphonse IX of León in 1218. Legend has it that if you can find the frog (perched atop a skull) in the facade without assistance, then you will receive good luck and marriage. Inside the university you can view the historical library, which holds 40,000 precious volumes including priceless manuscripts like *El Libro de Buen Amor* by the archpriest of Hita. You can also see the classroom where Fray Luis de León used to teach. While you're here, look for the red marks covering the sides of the building—when students graduated and became doctors, they used to stamp the walls with a mixture of bull's blood and oil.

▶ ✈ Next to Pl. Mayor. ⑤ €4, students and over 65 €2, under 12 and M morning free. Cash only. ⏰ Open Tu-F 10:30am-12:45pm and 5-7pm, Sa 9:30am-1:30pm and 3-7pm, Su 10am-1:30pm.

Cathedrals of Salamanca   CATHEDRAL

Pl. de Anaya

☎92 321 74 76

What could be cooler than a giant cathedral? How about two giant cathedrals stuck together? This was the attitude of the Spanish Catholic church in 1513 when it began constructing the massive New Cathedral right next to the original. Exactly when construction began on the original cathedral is unclear, but records suggest sometime in the second half of the 12th century. Today the most artistically renowned part of the Old Cathedral is its altarpiece, which is made of 53 panels conveying the life of Jesus Christ in the style of the Florentine Renaissance. The New Cathedral isn't new by any measure—work started in 1513, and it took two centuries to build. While predominantly Gothic in style, it also incorporates Baroque and Renaissance ornament. When you enter, be sure to look for the astronaut and lion with an ice cream cone carved into the stone by mischievous artists during renovations in 1992. In the Old Cathedral, it is said that if you visit the Santa Barbara chapel and place your feet on the tombstone of the bishop Juan Lucero, wisdom will surge from your feet to your head. Whether or not this will actually happen is questionable, but you're reading *Let's Go,* so chances are you're pretty wise already.

▶ ✚ From Pl. Mayor, exit south to C. de Rua Mayor and follow it south to Pl. de Anaya. The New Cathedral is on the plaza; the Old Cathedral is directly behind. *i* Purchase tickets to the Old Cathedral in the New Cathedral. ⑤ New Cathedral free. Old Cathedral €4.75, students €3.25. Tu 10am-noon free. Cash only. ⏰ New Cathedral open daily 9am-8pm. Old Cathedral open daily 10am-7:30pm.

Plaza Mayor
PLAZA

Salamanca's Plaza Mayor is one of the most beautiful plazas in Spain. Built by Alberto de Churriguera in 1775, the plaza is a popular social hub that has historically been the center of Salamanca's political, economic, and religious activities. At different times in its history it has served as a market, concert hall, bullring, and theater. Today it is home to dozens of restaurants and tourist shops. Stop by in the early evening (8-9pm) when locals convene to chat before heading off to dinner.

▶ ✚ From the New Cathedral, follow C. de Rua Mayor north. ⑤ Free.

Casa de las Conchas
LIBRARY, PALACE

C. de la Compañía, 2

☎92 326 93 17

Built by Rodrigo Arias Maldonado at the end of the 15th century, the "House of Shells" is dotted with 365 shells on its facade, one for each day of the year. They represent Maldonaldo's love for his wife (her family symbol was the shell) and his dedication to the Order of Santiago. Today the former palace is free to the public, but there's not much happening in the interior. There's a nice courtyard, and the building now stands as the city's public library.

▶ ⚐ Across the street from the university. From Pl. Mayor, exit south and take a right onto C. de Meléndez. This street dead-ends into the university building. Casa de las Conchas will be on your right. Ⓢ Free. Ⓩ Open M-F 9am-9pm, Sa 9am-2pm and 3-7pm, Su 10am-2pm and 3-7pm.

Museo de la Historia de la Automoción   MUSEUM
Pl. del Mercado Viejo, s/n
☎92 326 02 93; www.museoautomocion.com

This museum showcases a car collection, most of which belong to Gomez Planche. With over 100 vehicles, thousands of parts, and scores of car accessories, the collection is an impressive ode to the car's place in history. The collection ranges from awkward-looking spoke-wheel contraptions to modern sports cars straight out of *2 Fast 2 Furious*.

▶ ⚐ Just south of the Cathedral. From Pl. de Anaya, head west on El Tostado to C. de San Pablo. Take C. de San Pablo 100m to Paseo del Rector Esperabé, cross to the southern side of the street and head west another 100m. Ⓢ €3, students and over 65 €2, 1st Tu of each month 5-8pm free. Ⓩ Open Tu-Su 10am-2pm and 5-8pm.

Food

Salamanca offers plenty of great budget options for travelers. Avoid the two major thoroughfares of Pl. Mayor and C. de Rua Mayor, which offer picture menus, *menús del día* and alluring terrace seating, and follow our lead for the best local food.

▨ Zazu Bistro   ITALIAN, MEDITERRANEAN $$
Pl. de la Libertad, 8
☎92 326 16 90

Located in a restored townhouse along Pl. de la Libertad, the setting of Zazu Bistro cannot be beat. Unlike busy C. de Rua Mayor, Pl. de la Libertad remains calm through the night, which makes it more like dining in a sleepy European town than in a major tourist destination. The menu draws heavily on traditional Italian fare like the pizza with goat cheese, tomato, basil, and bacon (€11), and also includes Mediterranean-inspired salads and entrees. The setting on two floors of a restored town house makes Zazu Bistro a memorable dining experience. The top floor, with its vaulted ceilings and living

Excursions

room with couches, is a popular spot later in the evening for cocktails and dessert.

▶ ⚔ From Pl. Mayor, walk north along C. del Concejo (on the west side of plaza) to Pl. de la Libertad. The restaurant is on the south side of the plaza. ⑤ Entrees €10-20. ⏰ Open daily 2-4pm and 8:30pm-midnight.

Delicatessen and Cafe   MEDITERRANEAN $$

C. de Meléndez, 25

☎92 328 03 09

Located just a few steps from one of the oldest universities in the world, Delicatessen and Cafe has figured out how to please its student clientele. The menu here is dominated by large portions of Mediterranean staples and the occasional stateside favorite, like its steak, the Continental (with fried eggs, salad, and homefries; €10). Simple pizzas (€10-12), pasta (€10), and risotto (€11) are popular, as are combination entrees like the *estudiante* (grilled chicken, grilled vegetables, salad, and potatoes; €10). The food isn't particularly inventive, but it's satisfying. The restaurant's heated outdoor terrace has large tropical plants and a massive dome glass roof. At night, local DJs spin pop tunes and music videos play on the big screen projector.

▶ ⚔ Exit Pl. Mayor through the southwest corner, walk past Iglesia de San Martín until you reach C. de Meléndez. The restaurant is just around the bend on the left. ⑤ Entrees €10-15. ⏰ Open daily 10am-3am. Kitchen open 1-4pm and 8:30pm-midnight.

Cafe Bar Mandala   CAFE, BAR $

C. de Serrano, 9

☎92 312 33 42

Cafe Bar Mandala is a popular student hangout right across from the university. The drink variety here is endless, with each of the six menus dedicated to a different kind of beverage: there is a menu exclusively for loose leaf tea, regular tea, iced tea, Arabic coffee, milk shakes, and Italian sodas. If you leave this place and don't need to pee, you did something wrong. If you are looking for the same variety in food, you just won't find it. The menu is limited to a simple selection of *bocadillos* (€2-4), salads (€4-6), and international staples like lasagna and quiche.

▶ ⚔ Walk southeast along the southern edge of the university to C. de Serrano. The restaurant is just past C. de los Libreros. ⑤ Meals €5-10. Drinks €2-4. ⏰ Open daily 9am-1am.

Nightlife

Because of Salamanca's year-round student population, the city has a number of fairly steady nightlife options.

Gatsby
BAR, DISCO

C. de los Bordadores, 16

☎92 321 72 74

With old farming tools, tribal masks, and wooden chandeliers hanging from the ceiling, Gatsby is more Westphalia than West Egg. With a good mix of Spanish and American clientele and music, Gatsby is loved by everyone (except maybe Daisy). This club has been around since 1985 and continues to deliver on the same booze specials and themed parties. Deals like five shots for €5 sit well with university students, as do themed parties like "The Lollipop Party" and "The Galactic Party."

▶ ✱ From Pl. Mayor, walk west down C. del Prior and make a right onto C. de los Bordadores. ⑤ Beer and cocktails €3-8. ⓩ Open M-Th 5:30pm-3:30am, F-Sa 5:30pm-5am.

Camelot
BAR, DISCO

C. de los Bordadores, 3

☎92 321 21 82; www.camelotsalamanca.es

Decorated like an ancient castle, Camelot is your best bet for a round table round or Dark (Ages) dance floor. With a wrought-iron balcony, the second floor is a perfect place to party like its 1299. Occasional free flamenco shows get the crowd moving early in the night. They don't serve mead, so pretend your sangria is slightly less fruity and significantly more disgusting for the full medieval effect.

▶ ✱ From Pl. Mayor, walk west down C. del Prior and make a right onto C. de los Bordadores. ⑤ Beer €3-4. Cocktails €6. ⓩ Open M-W 9pm-4:30am, Th 9pm-5:30am, F-Sa 9pm-6:30am, Su 9pm-4:30am.

Arts and Culture

Named the European Capital of Culture in 2002, Salamanca has plenty to offer visitors beyond traditional sights. As one of Spain's primary university cities, Salamanca has a thriving music, dance, theater, and film scene. Pick up the seasonal program of cultural events *Culture Aqui* from the tourist office in Pl. Mayor (see **Essentials**) or check out nightly events at **www.salamancaciudaddecultura.org.** Like everywhere else in Spain,

Salamanca is serious about tradition. Look out for seasonal festivals and bullfighting events taking place in Salamanca's famous **La Glorieta.**

Plaza de Toros de Salamanca "La Glorieta" BULLFIGHTS

Pl. de Toros La Glorieta

☎92 322 12 99

The area around Salamanca is the most prominent bull-breeding territory in Spain, so you can expect some wicked fights and even wilder fans. Every June and September, the famous Pl. de Toros de Salamanca (also known as "La Glorieta") hosts the most famous matadors and fiercest bulls. Bullfights took place in Pl. Mayor until La Glorieta was completed in 1893. Today it holds up to 10,000 spectators and hosts cultural events and concerts when bullfighting isn't in season. If you happen to be in Salamanca during February, make the 45min. trip to **Ciudad Rodrigo,** where the Carnaval del Toro shakes the city up with street dancing, festivities, music, and bullfighting.

▶ ⚲ A 15min. walk from Pl. Mayor. Exit the plaza through from the northwest corner onto C. del Concejo, which becomes C. de Zamora. Follow C. de Zamora north to Paseo del Doctor Torres Villarroel and merge right onto Av. de San Agustín. This dead-ends into Pl. de de Toros La Glorieta. *i* For more info on the Carnaval del Toro, visit www.aytociudadrodrigo.es. Buses leave every hr. from Estación de Autobuses de Salamanca.

Museo Taurino BULLFIGHTS

C. del Doctor Piñuela, 5-7

☎92 321 94 25; www.museotaurinosalamanca.es

To learn more about this fierce sport, check out the bullfighting museum, Museo Taurino, where you'll find exhibits on everything from matador fashion to bullfighting in Spanish popular culture.

▶ ⚲ From Pl. Mayor, exit the plaza on the northwest corner and take C. del Toro north ½ a block to C. del Doctor Piñuela. The museum is on the left. Ⓢ €3. 🕐 Open Tu-F 6-9pm, Sa noon-2pm and 6-9pm, Su noon-2pm.

Teatro Liceo THEATER

C. del Toro, 23

☎92 328 06 19

Built on the ruins of the convent of San Antonio del Real, this theater was renovated in 2002 and has an impressive 565-person auditorium with the look and feel of Carnegie Hall. Teatro Liceo is the city's most impressive venue for classical

Excursions

and contemporary theater, dance, music, and Baroque opera. The space also hosts a popular film series throughout the year. Tickets vary in price, but most events do not exceed €15.

▶ ⚔ From Pl. Mayor, exit the northwest corner onto C. del Toro and walk 2 blocks north. The theater is on the left. *i* For a performance schedule, consult the tourist office. Tickets can be purchased at the box office or through El Corte Inglés (☎90 240 02 22; www.elcorteingles.es). ⏰ Ticket office open M-F 11am-2pm, Sa noon-2pm. The ticket office also opens 2hr. before each performance.

Teatro Juan de Enzina   THEATER

C. de Tostado, 2
☎92 329 45 42

This university-sponsored theater offers some of the cheapest seats in all of Spain and focuses on contemporary theater, dance, and music performances.

▶ ⚔ From the Cathedrals, follow C. de Tostado just west of Pl. de Ayana. ⏰ Shows year-round.

Festivals

Reyes Magos

Like most Spanish cities, Salamanca needs little excuse to party. Every year on January 5th, residents, students, and tourists celebrate the arrival of the Three Kings during Cabalgata de los Reyes Magos, an evening parade that features dancing, music, and costumes. The day after is similar to Christmas Day in the United States, with feasts and the exchange of gifts.

▶ ⏰ Jan 5-6.

FACYL: International Arts Festival of Castilla and León

During the first two weeks of June, this arts festival takes over every cultural establishment in the city. Plazas, museums, and major performance spaces become venues for the latest in contemporary art, music, theater, and dance.

▶ *i* For more info, check out www.facyl-festival.com. ⏰ 1st 2 weeks of June.

Corpus Christi

On June 18th, the Corpus Christi celebration is in full force around the Old Cathedral. Salamanca residents celebrate with street performances and parties.

▶ ⏰ June 18th.

Essentials

Practicalities

- **TOURIST OFFICES:** The **Municipal Tourist Office** distributes free maps and pamphlets. (Pl. Mayor, 32 ☎92 321 83 42 ☷ Open June-Sept M-F 9am-2pm and 4:30-8pm, Sa 10am-8pm, Su 10am-2pm; Oct-May M-F 9am-2pm and 4-6:30pm, Sa 10am-6:30pm, Su 10am-2pm.) The **Regional Tourist Office** also has free information. (C. de Rua Mayor ☎92 326 85 71 ☷ Open July-Sept M-Th 9am-8pm, F-Sa 9am-9pm, Su 9am-8pm; Oct-June daily 9am-2pm and 5-8pm.) Look out for **DGratis,** a free listing of goings-on distributed every F, available at tourist offices and distributors in Pl. Mayor. For details, visit www.salamanca.es.

- **TOURS:** A **walking tour** departs from the tourist office in Pl. Mayor and covers Pl. Mayor, Casa de las Conchas, Clerecía, Universidad Civil, and the Cathedrals. (☎65 375 96 02 *i* In English. Min. 10 people. ⑤ €15; includes admission to sights. ☷ 2hr.; M, W.)

- **CURRENCY EXCHANGE:** **EuroDivisas** has ATMs and currency exchange. (C. de Rua Mayor, 2 ☎923 21 21 80 ☷ Open M-F 8:30am-10pm, Sa-Su 10am-7pm.)

- **LUGGAGE STORAGE:** At the **train station.** (⑤ €3-4.50.) At the **bus station.** (⑤ €2. ☷ 7am-7:45pm.)

- **LAUNDROMAT:** Pasaje Azafranal, 18 ☎92 336 02 16 ⑤ Wash and dry €4. ☷ Open M-F 9:30am-2pm and 4-8pm, Sa 9:30am-2pm.

- **INTERNET ACCESS:** The **Biblioteca Pública** offers free internet access. (Casa de Las Conchas, C. de la Compañía, 2 ☎92 326 93 17 ☷ Open July-Aug M-F 9am-3pm, Sa 9am-2pm; Sept-June M-F 9am-9pm, Sa 9am-2pm.) **Cyber Place Internet** is busy, but has good rates for internet access. (Pl. Mayor, 10, 1st fl. ⑤ €1 per hr. ☷ Open M-F 11am-midnight, Sa-Su noon-midnight.) **Cyber Anuario.** (C. de Traviesa, 16 ☎92 326 13 54 ⑤ €1.50 per hr. ☷ Open M-Sa 11am-2:30pm and 4:30-11pm.)

- **POST OFFICE:** C. de la Gran Vía, 25-29 ☎92 328 14 57 🕗 Open M-F 8:30am-8:30pm, Sa 9:30am-2pm.

- **POSTAL CODE:** 37001.

Emergency

- **EMERGENCY NUMBER:** ☎112.

- **POLICE:** Ayuntamiento, Pl. Mayor 2 ☎92 326 53 11.

- **CRISIS LINES: Red Cross.** (C. Cruz Roja, 1 ☎92 322 22 22.)

Getting There

By Plane

Flights arrive at the **Aeropuerto de Salamanca.** (Ctra. Madrid, 14 km from the city. ☎92 332 96 00.)

By Train

Trains arrive at the **Vialia Estación de Salamanca** (Paseo de la Estación ☎90 224 02 02) from Lisbon (⑤ €47. 🕗 6hr., 4:51am.) and Madrid (⑤ €18. 🕗 2½hr., 6-7 per day 6am-7:53pm).

By Bus

The **Estación de Autobuses de Salamanca** (Av. Filiberto Villalobos, 71 ☎92 323 67 17) has express buses to Madrid (⑤ €22. 🕗 2½hr., every hr. 6am-9:30pm.) and local bus routes to Madrid. (⑤ €16. 🕗 3hr., every hr. 7:30am-8:30pm.)

Getting Around

Salamanca is easily walkable; most sights are concentrated around Pl. Mayor. The trip from the train station to the city center is 15-20min. on foot or 5min. by taxi. (Radio Taxi. ☎92 325 00 00 ⑤ €5.) To walk from the Vialia Estación de Salamanca, walk southwest down Paseo de la Estación three blocks to Pl. de España and make a right onto Paseo de las Canalejas. Walk half a block and make a left onto C. del Toro (this street dead-ends into the northern end of the plaza). To get to the city center from the bus station, exit the station and follow Av. de Filiberto Villalobos four blocks southwest. Cross Pl. de las Carmelitas, at which point Av. de Filiberto Villalobos becomes C. de Ramón y Cajal. Follow for two blocks, at which point this street becomes C. del Prior. This dead-ends into the western edge of Pl. Mayor.

SEGOVIA

Set above rolling hills and country pasture just 60km from Madrid, Segovia is a getaway. The city's Roman aqueduct and imposing medieval castle situated in the middle of town are undoubtedly its greatest attractions, and they don't fail to impress. The 2000-year-old granite aqueduct has stood virtually unchanged since Roman times and was even functional until recently. Meanwhile the 12th-century Alcázar remains intact. But Segovia is more than any single monument: it's a sleepy, comforting town that calls to travelers when they tire of big-city life in Madrid. It is definitely a tourist destination, and you will see people who look just like your grandparents, but at a certain point, we're all tourists. Segovia is easy to get to, it's beautiful, and it has some of Spain's most interesting historical monuments.

Orientation

The best way to orient yourself in Segovia is to get a **free map** at the visitors' reception center; you'll need it to navigate the labyrinth of winding roads in the **Old City.** To get to the visitors' reception center from the train station, take bus #8 to Acueducto (7min.). If you are arriving from the bus station you can also take bus #4 to Acueducto or take a short taxi ride (€4). The visitors' center is on the northwest corner of the Pl. del Azoguego. The best way to get around the city once you have gotten a hold of a map is to stick to **Calle Juan Bravo** east to west from Pl. Mayor. To get to C. de Juan Bravo, take a left at the tourist office onto C. de Cervantes and follow it for one block. C. de Cervantes becomes C. de Juan Bravo.

Accommodations

Segovia has plenty of high-end hostels, all offering the conveniences of budget hotels at a reasonable cost. While many travelers choose to make a quick daytrip to Segovia and head back to Madrid for the evening, a night in the small village can make for a restful break. All of the hostels within the old city are just a few blocks apart, making quality and price fairly standard; *pensiones* can be significantly cheaper than hotels. Segovia's many sights and its proximity to Madrid and La Granja make rooms scarce during the summer, so be sure to book in advance if you want to stay overnight.

Natura La Hostería   HOSTEL $$$

C. de Colón, 5 and 7
☎92 146 67 10; www.naturadesegovia.com

Natura La Hostería is located in Pl. de los Huertos, one of the few green businesses in the Old City. Many of the rooms look out onto the plaza, and all of the rooms, including the smaller singles, have queen-sized beds, air-conditioning, flatscreen TVs, and ensuite bathrooms. The downstairs Cafe Natura offers a simple breakfast (coffee, tea, toast, and juice; €4).

▶ ⚐ From Pl. Mayor (facing Teatro Bravo) take C. del Cronista Lecea from Pl. de la Rubia to Pl. de los Huertos, C. de Colón is on the southern border of the plaza. ⑤ Singles €35-40; doubles €50-80.

Hostal Don Jaime   HOSTAL $$

C. de Ochoa Ondátegui, 8
☎92 144 47 87; hostaldonjaime@hotmail.com

Hostal Don Jaime is a pleasant family-run *hostal* one block up the hill from the aqueduct. They offer some of the most afford-able rooms in old Segovia, with some singles as cheap as €20 per night. Located on a quiet road with little activity, Don Jaime is a great place to crash. The downstairs cafe serves a simple breakfast (juice, coffee, and toast; €3), and while the *hostal* has a computer with internet, at €0.50 for every 15min., it can be an expensive habit if you spend all of your time in Segovia on Second Life.

▶ ⚐ From the tourist office in Pl. del Azoguejo, walk west through the aq-ueduct past the long promenade of stairs (C. de Fernán García), make an immediate right onto C. de Ochoa Ondátegui, walk uphill 2min., and look for the "Don Jaime" sign. ⑤ Singles M-Th €20-30, F-Su €35; doubles €45/50.

Hotel San Miguel   HOTEL $$

C. de la Infanta Isabel, 6
☎92 146 36 57; www.sanmiguel-hotel.com

Hotel San Miguel is located in the dead center of the city, one block from the restaurants and attractions around Pl. Mayor. Rooms here are simple, with queen-size beds, large private bathrooms with fresh towels, and flatscreen TVs. Second-floor rooms have nice balconies overlooking the street, and run €5-10 cheaper per night.

▶ ✇ From Pl. Mayor (facing Teatro Bravo) head east on C. de la Infanta Isabel for ½ a block. *i* Breakfast €3. Ⓢ Singles €30-35; doubles €60-70.

Sights

As you walk through the city, look for blue information placards, which mark historically important buildings, churches, private homes, and museums.

▨ Aqueduct   MONUMENT

The Romans built Segovia's aqueduct around 50 BCE with 20,000 blocks of granite and not a drop of mortar. Two tiers of arches (that's 166 arches in total) span 813m, reaching a height of 29m near Pl. del Azoguejo. This spectacular feat of engineering piped water in from the Fuente Fría river, 17km away, and was capable of transporting 30L of water per second to the Alcázar. In use until 60 years ago, today the aqueduct primarily pipes in tourists from Madrid.

▨ Alcázar   PALACE

☎92 146 07 59

Walt Disney reportedly modeled the Disney castle on the Alcázar's spiral towers and pointed turrets; you may experience a magical sense of déjà vu. Alfonso X beautified the original 11th-century fortress in the 13th century. Successive monarchs increased the grandeur; final touches were added for the coronation of Isabel I in 1474. In the **throne room,** the inscription above the throne reads *"tanto monta,"* a phrase that suggests that Ferdinand and Isabella had equal authority to rule. Process through various luxurious royal bedrooms and halls. The **tower of Juan II,** 152 steps up, offers incredible views of Segovia and the surrounding hills.

▶ *i* Buy tickets in the Real Laboratorio de Chimia, to the left of the Alcázar. Ⓢ Palace €4, seniors and students €3. Tower €2. Audio tours in English €3. ☯ Palace open daily Apr-Sept M 10am-7pm, W-Su 10am-7pm; Oct-Mar M 10am-6pm, W-Su 10am-6pm.

Catedral de Nuestra Senora de la Asunción   CATHEDRAL

Pl. Mayor

☎92 146 22 05

In 1525, Carlos V commissioned a cathedral in Pl. Mayor to replace the 12th-century edifice that was destroyed in the Revuelta de las Comunidades, a political uprising against the crown from 1520 to 1521. When the cathedral was finally finished 200 years later, its impressive 23 chapels topped with stained glass earned Nuestra Senora de la Asunción the nickname "The Lady of All Cathedrals." The altar was designed by Sabatini, creator of the gardens in Madrid, and features the four saints of Segovia. The **Sala Capitular,** hung with 17th-century tapestries, displays an ornate silver-and-gold chariot. Off the cloister (moved from the Alcázar) is the **Capilla de Santa Catalina,** filled with crosses, chalices, and candelabra. A framed coin collection on the cloister wall has currency from the royal mint going back five centuries.

▶ *i* Guided tours leave from the entrance. Ⓢ €3, under 14 free. ⏲ Open daily Apr-Oct 9am-6:30pm; Nov-Mar 9:30am-5:30pm. Last entry 30min. before close. Tours 11am, 4:30, 5:30pm. Mass M-Sa 10am, Su 11am and 12:30pm.

La Granja de San Ildefonso   PALACE, MUSEUM

Pl. de España, 17, Real Sitio de San Ildefonso

☎92 147 00 19

Eleven kilometers southeast of Segovia, La Granja is the most extravagant of Spain's royal summer retreats. Philip V, the first Bourbon king of Spain and grandson of Louis XIV, detested the Hapsburgs' austere Escorial. Nostalgic for Versailles, he commissioned La Granja in the early 18th century, choosing the site for its hunting and gardening potential. A fire destroyed the living quarters in 1918, but the structure was rebuilt in 1932. Today it houses the **Museo de Tapices,** one of the world's best collections of Flemish tapestries, which were popular in Spanish royal palaces. The usual marble clocks, Oriental porcelain, and paintings by Luca Giordano round out the palace's decor. French architect René Carlier designed the immense French **gardens** around the palace. Hedges surround impressive flowerbeds and lead to endless waterworks, including the decadent *cascadas nuevas,* an ensemble of illuminated fountains and pools that represents the continents and seasons. The **Baños de Diana** is a massive pool with a bronze statue of the goddess, backed by a wall meticulously inlaid with hundreds of seashells.

▶ ⚎ For transportation information, see **Essentials.** ⑤ €5; students and under 16 €3. ⏰ Palace open from mid-June to Aug 10am-9pm; Sept 10am-8pm; Oct 10am-6:30pm; Nov-Feb 10am-6pm; Mar 10am-6:30pm; Apr 10am-7pm; from May to mid-June 10am-8pm. Tours in Spanish every 15min. Gardens open daily 10am-9pm. Baños de Diana open July 22-Sept 2 Sa 10:30am-11:30pm.

Casa-Museo de Antonio Machado   MUSEUM
C. de los Desamparados, 5
☎92 146 03 77

Antonio Machado (1875-1939), literature professor, playwright, and, above all, poet, never made much money. The poet rented this small *pensión* from 1919 to 1932 for three *pesetas* per day while he taught French at the nearby university. A short, informative tour details major influences on Machado's poetry, including the 1909 death of his teenaged wife and his affair with a married woman. The poet's room, filled with manuscripts and portraits (including one by Picasso), has been left untouched.

▶ *i* Mandatory guided tour in Spanish every 30min. ⑤ M-Tu €1.50, W free. ⏰ Open daily M-Tu 4:30-7:30pm, W-Su 11am-2pm and 4:30-7:30pm.

Food

The restaurants in the larger plazas cater to tourists and jack up their prices accordingly—steer clear of any menu printed on "parchment." *Sopa castellana* (soup with eggs and garlic), *cochinillo asado* (roast suckling pig), *ponche* (egg yolk pastry), and lamb dishes are regional specialties worth trying. There's a fresh fruit and vegetable market on **Plaza Mayor** on Thursdays and **Avenida de la Constitución** on Saturdays (9am-2:30pm). For basic groceries, head to **Día,** C. Gobernador Fernández Jiménez, 3, off Av. de Fernández Ladreda. (⏰ Open M-Sa 9am-9pm.)

▧ Restaurante La Almuzara   MEDITERRANEAN $$
C. del Marqués del Arco, 3
☎92 146 06 22

Almuzara is a quiet family-owned restaurant that specializes in vegetarian pizza and pasta. While many of the upscale restaurants throughout town go for the wooden coffin-like interiors, La Almuzara keeps it cool and calm with pastoral murals on the walls and fresh flowers on the tables. In addition to vegetarian specialties like vegetable lasagna (€9.50) and pizza (€10-12), they also offer Italian staples like pasta

Bolognese (€10), and they do a fine job with local dishes like *sopa de ojo* (garlic soup with poached egg; €5). This is one of only a handful of places in town where you can get a nice meal on a budget.

▶ ⚔ From Pl. Mayor take C. del Marqués del Arco west just past the Catedral de Nuestra Señora. Ⓢ Salads €5-8. Entrees €9-14. ⏰ Open Tu 8-11:30pm, W-Su 12:45-4pm and 8-11:30pm.

Bar-Mesón Cueva de San Esteban   TABERNA $$

C. de Valdeláguila, 15
☎92 146 09 82

The owner knows his wines: he's still celebrating his 2002 victory in the national "nose of gold" competition, and he uses this schnozz to serve a stellar selection of wines. While Bar-Mesón serves Segovian specialties like suckling pig and roasted lamb, they also have a number of good options for budget travelers, such as the freshly prepared *tortillas*. The *tortilla con gambas fritas* (Spanish omelette with fried shrimp; €6.50) is particularly good. And with such a highly regarded wino at the helm, there are often a number of great choices served by the glass (€2-4).

▶ ⚔ From Pl. Mayor (facing Teatro Juan Bravo) take a left onto Pl. del Potro north. This quickly merges into C. de Valdeláguila. Take C. de Valdeláguila ½ a block down the narrow alley. Ⓢ *Menú* M-F €9, Sa-Su €10. Meat dishes €12-20. ⏰ Open daily 11am-midnight.

Restaurante-Mesón José María   TABERNA $$$

C. del Cronista Lecea, 11
☎92 146 11 11; www.rtejosemaria.com

While this restaurant lacks the pomp and overdone interiors of so many *asadors* in town, Mesón José María is still a destination for local specialties like suckling pig (€23) and roasted lamb (€44). All of Mesón José María's best meat dishes come in mammoth servings made for two. For those less interested in shelling out for the most expensive entrees, Mesón José María is also known for *papas con huevas rotas* (€10) served with pork loin.

▶ ⚔ From Pl. Mayor (facing Teatro Juan Bravo) take C. del Cronista Lecea northwest ½ a block. ⏰ Open M-W 1-4pm and 8:30-11pm, Th-Sa 1-4pm and 8:30pm-12:30am, Su 1-4pm and 8:30-11pm.

Excursions

La Bodega del Barbero

BAR $

C. Alhóndiga, 2

☎92 146 27 70

La Bodega del Barbero is an easy-to-miss wine bar with terrace seating just off C. de Juan Bravo. The selection of wines changes daily, but you should always be able to get a decent glass at a reasonable price (€1.50-3). They also serve salads (€5.80-9), *bocadillos* (€4-8), and a *menú del día* (€10).

▶ ⚡ From Pl. Mayor, take C. de Isabel 'La Católica' to C. de Juan Bravo and follow 2 blocks to C. Alhóndiga. Take a right down the small flight of stairs and look for the yellow awning. ⑤ Food €5-10. Drinks €1.50-3. ⏰ Open Tu 11am-3:30pm, W-Su 11am-3:30pm and 7:30-11:30pm.

Nightlife

Segovia is a small sleepy village; if you came here to grab a stranger's ass on the dance floor, you are in the wrong place. (Madrid is just a short train ride away...) That said, if you are with a group of friends and looking for a place to hear live music or get on the dance floor, there are a handful of options. The best bet is to head to **Calle de la Infanta Isabel** just off Pl. Mayor. While there are a few other bars and clubs throughout the Old City, places shut down and streets get pretty quiet by midnight, so best to roll out with a posse.

Bar Santana

BAR, LIVE MUSIC

C. de la Infanta Isabel, 18

☎92 146 35 64

Santana is one of the few live music bars in town, and they draw local acts every Friday. Tasty tapas and rock music draw a casual older crowd, who loiter with drinks at the exterior bar. Photo and poetry exhibits line the back wall.

▶ ⚡ Across the street from Geographic Chic. ⑤ Beer €1.10. Cocktails €4.50. ⏰ Open Th-Sa 10:30pm-3:30am.

Toys

CLUB

C. de la Infanta Isabel, 13

☎92 146 31 27

Toys looks something like your favorite trashy club in your favorite trashy college town. Drinks are cheap, the music is loud, and the room is 🔲**dark.** This is one of the few venues open late, along with neighbor Geographic Chic.

▶ ⚡ 1 block east from Pl. Mayor. ⑤ Beer €1. Cocktails €4.50-5.50. ⏰ Open daily 10pm-4am.

Geographic Chic   CLUB

C. de la Infanta Isabel, 13

☎92 146 30 38

Mannequins line the windows and cherubs smile on the bar. Drinks are cheap and American pop is the norm. Come late if you choose to come at all; this place is often empty until 1am.

▶ ⚰ Adjacent to Toys. Ⓢ Cocktails €5. 🕗 Open W-Sa 10:30pm-4am.

Festivals

Fiestas de San Juan y San Pedro

In the month of June, Segovia holds a fiesta in honor of San Juan and San Pedro, with free open-air concerts on Pl. del Azoguejo, a pilgrimage to the hermitage of Juarrillos (5km away), and dances and fireworks on June 29.

▶ ⚰ In Pl. del Azoguejo. *i* June 23-29.

Fiestas de Santa Águeda

The town of Zamarramala hosts the Fiestas de Santa Águeda. Women take over the town for a day and dress in period costumes to commemorate a |**sneak attack** on the Alcázar in which women distracted the castle guards with wine and song. The all-female local council takes advantage of its temporary authority to ridicule men, burning a male effigy at the festival's end.

▶ ⚰ In Zamarramala, 3km northwest of Segovia. *i* 1st Su in Feb.

Essentials

Practicalities

- **TOURIST OFFICES: Regional office.** (Pl. Mayor, 10 ☎92 146 03 34 🕗 Open July-Sept 15 M-Th 9am-8pm, F-Sa 9am-9pm, Su 9am-8pm; Sept 16-June daily 9am-2pm and 5-8pm.) **Visitor's Reception Center.** (Centro de Recepción de Visitantes. Pl. del Azoguejo, 1 ☎92 146 67 20 🕗 Open M-F 10am-7pm, Sa 10am-8pm, Su 10am-7pm.)

- **CURRENCY EXCHANGE: Banco Santander Central Hispano.** (Av. de Fernández Ladreda, 12 🕗 Open Apr-Sept M-F 8:30am-2pm; Oct-Mar M-F 8:30am-2pm, Sa 8:30am-1pm.)

ATMs and other banks, which also change cash, line Av. de Fernández Ladreda.

- **LUGGAGE STORAGE:** At the **train station.** (☎90 224 02 02 ⑤ €3 per day. ☒ Open daily 6am-10:30pm.)

- **INTERNET ACCESS: Biblioteca Pública.** (C. de Juan Bravo, 11 ☎92 146 35 33 *i* Passport required. Max. 30min. ⑤ Free. ⑤ Open Sept-June M-F 9am-9pm, Sa 9am-2pm; July-Aug M-F 9am-3pm, Sa 9am-2pm.) **Locutorio Aceducto.** (C. de San Francisco, 6 *i* Off Pl. del Azoguejo. ☒ €1 per hr. ☒ Open daily noon-11pm.)

- **POST OFFICE:** Pl. del Doctor Laguna, 5 ☎92 146 16 16 ⚑ Up C. del Cronista Lecea from Pl. Mayor. ☒ Open M-F 8:30am-8:30pm, Sa 9:30am-2pm.

- **POSTAL CODE:** 40001.

Emergency

- **EMERGENCY NUMBERS:** ☎091. **Ambulance:** ☎112.

- **POLICE: City Police.** (C. de Guadarrama, 24 ☎92 143 12 12) **National Police.** (☎92 141 47 00)

- **HOSPITALS: Hospital General de Segovia.** (Carretera de Ávila s/n ☎92 141 91 00 ⚑ A 10min. walk from the police station on the road to Carretera de Ávila, on the left.)

Getting There

By Train

The train station is at Av. del Obispo Quesada, 1. (☎90 224 02 02) There's a high-speed train (☒ 27min.; 8, 8:45am, every 1½hr. 2-8pm.) and a regional train (⑤ €5.90. ☒ Every 2hr. M-F 5:55am-8:55pm, Sa-Su 8:55am-8:55pm.) to Madrid. There's also a regional train to Vilalba (⑤ €3.90. ☒ 1hr., 7-9 per day M-F 5:55am-8:55pm.), with transfers to Ávila, El Escorial, León, and Salamanca.

By Bus

The bus station, **Estación Municipal de Autobuses** offers two bus options. (Paseo Ezequiel González, 12 ☎92 142 77 07) **La Sepulvedana** (☎92 142 77 07) heads to Ávila (Ⓢ €4.25. ⏰ 1hr.; M-Sa 7:45am, 6pm.), La Granja (Ⓢ €1.05. ⏰ 20min.; 9-15 per day M-Sa 7:40am-9:30pm, Su 10:30am-10:30pm.), and Madrid. (Ⓢ €6.43. ⏰ 1hr.; M-F every 30min. 6:30am-10:30pm, Sa every 30min. 8am-10:30pm, Su every hr. 8am-10:30pm.) **Linecar** (☎92 142 77 06) goes to Valladolid. (Ⓢ €6.85. ⏰ 2hr.; M-F 12 per day 6:45am-9pm, Sa 8 per day 6:45am-9pm, Su 6 per day 9am-9pm.)

Getting Around

By Bus

Transportes Urbanos de Segovia, is in the Centro Comercial Almuzara. (C. de Juan Bravo ☎92 146 27 27 Ⓢ €0.80, discounted electronic passes available.)

By Taxi

Taxi stands are in the train and bus stations, in Pl. Mayor, and just beyond Pl. Azoguejo. **Radio Taxi** (☎92 144 50 00) is a good bet.

Essentials

You don't have to be a rocket scientist to plan a good trip. (It might help, but it's not required.) You do need to be well prepared—that's where we come in. Essentials is the chapter that gives you all the nitty-gritty that you will need for your trip: the hard information gleaned from 50 years of collective wisdom and several months of furious fact-checking. Planning your trip? Check. Where to find Wi-Fi? Check. The dirt on public transportation? Check. We've also thrown in communications info, safety tips, and a phrase-book, just for good measure. For overall trip-planning advice from what to pack (money and as little underwear as possible) to how to take a good passport photo (it's physically impossible; consider airbrushing), visit the Essentials section of www.letsgo.com.

So, flip through this chapter before you leave so you know what documents to bring, while you're on the plane so you know how you'll be getting from the airport to your accommodation, and when you're on the ground so you can find a laundromat when you run out of underwear. This chapter may not always be the most scintillating read, but it just might save your life.

RED TAPE

Documents and Formalities

We're going to fill you in on visas and residence permits, but don't forget the most important ID of all: your **passport. Don't forget your passport!**

Entrance Requirements

- **PASSPORT:** Required for citizens of all countries, except EU citizens (who can show their national ID).

- **VISA:** Required by those who wish to stay longer than 3 months.

- **WORK PERMIT:** Required for all foreigners planning to work in Spain.

Visas

Those lucky enough to be EU citizens do not need a visa to travel to Spain. Citizens of Australia, Canada, New Zealand, the US, and other non-EU countries do not need a visa for stays of up to 90 days, but this three-month period begins upon entry into any of the countries that belong to the EU's **freedom of movement** (see **One Europe,** below.) Those staying for more than 90 days should apply for a long-term visa; consult an embassy or consulate for more information. Double-check entrance requirements at the nearest embassy or consulate of Spain for up-to-date information before departure. US citizens can also consult **http://travel.state.gov.**

Entering Spain to study requires a special visa. For more information, see the **Beyond Tourism** chapter.

Work Permits

Entry into Spain as a traveler does not include the right to work, which is authorized only by a work permit. For more information, see the **Beyond Tourism** chapter.

Embassies and Consulates

At Home

- **AUSTRALIA: Consulate General.** (Level 24, St-Martins Tower, 31 Market St., Sydney NSW 2000 ☎+61 292 612 433; www.ambafrance-au.org ☒ Open M-F 9am-1pm.)

- **CANADA: Embassy.** (74 Stanley Ave., Ottawa, Ontario, K1M 1P4 ☎+1-613-747-2252; embespca@mail.mae.es ☒ Open M-Th 8:30am-5pm, F 8:30am-2:15pm.)

- **IRELAND: Embassy.** (17 A, Merlyn Park, Ballsbridge, Dublin 4 ☎+353 126 08 066; www.mae.es/Embajadas/dublin ☒ Open M-F 9:30am-1:30pm.)

- **NEW ZEALAND: Consulate.** (Ste. 1, The Arcade, 13 Victoria Road, Devonport, Auckland 0624 ☎+64 09 923 71 44; spanish.consulate@gmail.com ☒ Open M-F 9am-5 pm.)

- **UK: Embassy.** (39 Chesham Place, London SW1X 8SB ☎+44 20 723 55 555; www.maec.es/Embajadas/Londres ☒ Open M-F 9:30am-noon.)

- **USA: Embassy.** (2375 Pennsylvania Ave., Washington DC 20037 ☎+1-202 452-0100; www.maec.es/embajadas/Washington ☒ Open M-F 9am-1pm.)

In Madrid

- **AUSTRALIAN EMBASSY:** Torre Espacio, Paseo de la Castellana, 259D, Planta 24 ☎91 353 66 00; www.spain.embassy.gov.au ☒ Open M-F 8:30am-4:30pm.

- **CANADIAN EMBASSY:** Torre Espacio, Paseo de la Castellana, 259D ☎91 382 84 00; www.canadainternational.gc.ca/spain-espagne ☒ Open Sept-July M-Th 8:30am-2pm and 3-5:30pm, F 8:30am-2:15pm; Aug M-F 8:30am-2:15pm.

- **IRISH EMBASSY:** Ireland House, Paseo de la Castellana, 46-4

☎91 436 40 93; www.irlanda.es 🕐 Open M-Th 10am-2pm, F 8:30am-2:15pm.

- **NEW ZEALAND EMBASSY:** C. del Pinar 7, 3rd fl. ☎91 523 02 26; www.nzembassy.com/spain 🕐 Open Sept-June M-F 9am-2pm and 3-5:30pm; July-Aug M-F 8:30am-1:30pm and 2-4:30pm.

- **UK EMBASSY:** Torre Espacio, Paseo de la Castellana, 259D ☎91 714 63 00; www.mae.es/Embajadas/Ottawa/en/Home 🕐 Open M-Th 8:30am-5pm, F 8:30am-2:15pm.

- **US EMBASSY:** C. de Serrano 75 ☎91 587 22 00; http://madrid.usembassy.gov 🕐 Open M-F 8:30am-1pm.

One Europe

The EU's policy of **freedom of movement** means that most border controls have been abolished and visa policies harmonized. Under this treaty, formally known as the Schengen Agreement, you're still required to carry a passport (or government-issued ID card for EU citizens) when crossing an internal border, but, once you've been admitted into one country, you're free to travel to other participating states. Most EU states (the UK is a notable exception) are already members of Schengen, as are Iceland and Norway.

In recent times, fears over immigration have led to calls for suspension of this freedom of movement. Border controls are being strengthened, but this shouldn't affect casual travelers.

MONEY

Getting Money from Home

Stuff happens. When stuff happens, you might need some money. When you need some money, the easiest and cheapest solution is to have someone back home make a deposit to your bank account. Otherwise, consider one of the following options.

Wiring Money

Arranging a **bank money transfer** means asking a bank back home to wire money to a bank in Madrid. This is the cheapest way to transfer cash, but it's also the slowest and most agonizing, usually taking several days or more. Note that some banks may only release your funds in local currency, potentially sticking you with a poor exchange rate; inquire about this in advance. International bank transfers normally take two to four days to complete.

Money transfer services like **Western Union** are faster and more convenient than bank transfers—but also much pricier. Western Union has many locations worldwide. To find one, visit www.westernunion.com or call: in Australia }1800 173 833, in Canada }800-235-0000, in the UK }0808 234 9168, in the US }800-325-6000, or in Spain }900 983 273. Money transfer services are also available to **American Express** cardholders and at select **Thomas Cook** offices.

US State Department (US Citizens Only)

In serious emergencies only, the US State Department will help your family or friends forward money within hours to the nearest consular office, which will then disburse it according to instructions for a US$30 fee. If you wish to use this service, you must contact the **Overseas Citizens Services** division of the US State Department. (☎+1-202-501-4444, from US ☎888-407-4747).

Withdrawing Money

To use a debit or credit card to withdraw money from a **cash machine** (ATM) in Europe, you must have a four-digit Personal Identification Number (PIN). If your PIN is longer than four digits, ask your bank whether you can just use the first four or whether you'll need a new PIN. Credit cards don't usually come with PINs, so if you intend to hit up ATMs in Europe with a credit card, call your credit card company before leaving to request one.

ATMs are relatively well distributed throughout Madrid. Almost all ATMs accept all networks, and Visa and Mastercard will almost certainly be accepted anywhere. Check with your bank to see if they charge a conversion fee for withdrawing from a euro-dispensing ATM.

The Euro

Despite what many dollar-possessing Americans might want to hear, the official currency of 16 members of the European Union—Austria, Belgium, Cyprus, Finland, France, Germany, Greece, Ireland, Italy, Luxembourg, Malta, the Netherlands, Portugal, Slovakia, Slovenia, and Spain—is the **euro.**

The currency has some positive consequences for travelers hitting more than one eurozone country. For one thing, money-changers across the eurozone are obliged to exchange money at the official, fixed rate and at no commission (though they may still charge a small service fee). Second, euro-denominated traveler's checks allow you to pay for goods and services across the eurozone at the official rate and commission-free. For more info, check a currency converter (such as **www.xe.com**) or **www.europa.eu.int.**

Tipping and Bargaining

Native Spaniards rarely tip more than their spare change, even at expensive restaurants. If you make it clear that you're a tourist—especially an American one—they might expect you to tip more. No one will refuse your money, but don't ever feel like you have to tip as the server's pay is almost never based on tips.

Bargaining is common and necessary in open-air and street markets. Especially if you are buying a number of things, like produce, you can probably get a better deal if you haggle. Do not barter in malls or established shops.

Taxes

Spain has a 7-8% value added tax (IVA) on all means and accommodations. The prices listed in *Let's Go* include IVA unless otherwise mentioned. Retail goods bear a much higher 16% IVA, although the listed prices generally include this tax. Non-EU citizens who have stayed in the EU fewer than 180 days can claim back the tax paid on purchases at the airport. Ask the shop where you have made the purchase to supply you with a tax return form, but stores will only provide them for purchases of around €50-100.

GETTING THERE

By Plane

All flights come in through the **Aeropuerto Internacional de Barajas** (☎902 404 704; www.aena.es). The **Barajas** Metro stop connects the airport to the rest of Madrid (Ⓢ €2.). To take the subway into the city center, take the number 8 toward Nuevo Ministerios, transfer to the #10 toward Puerta del Sur, get off at ĆTribunal (3 stops), transfer to the #1 toward Valdecarros, and get off at ĆSol. The journey should take 45-60min. By bus, the **Bus-Aeropeurto 200** leaves from the national terminal T2 and runs to the city center through ĆAvenida de América. (☎90 250 78 50 ⌚ Every 15min. 5:20am-11:30pm.) **Taxis** (Ⓢ €35. ⌚ 30min.) are readily available outside of the airport. For more info on ground transport, visit **www.metromadrid.es**.

By Train

Trains (☎90 224 02 02; www.renfe.es) from northern Europe and France arrive on the north side of the city at Chamartín. Trains to and from the south of Spain and Portugal use Atocha. Buy tickets at the station or online. There is a **RENFE** information office at the main terminal. (☎90 224 02 02 ⌚ Open daily 7am-7pm.) **AVE** trains offer high-speed service throughout Spain, including Barcelona, Salamanca, Segovia, Sevilla, and Toledo. (Estación Chamartín, C. de Agustín de Foxá ☎91 300 69 69; 91 506 63 29.) Be sure to keep your ticket, or you won't be able to pass the turnstiles. Call RENFE for both international destinations and domestic travel. (☎90 224 34 02 for international destinations; ☎90 224 02 02 for domestic.) Ticket windows are open daily 6:30am-9pm; when they're closed, you can buy tickets at vending machines.

By Bus

If you prefer four wheels, many private bus companies run through Madrid, and most pass through **Estación Sur de Autobuses.** (C. de Méndez Álvaro ☎91 468 42 00; www.estacionautobusesmadrid. com. *i* Info booth open daily 6:30am-1am.) National destinations include Algeciras, Alicante, Oviedo, and Toledo. Inquire at the station, online, or by phone for specific information on routes and schedules.

GETTING AROUND

By Metro

The Madrid Metro system is by far the easiest, cheapest way to get you almost anywhere you need to go in the city. It is clean, safe, and recently renovated. Service begins Monday through Saturday at 6am—Sunday at 7am—and ends daily around 1:30am. Try to avoid rush hours (8-10am, 1-2pm, and 4-6pm). You can buy either a one-way ticket (€1), or, if you're making multiple trips, you can save by purchasing a combined **10-in-one metrobus ticket** (€9.30). Trains run frequently, and green timers above most platforms show approaching train times. Be sure to grab a free Metro map (available at any ticket booth or tourist office). **Abonos mensuales,** or monthly passes, grant unlimited travel within the city proper for €47.60, while **abonos turísticos** (tourist passes) come in various lengths (1, 2, 3, 4, or 7 days) and sell for €6-25 at the Metro stations or online. For Metro information, visit **www.metromadrid.es** or call ☎90 244 44 03.

By Bus

Buses cover areas that are inaccessible by the Metro and are a great way to see the city. The pamphlet "Visiting the Downtown on Public Transport" lists routes and stops. (Ⓢ Free at any tourist office or downloadable at **www.madrid.org.**) Tickets for the bus and Metro are interchangeable. The Búho (owl), or night bus, travels from Pl. de Cibeles and other marked routes along the outskirts of the city. (Ⓞ M-Th every 30min. midnight-3am, every hr. 3-6am; F-Sa every 20min midnight-6am; Su every 30 min. midnight-3am.) These buses, marked on the essential **Red de Autobuses Nocturnos** (available at any tourist office) run along 26 lines covering regular daytime routes. For info, call **Empresa Municipal de Transportes** (☎90 250 78 50; www.emtmadrid.es). **Estación Sur** (C. de Méndez Álvaro ☎91 468 42 00) covers mainly southern and southeastern destinations outside Madrid such as Granada, Málaga, Sevilla, and Valencia. Visit **www.avanzabus.com** for timetables and routes.

By Taxi

Registered Madrid taxis are black or white and have red bands and small insignias of a bear and *madroño* tree (symbols of

Madrid). Hail them on the street or at taxi stands all over the city. A green light means they're free. The fare starts at €1.75 and increases by €1 every kilometer thereafter. To call a city taxi, dial ☎91 447 51 80.

By Moped and Bike

Biking in the city is ill-advised, but Casa de Campo and Dehesa de la Villa both have easily navigable bike trails. You can rent a bike from **Karacol Sport**. (C. de Tortosa, 8 ☎91 539 96 33; www.karacol.com *i* Cash deposit of €50 and photocopy of your passport required, €18 per day. ⏰ Open M-W 10:30am-3pm and 5-8pm, Th 10:30am-3pm and 5-9:30pm, F-Su 10:30am-3pm and 5-8pm.) **Motocicletas Antonio Castro** rents mopeds for €23-95 per day including unlimited mileage and insurance, but you'll need your own lock and helmet. You must be at least 25 years old and have a driver's license for motorcycles. (C. de Clara del Rey, 17 ☎91 413 00 47; www.blafermotos.com ⏰ Open M-F 8am-6pm, Sa 10am-1:30pm.)

PRACTICALITIES

For all the hostels, cafes, museums, and bars we list, some of the most important places you'll visit during your trip may be more mundane. Whether it's a tourist office, currency exchange, or post office, these practicalities are vital to a successful trip, and you'll find all you need right here.

- **TOURIST OFFICES:** The **Madrid Tourism Centre** in Pl. Mayor (☎91 588 16 36; www.esmadrid.com) is a good place to start, where you'll find city and transit maps as well as suggestions for activities, food, and accommodations. English is spoken at most tourist offices throughout the city. There are additional tourist offices and stands throughout the city; look for large orange stands with exclamation marks: **Calle del Duque de Medinaceli, 2** (☎91 429 49 51 ⏰ Open M-Sa 9:30am-8:30pm, Su and holidays 9:30am-2pm.); **Estación de Atocha** (☎91 528 46 30 ⏰ Open M-Sa 9:30am-8:30pm, Su and holidays 9:30am-2pm.); **Madrid-Barajas Airport Terminal 1** (☎91 305 86 56); **Terminal 4** (☎90 210 00 07 ⏰ Open daily 9:30am-8:30pm). Also, there is a tourist office at the **airport train station** (☎91 315 99 76 ⏰ Open M-Sa 8am-8pm, Su 9am-2pm.)

- **TOURS:** Themed tours leave regularly from the Madrid Tourism Centre. For dates, times, and more info, visit **www.esmadrid.com.** Many youth hostels host tapas tours, pub crawls, and walking tours for reasonable prices. Check out **www.toursnonstop.com** (⑤ €10 tapas and pub tours). **LeTango Tours** is run by a Spanish-American husband-wife team; their tours that take you to local bars, give fun city facts, and explain Spanish traditions. (☎91 369 47 52; www.letango.com). Run by historian and writer Stephen Drake-Jones, the **Wellington Society** (☎60 914 32 03; www. wellsoc.org) offers different themed tours of Madrid and daytrips to Toledo and Segovia. Another option is **Madrid Vision** (☎91 779 18 88; www.madridvision.es), which runs the double-decker red buses that you see throughout the city. Choose between the *historicó* and *moderno* routes. Each route makes 15-20 stops around the city. (⑤ €17; discounts online.)

- **CURRENCY EXCHANGE:** The most convenient place to change your money—although not always the cheapest—is the airport. There are also currency exchanges in Puerta del Sol and Gran Vía (look for booths that say "change"), but try to use these as a last resort, as rates are bad and commission charges are high. Most *hostales* and hotels will also be able to change your money; rates vary by location. Another option is **Banco Santander Central Hispano,** which charges €12-15 commission on non-American Express Travelers Cheques (max. exchange €300). Wherever you go, be sure to bring your passport as identification.

- **LUGGAGE STORAGE:** Store your luggage at the **Aeropuerto Internacional de Barajas** (☎91 393 68 05 ⑤ 1-day €3.70; 2-15 days €4.78 per day. ⌚ Open 24hr.) or at the **bus station.** (⑤ €1.40 per bag per day. ⌚ Open M-F 6:30am-10:30pm, Sa 6:30am-3pm.)

- **POST OFFICES:** Buy **stamps** *(sellos)* from a post office or tobacco stand. Madrid's **central post office** is at Pl. de Cibeles. (☎91 523 06 94; 90 219 71 97 ⌚ Open M-F 8:30am-9:30pm.) Mailboxes are usually yellow with one slot for "Madrid" and another for everywhere else.

- **POSTAL CODE:** 28008.

Emergency

Hopefully you won't need any of these things, but in case you do, it's best to be prepared.

- **EMERGENCY NUMBERS:** In case of a **medical emergency,** dial ☎061 or ☎112.

- **POLICE: Servicio de Atención al Turista Extranjero (SATE)** are police who deal exclusively with tourists and help with contacting embassies, reporting crimes, and canceling credit cards. (C. Legantos, 19 ☎91 548 85 27; 90 210 21 12 🕐 Open daily 9am-midnight.)

- **MEDICAL SERVICES:** For non-emergency medical concerns, go to **Unidad Medica Angloamericana,** which has English-speaking personnel on duty by appointment. (C. del Conde de Aranda, 1, 1st fl. ☎91 435 18 23 🕐 Open M-F 9am-8pm, Sa 10am-1pm.)

SAFETY AND HEALTH

General Advice

In any type of crisis, the most important thing to do is **stay calm.** Your country's embassy is usually your best resource in an emergency; it's a good idea to register with the embassy upon arrival. The government offices listed in **Travel Advisories** can provide information on the services they offer their citizens in case of emergencies abroad.

Local Laws and Police

Travelers are not likely to break major laws unintentionally while visiting Spain. You can contact your embassy if arrested, although they often cannot do much to assist you beyond finding legal counsel. You should feel comfortable approaching the police, although few officers speak English. There are three types of police in Spain. The **policía nacional** wear blue or black uniforms and white shirts; they guard government buildings, protect dignitaries, and deal with crime investigation (including theft). The **policía local** wear blue uniforms, deal more with local issues, and report to the mayor or town hall in each municipality. The

Travel Advisories

The following government offices provide travel information and advisories:

- **AUSTRALIA: Department of Foreign Affairs and Trade.** (☎+61 2 6261 1111; www.smartraveller.gov.au)

- **CANADA: Department of Foreign Affairs and International Trade.** Call or visit the website for the free booklet *Bon Voyage, But...* (☎+1-800-267-6788; www.international.gc.ca)

- **NEW ZEALAND: Ministry of Foreign Affairs and Trade.** (☎+64 4 439 8000; www.safetravel.govt.nz)

- **UK: Foreign and Commonwealth Office.** (☎+44 845 850 2829; www.fco.gov.uk)

- **US: Department of State.** (☎888-407-4747 from the US, +1-202-501-4444 outside the US; http://travel.state.gov)

guardia civil wear olive-green uniforms and are responsible for issues more relevant to travelers: customs, crowd control, and national security.

Drugs and Alcohol

Recreational drugs are illegal in Spain, and police take these laws seriously. The legal **drinking age** is 18. Spain has the highest road mortality rate and one of the highest rates of drunk driving deaths in Europe. Recently, Spanish officials have started setting up checkpoints on roads to test drivers' blood alcohol levels (BAC). Do not drive while intoxicated, and be cautious on the road.

Specific Concerns

Basque terrorism concerns all travelers in Spain, with the active presence of a militant wing of Basque separatists called the Euskadi Ta Askatasuna (ETA; Basque Homeland and Freedom). In March 2006, ETA declared a permanent cease-fire that officially ended in June 2007. ETA's attacks are generally targeted politically and are not considered random terrorist attacks that endanger regular civilians. The March 11, 2004 train bombings linked to al-Qaeda are viewed by Spaniards in the same way that Americans view September 11.

Pre-Departure Health

Matching a prescription to a foreign equivalent is not always easy, safe, or possible, so if you take **prescription drugs,** carry up-to-date prescriptions or a statement from your doctor stating the medications' trade names, manufacturers, chemical names, and dosages. Be sure to keep all medication with you in your carry-on luggage. It is also a good idea to look up the Spanish names of drugs you may need during your trip.

Immunizations and Precautions

Travelers over the age of two should make sure that the following vaccines are up to date: MMR (for measles, mumps, and rubella); DTaP or Td (for diphtheria, tetanus, and pertussis); IPV (for polio); Hib (for *Haemophilus influenzae* B); and HepB (for Hepatitis B). For recommendations on immunizations and prophylaxis, check with a doctor and consult the **Centers for Disease Control and Prevention (CDC)** in the US (☎+1-800-232-4636; www.cdc.gov/travel) or the equivalent in your home country.

KEEPING IN TOUCH

By Email and Internet

Hello and welcome to the 21st century, where you're rarely more than a 5min. walk from the nearest **Wi-Fi hot spot,** even if sometimes you have to pay a few bucks or buy a drink for the privilege of using it. Hostels in Madrid generally have free Wi-Fi, and chains like McDonalds and Starbucks do too, though you'll generally have to purchase food to access it. For lists of additional cybercafes in Madrid check out **www.cybercaptive.com.**

Wireless hot spots make internet access possible in public and remote places. Unfortunately, they also pose security risks. Hot spots are open, public networks that use unencrypted, insecure connections. They are susceptible to hacks and "packet sniffing," the theft of passwords and other private information. To prevent problems, disable "ad hoc" mode, turn off file sharing and network discovery, encrypt your email, turn on your firewall, beware of phony networks, and watch for over-the-shoulder creeps.

By Telephone

Calling Home from Madrid

If you have internet access, your best—i.e., cheapest, most convenient, and most tech-savvy—means of calling home is our good friend **Skype** (www.skype.com). You can even videochat if you have a webcam. Calls to other Skype users are free; calls to landlines and mobiles worldwide start at US$0.023 per minute, depending on where you're calling.

For those still stuck in the 20th century, **prepaid phone cards** are a common and relatively inexpensive means of calling abroad. Each one comes with a Personal Identification Number (PIN) and a toll-free access number. You call the access number and then follow the directions for dialing your PIN. To purchase prepaid phone cards, check online for the best rates; **www.callingcards.com** is a good place to start. Online providers generally send your access number and PIN via email, with no actual "card" involved. You can also call home with prepaid phone cards purchased in Madrid.

Another option is a **calling card,** linked to a major national telecommunications service in your home country. Calls are billed collect or to your account. Cards generally come with instructions for dialing both domestically and internationally.

Placing a **collect call** through an international operator can be expensive but may be necessary in case of an emergency. You can frequently call collect without even possessing a company's calling card just by calling its access number and following the instructions.

Cellular Phones

Cell phones are the norm for both locals and temporary residents in Spain. You can either get an internationally capable SIM card for your normal cell phone, or purchase a cheap phone on a pay-as-you-go style plan from a wireless company in Madrid. If you choose to go the latter route, **Movistar, Yoigo,** and **Orange** are usually safe bets.

The international standard for cell phones is **Global System for Mobile Communication (GSM).** To make and receive calls in Spain, you will need a GSM-compatible phone and a **SIM (Subscriber Identity Module) card,** a country-specific, thumbnail-size chip that gives you a local phone number and plugs you into the local network. Many SIM cards are prepaid, and incoming calls are often free. You can buy additional cards or vouchers (usually available at convenience stores) to "top up" your phone. For more information on GSM phones, check out **www.telestial.com.** Companies like **Cellular Abroad** (www.cellularabroad.com) and **OneSimCard** (www.onesimcard.com) rent cell phones and SIM cards that work in a variety of destinations around the world.

International Calls

To call Spain from home or to call home from Spain, dial:

1. **THE INTERNATIONAL DIALING PREFIX.** To call from Spain dial ☎00, from Australia ☎0011; from Canada or the **US** ☎011; and from Ireland, New Zealand, or the UK ☎00.

2. **THE COUNTRY CODE OF THE COUNTRY YOU WANT TO CALL.** To call Spain dial ☎34; for Australia ☎61; Canada or the US ☎1; Ireland ☎353; New Zealand ☎64; and for the UK ☎44.

3. **THE LOCAL NUMBER.** If the area code begins with a zero, you can omit that number when dialing from abroad.

By Snail Mail

Sending Mail from Madrid

Airmail is the best way to send mail home from Madrid. Write "airmail," *"par avion,"* or *"correo aéreo"* on the front. For simple letters or postcards, airmail tends to be surprisingly cheap, but the price will go up sharply for packages. Surface mail is by far the cheapest, slowest, and most antiquated way to send mail. It takes one to two months to cross the Atlantic and one to three to cross the Pacific—good for heavy items you won't need for a while, like souvenirs that you've acquired along the way.

Receiving Mail in Madrid

There are several ways to arrange pickup of letters sent to you while you are in Madrid, even if you do not have an address of your own. Mail can be sent via **Poste Restante** (General Delivery;

Lista de Correos in Spanish) to Madrid, and it is pretty reliable. Address Poste Restante letters like so:

> Penélope Cruz
> Lista de Correos
> Madrid, Spain

The mail will go to a special desk in the central post office at **Plaza de Cibeles** unless you specify a local post office by street address or postal code. It's best to use the largest post office, since mail may be sent there regardless. Bring your passport (or other photo ID) for pickup; there may be a small fee. If the clerks insist that there is nothing for you, ask them to check under your first name as well. *Let's Go* lists the information for the main post office in **Practicalities.** It's usually safer and quicker, though more expensive, to send mail express or registered. If you don't want to deal with Poste Restante, consider asking your hostel or other accommodation if you can receive mail there. Of course, if you have your own mailing address or a reliable friend to receive mail for you, that may be the easiest solution.

TIME DIFFERENCES

Spain is 2hr. ahead of Greenwich Mean Time (GMT) and observes Daylight Saving Time. This means that it is 9hr. ahead of Los Angeles, 6hr. ahead of New York City, 1hr. ahead of the British Isles, 8hr. behind Sydney, and 10hr. behind New Zealand.

CLIMATE

Madrid's climate is basically Mediterranean, with hot summers and relatively cold winters due to its altitude. Fortunately for most travelers, most precipitation occurs during the fall and spring and very minimally in the summer. It's still always a good idea to bring a *paraguas* (umbrella)—you never know.

MONTH	AVG. HIGH TEMP.		AVG. LOW TEMP.		AVG. RAINFALL		AVG. NUMBER OF WET DAYS
January	9°C	48°F	2°C	36°F	39mm	1.5 in.	8
February	11°C	52°F	2°C	36°F	34mm	1.3 in.	7
March	15°C	59°F	5°C	41°F	43mm	1.7 in.	10
April	18°C	64°F	7°C	45°F	48mm	1.9 in.	9
May	21°C	70°F	10°C	50°F	47mm	1.9 in.	10
June	27°C	81°F	15°C	59°F	27mm	1.1 in.	5
July	31°C	88°F	17°C	63°F	14mm	.6 in.	2
August	30°C	86°F	17°C	63°F	15mm	.6 in.	3
September	25°C	77°F	14°C	57°F	32mm	1.3 in.	6

October	19°C	66°F	10°C	50°F	53mm	1.3 in.	8
November	13°C	55°F	5°C	41°F	47mm	1.9 in.	9
December	9°C	48°F	2°C	36°F	48mm	1.9 in.	20

To convert from degrees Fahrenheit to degrees Celsius, subtract 32 and multiply by 5/9. To convert from Celsius to Fahrenheit, multiply by 9/5 and add 32. The mathematically challenged may use this handy chart:

°CELSIUS	-5	0	5	10	15	20	25	30	35	40
°FAHRENHEIT	23	32	41	50	59	68	77	86	95	104

MEASUREMENTS

Like the rest of the rational world, Spain uses the metric system. The basic unit of length is the meter (m), which is divided into 100 centimeters (cm) or 1000 millimeters (mm). One thousand meters make up one kilometer (km). Fluids are measured in liters (L), each divided into 1000 milliliters (mL). A liter of pure water weighs one kilogram (kg), the unit of mass that is divided into 1000 grams (g). One metric ton is 1000kg.

MEASUREMENT CONVERSIONS	
1 inch (in.) = 25.4mm	1 millimeter (mm) = 0.039 in.
1 foot (ft.) = 0.305m	1 meter (m) = 3.28 ft.
1 yard (yd.) = 0.914m	1 meter (m) = 1.094 yd.
1 mile (mi.) = 1.609km	1 kilometer (km) = 0.621 mi.
1 ounce (oz.) = 28.35g	1 gram (g) = 0.035 oz.
1 pound (lb.) = 0.454kg	1 kilogram (kg) = 2.205 lb.
1 fluid ounce (fl. oz.) = 29.57mL	1 milliliter (mL) = 0.034 fl. oz.
1 gallon (gal.) = 3.785L	1 liter (L) = 0.264 gal.

LANGUAGE

Spanish

Thanks to a maniacal desire for gold and the fountain of youth (both on Earth and in the Catholic hereafter), Spain spread its language across the globe during its imperial heyday. Today, it is the third most widely spoken language in the world after English and Mandarin. Spain's Spanish, though, differs notably from the rest of the Spanish-speaking world by the tell-tale "theta": changing the pronunciation of *c*'s and *z*'s from an "*s*"-sound to a "*th*"-sound. Be careful not to do this with *s*'s, because saying "Buenath

Nocheth" will make people think you have a speech impediment. In general, Spanish is a very easy language to pronounce since all letters (except h) are pronounced and have a consistent sound.

Pronunciation

All of the phonetic sounds in Spanish are found in English but are represented differently. The *h* is silent in all words. An accent on a letter indicates that the emphasis of the word should be placed on that letter.

PHONETIC UNIT	PRONUNCIATION	PHONETIC UNIT	PRONUNCIATION
a	aw, as in "law"	u	oo, as in "boo"
e	ey as in "ray"	ll	y-, as in "year"
i	ee as in "fee"	j	h- as in "hat"
o	oh as in "oval"	v	a mixture of v/b

Phrasebook

ENGLISH	SPANISH	PRONUNCIATION
Hello!/Hi!	¡Hola!	Oh-lah
Goodbye!	¡Adiós!	Aw-dee-ose
Yes.	Sí.	See
No.	No.	samesies
Please.	Por favor.	pohr fa-VOHR
Sorry!/Excuse me!	¡Perdón!	pehrd-OWN
Good morning.	Buenos días.	BWEH-nos DEE-as
Good evening.	Buenas noches.	BWEH-nas DEE-as
How are you?	Cómo estás?	CO-mo ays-TAS
I'm fine, thanks, and you?	Bién, gracias, ¿y tú?	Bee-AYN, GRA-thi-as, ee too
What time is it?	¿Qué hora es?	Kay ora es
It's 5 o'clock.	Son las cinco!	Sown las SEEN-ko
Wait!	¡Espera!	Ace-PEHR-a
EMERGENCY		
Go away!	¡Vete!	VAY-tay
Help!	¡Socorro!	So-CO-ro
Call the police!	¡Llama a la policia!	YA-ma ah la po-lee-SEE-a
Get a doctor!	¡Llama al médico!	YA-ma ahl MAY-dee-co

FOOD AND DRINK		
Waiter/waitress	camarero/a	Cama-RAY-roh/rah
I'd like...	Me gustaría...	May goost-er-EE-a
Is there meat in this dish?	¿Tiene carne este plato?	Tee-YEN-ay CAR-nay ES-tay plah-to
salad	ensalada	en-sa-LAHD-a
wine (sherry)	vino (jerez)	VEE-no (hay-rayth)
shots	chupitos	choo-PEE-tos
Spanish cured ham	jamon serrano	ha-MONE serr-AH-no
Can I buy you a drink?	¿Te compro una copa?	Tay COM-pro OO-na CO-pa
Is the bread free?	¿Está gratis el pan?	Es-TAH GRA-tees el pan
How much does it cost?	¿Cuánto cuesta?	KWAHN-to KWEH-stah
FOR KICKS		
I believe that David Bowie is my soumate.	Creo que David Bowie es mi alma gemela.	CRAY-o kay David Bowie es mi AL-ma HEH-meh-la
Do you have anything a little sexier?	¿Tienes algo un poco mas sexy?	Tee-YEN-ays AL-go un PO-co mas SEH-xy
These grapes taste funny.	Estas uvas tienen un sabor raro.	AYS-tas OO-bas tee-YEN-en OO-na sah-BOOR RAH-ro
Will you marry me?	¿Te casarás conmigo?	TAY cah-sah-RAHS con-MEE-go
I would like eight kilograms of french fries, please.	Póngame ocho kilos de patatas fritas, por favor.	POHN-gah-may OH-cho KEE-lohs day pah-TAH-tahs FREE-tahs, por fah-VOOR

Madrid 101

Ready for over 1000 years of history in fewer than three pages? *Let's Go* has thrown away the boring bits and stuffed what's left into bite-size nuggets just for you, complete with jokes, violence, and more violence, because Spain's history is certainly bloody. The latest studies all show that not reading the *Let's Go* 101 section before visiting Madrid could be hazardous to your health, so have at it!

Facts and Figures

- **NUMBER OF BULLS KILLED EACH YEAR AT THE PLAZA DE TOROS DE LAS VENTAS:** Over 400
- **TIME MADRILEÑOS SPEND TAKING SIESTAS (APPROXIMATE):** 1.75 billion hours per year
- **ANCIENT EGYPTIAN TEMPLES IN THE CITY:** 1
- **NUMBER OF METRO STOPS:** 270
- **RELATIVE AREA OF MADRID'S PLAZA MAYOR:** 2.3 American football fields

HISTORY

Ain't No There There (Big Bang–939 CE)

It's hard to imagine while exploring today's Madrid, but there was a time when the land on which the capital sits was an empty plain, sparsely inhabited by livestock, Neanderthals, Romans, and dinosaurs, though not necessarily in that order. The eighth century saw the invasion of Moorish armies from North Africa, who conquered nearly all of the Iberian Peninsula. The **Moors** brought the region an era of enlightenment and relative religious tolerance, which the Christian armies to the north found wholly unacceptable. At the time, Madrid was but a small village in the shadow of a ninth-century fortress erected by **Muhammad I** of Córdoba. Though often a source of confusion, the city of Madrid actually takes its name from the locale's Arabic name, **Majerit,** not from the town of New Madrid, Missouri.

This Land is Your Land, This Land is My Land (939–1469)

As the first millennium drew to a close, the various Christian kingdoms of the Iberian north began the nearly 800-year-long campaign to push their Moorish neighbors back across the Strait of Gibraltar. This gradual wave of **Reconquista** (Reconquest) arrived at Majerit's doorstep in 939, when Don Ramiro II of León razed the town. The fortress and humble town sat near the frontier between the warring groups and was attacked several times, until **Alfonso VI** of León and Castile finally took the city in 1085 on his way to the Moors' stronghold at **Toledo.**

Madrid obtained its charter in 1200 and became a favorite retreat of Castilian royals, who used it as a hunting ground. But the town remained more rustic-backwater-with-big-castle than metropolis. That all changed when a sudden need for a cosmopolitan capital with an even bigger castle arose.

Age of Empires (1469–1561)

Until the marriage of **Isabella of Castile** and **Ferdinand of Aragón** in 1469, the Iberian Peninsula was a collection of many kingdoms, united only by their shared enthusiasm for crusades. Isabella and

Ferdinand's marriage brought the two most powerful kingdoms under the same crown, laying the foundations for a dominant state that controlled much of the peninsula and nearly all of its center. By 1500, the Moors were gone, the New World was being conquered and its riches plundered for the crown, and the Inquisition was going strong, uniting the peninsula in religion as well as political dominion. All those Spanish royals needed was a capital to call their own. In 1524, **Charles V** came to Madrid to recover from a fever (the cure, oddly enough, was more cowbell), and in 1561 his son, **Philip II,** declared Madrid his capital and moved his court there from Toledo. The rationale was that the new capital was not associated with any one former kingdom, but could instead serve as a neutral center of a new, unified nation.

Capital Gains (1561–1650)

Except for four wild years when **Philip III** moved the capital to Valladolid, Madrid remained the seat of Spanish power and flourished. The old Moorish fortress was replaced with the **Palácio Real,** luxurious churches and convents were put up all over the city, and literature and the arts thrived. Wealth poured into the city from the farthest reaches of the vast and still-expanding empire, but the prosperity was short-lived.

It's a Mad, Mad, Mad, Madrid (1650–1759)

Financial mismanagement and massive foreign debts caused much of the silver and gold of Nuevo España to pass straight through Spain and into the coffers of other European powers and creditors. This age of decadence saw poverty across the nation, and Madrid went through a period of starvation, destitution, and lawlessness. The shift from Austrian to Bourbon rule in 1700 began the revitalization of the state and the city, and this comeback culminated in the rule of **Charles III.**

One Borbón, One Scotch, One Beer (1760–1808)

Though he was king of one of the largest empires the world has ever known, you'd think Charles III never set his sights beyond Madrid's walls, given everything he did for the city. The **"best mayor of Madrid"** was an enlightened ruler with liberal policies, to whom Madrid owes dozens of schools, colleges, parks, promenades, public buildings, and museums, including the **Museo del Prado.** One of his most celebrated actions was urging the citizens of Madrid to stop throwing their waste out their windows; passersby remain grateful to this day.

War, War, and More War (1808-1939)

The salad days of the Bourbons ended with the **Peninsular Wars,** the violent French invasion of Spain in 1808. **Napoleon's** ruthless troops took Madrid in May 1808, and the city's citizens revolted, which didn't end so well for them (cf. Goya's *Dos de Mayo, 1808* and *Tres de Mayo, 1808,* both in the Prado). Spain regained its independence from France in 1814 and restored its monarchy, but three wars over royal succession in the 19th century tore the nation apart, and the 1898 Spanish-American War left Spain at an **all-time low.** Spain stayed neutral during WWI, but another war of its own was not far off.

At the start of the 1930s, leftists saw huge gains, but—surprise, surprise—the anarcho-syndicalists did not govern very effectively. In 1934, a conservative government was established, and revolts broke out in Oviedo, Gijón, and Barcelona. These outbreaks were quelled by the army, led by **General Francisco Franco.** In 1936, a coalition of **Republicans** narrowly won parliamentary elections, and Franco led an insurgency in a **Civil War** that lasted three years. Madrid stayed loyal to the Republic until it fell to Franco's forces in March 1939.

Generalísimo Francisco Franco… (1939–75)

Madrid was Generalísimo Franco's seat of power. Before the 20th century, Madrid had served mainly as a bureaucratic hub, but Franco's regime brought about much **internal migration** and the capital grew in population and socio-economic diversity. Intense **industrialization** characterized Madrid under Franco's often brutal rule. Today the Franco era continues to divide Spaniards who lived through it and their descendants; it should probably be avoided as a topic of conversation.

…is Still Dead (1975–Today)

After Franco's death in 1975, Spain transitioned to a democratic government, and the modernizing city of Madrid benefited from the ensuing economic prosperity. Today, Madrid is a cultural and tourist center of Europe, a gleaming city of parks, fountains, and some of the best professional *fútbol* the world has ever seen.

CUSTOMS AND ETIQUETTE

Greetings and Addresses

When meeting for the first time, two men usually shake hands, two women usually exchange a kiss on each cheek, and a man and woman will, well, you know. (Just kidding—depending on circumstances and age range, either the handshake or double-kiss is appropriate, though a handshake is safer.) Acquaintances will generally greet each other with a double-kiss, hug, or "man-hug." It is polite to address men as *señor* and women as *señora* (if married) or *señorita* (if unmarried). *Usted* ("you") is only used in very formal situations or when speaking to someone from an older generation; the informal *tú* ("you") is much more common. If you find the *tú-usted* duality a source of confusion, don't worry: many young Spaniards do, too.

Naps and Noms

The Spanish schedule tends to confuse visitors, so here's a quick rundown. The workday usually starts around 9am—so far, so good. Around 1 or 2pm, most Spaniards will go home for lunch and a **siesta,** and stores and businesses usually close from around 2-5pm. Everything (except banks) reopens around 8pm. Dinner is usually from 9pm to midnight, with trendy *madrileños* dining on the later side.

Touchy Subjects

There are a few topics of discussion that can be rather delicate in Spain. The **Franco** era remains the elephant in the nation, and it's unwise to discuss it unless you know what you're talking about and know your audience agrees. **Bullfighting** is another divisive issue: some view it as a longstanding tradition that is a rich part of Spain's cultural heritage, while others see it as barbaric bloodsport. Finally, be careful when discussing certain regions' **separatist movements.** If you read the **history** section, you know that the unified nation of Spain is a relatively recent construct;

regional identities are still very strong. The Basque Country (País Vasco) has been trying for decades to gain independence from Spain, with the militant group ETA using terrorist tactics to try to reach this goal. The region of Catalonia (Catalunya), which includes Barcelona, also has a strong independence movement.

FOOD AND DRINK

In Spain, **el desayuno** (breakfast) is simple: a big **café con leche** (coffee with milk) and **pan tostada** (toast) with jam. **La comida** (lunch; literally "the meal") is the main meal of the day in Spain, though cosmopolitan *madrileños* tend to favor dinner, as the popularity and length of the beloved siesta has begun to decline. One of the most notable local dishes is the filling **cocido madrileño,** a massive beef, sausage, and vegetable stew available only at lunchtime. **Gambas al ajillo** (prawns in garlic) are also a popular midday repast in the capital, as are unshelled and heavily salted shrimp; some bars' floors are ankle-deep in shells and napkins by 2pm. The great thing about Madrid, though, is that in addition to the local dishes, you can get some of the best food from the farthest corners of Iberia and beyond. Beer and wine are commonly enjoyed with lunch. **La cena** (dinner) is sometimes a later, lighter version of *la comida* (lunch), sometimes a lengthy bar hop involving large amounts of tiny, inexpensive **tapas.**

SPORTS AND RECREATION

Let's Get Real

You can usually find a game of Spain's beloved pastime of soccer (also known as *fútbol*) in just about any open space in the country. Madrid's best games, though, are held in **Estadio Santiago Bernabéu,** where **Real Madrid** play their home matches. The club is often compared to the New York Yankees, since both teams spend exorbitant sums of money on their players and win championships with exceptional frequency (Real Madrid has 31 league titles; the Yankees have 27). **Atlético Madrid,** the city's other team, is often overshadowed by Real Madrid, even though their red-and-white-striped uniforms are much more eye-catching.

Grab Life By the Horns

Bullfighting tends to stir up more controversy than soccer. Some view it as a cruel and violent tradition that should be brought to an end, while others view it as a cruel and violent tradition that must endure. The region of Catalonia—one of Spain's largest and most populous—banned bullfighting in July 2010, and in January 2011 Spanish state TV banned broadcasts of live bull-fights because the network's policy forbids displaying violence against animals before 10pm. The attitude toward bullfighting is certainly shifting against the sport, but the ardent fans will be at **Las Ventas** every week until the bitter end.

ART AND ARCHITECTURE

The Big Three

The traditional view of premodern Spanish art focuses almost exclusively on El Greco, Velázquez, and Goya, and with good reason. Yes, **Zurbarán** did some striking still lifes, **Murillo** could paint a rosy-cheeked Virgin like nobody's business, and **Ribera's** use of light might have grabbed even Caravaggio's attention, but the works of the three masters are a level above. **El Greco** (born Domenikos Theotokopoulous; 1541-1614) was born in Crete, trained in Venice, opened up shop in Rome, and spent the rest of his life in Toledo. His vivid colors, heavy shadows, and expressively elongated figures are often seen as precursors to Cubism and Expressionism. El Greco never achieved the favor of the royals, but **Diego Velázquez** (1599-1660) was beloved at court in Madrid. Many of his paintings depict members of the court, from the king and queen to the dwarves and jesters. His most famous work, on display in the Prado, is *Las Meninas,* an enigmatic group portrait of the princess and her ladies-in-waiting, with the king and queen reflected in the mirror and the artist himself at the easel on the left. Velázquez is also celebrated for his marvelous ability to capture various textures and surfaces, such as the ceramics in *The Water Carrier of Seville.* **Francisco de Goya** (1746-1828) also spent much of his career painting royals and courtiers in Madrid, but exhibited an impressive range of subjects and styles. Many of his works are quite playful and humorous, while others, such as his Black Paintings, are downright nightmarish.

The New Guys

The 20th century saw a new crop of celebrated Spanish artists; . Few hailed from the capital, and nearly all spent a good part of their careers abroad, but many of their works now permanently reside in Madrid. The most famous is **Pablo Picasso** (1881-1973), illustrious pioneer of **Cubism** and **womanizing.** His manifesto *Guernica,* an enormous, emotional protest against the bombing of civilians during the Spanish Civil War, can now be seen in the Reina Sofía after a long stay at MoMA in New York City. Other modern Spanish artists include the Catalan **Joan Miró** (1893-1983), whose works are beautifully child-like; Madrid native and skillful cubist painter **Juan Gris** (1887-1927); and darkly zany Surrealist **Salvador Dalí** (1904-89), perhaps best known for his unique moustache and pet anteater.

HOLIDAYS AND FESTIVALS

HOLIDAY OR FESTIVAL	DESCRIPTION	DATE
Día de los Reyes Magos	Three Kings' Day/Epiphany. *Cabalgata* (parade) takes place the night before.	January 6
Día de la Candelaria	Celebrates the purification of the Virgin 40 days after Christ's birth. The holiday is known for mock bullfights, sangria, and candy.	February 2
Semana Santa	"Holy Week": the days leading up to Easter. Lots of hooded processions.	March 30 – April 8 (2012)
Labor Day	Workers of the world, unite!	May 1
Dos de Mayo	The city of Madrid commemorates the 1808 uprising against Napoleon's troops with concerts and various festivities.	May 2
Fiesta de San Isidro	The feast day of Madrid's patron saint is celebrated with pilgrimages to the meadow where he performed miracles.	May 15
Noche de San Juan	Revelers jump over bonfires in the Parque del Retiro and around the city.	June 23
La Paloma	Feast of the Assumption, and the feast of the Virgin of La Paloma in Madrid.	August 15
La Almudena	Celebrates an image of the Virgin that was hidden in a Madrid wall and survived the Moorish occupation.	November 9
Nochevieja	New Year's Eve. At midnight, one grape is eaten for each of the 12 strokes of the clock. There are huge televised celebrations at the Plaza del Sol and at other locations throughout Madrid.	December 31

Beyond Tourism

If you are reading this, then you are a member of an elite group—and we don't mean "the literate." You're a student preparing for a semester abroad. You're taking a gap year to save the trees, the whales, or the dates. You're an 80-year-old woman who has devoted her life to egg-laying platypuses and what the hell is up with that. In short, you're a traveler, not a tourist; like any good spy, you don't just observe your surroundings—you become an active part of them.

Your mission, should you choose to accept it, is to study, volunteer, or work abroad as laid out in the dossier—er, chapter—below. We leave the rest (when to go, whom to bring, and how many clubbin' tops to pack) in your hands. This message will self-destruct in five seconds. Good luck.

STUDYING

Whether your goal is to become fluent in Spanish, learn the unique fusion of Latin American and European culture, or master sexy flamenco dance moves, Madrid is the place for you. Here you can read about Goya, El Greco, and Velázquez in your textbook and then go check out their work in the city's art museums.

If a night at the museum doesn't sound like your ideal outing, how about watching the classic Spanish entertainment—bull-fighting—in Las Ventas? Or enjoying tapas while walking down the stone-paved streets of the city? Studying abroad in Madrid certainly presents exciting opportunities beyond the typical classroom setting—after all, you can't exactly bring a feisty bull to class…

Visa Information

As a member of the **Schengen Convention,** Spain doesn't require visas for legal residents of the European Union, Iceland, Norway, or Switzerland regardless of their purpose or length of stay. All **non-EU residents** entering Spain should contact a Spanish consulate to get a student visa, a process that takes a minimum of six weeks.

Since visas are not granted on the spot, you should apply for one at least four months before your planned departure. The cost of a student visa is $140, payable to the Consulate of Spain. Applications must be submitted in person at the diplomatic mission, the consular office, or at your local Spanish embassy. When you apply for a visa, make sure to bring your completed visa application form, a passport, and a proof of admission to your study abroad program in Spain. If you are going to be in the country for only a short visit, you can avoid the hassle, as US citizens need a visa only if they stay for a period of longer than 90 days.

Universities

Home to many prestigious universities, Madrid offers a wide array of studies for people interested in art, language, engineering, or business. Students wishing to study abroad can do so alongside more than 200,000 students in Madrid. Choose among many different areas of study, browse through a million volumes and 25,000 periodical publications at the universities' vast libraries, and interact with your Spanish-loving peers. Many classes are taught both in English and in Spanish, accommodating all skill levels.

International Programs

CEA Global Education

2005 W. 14th St., Ste. 113, Tempe, AZ 85281, USA

☎+1-800-266-4441; www.gowithcea.com

CEA offers small, interactive classes in a wide range of subjects, from the liberal arts and social sciences to international and cultural studies. Students have the option to study at the global campus in Madrid or at the Antonio de Nebrija University for a summer, semester, or year.

IES Abroad Madrid

33 N. LaSalle St., 15th fl., Chicago, IL 60602, USA

☎+1-800-995-2300; www.iesabroad.org

In addition to classes in art history, film studies, and business, IES Abroad Madrid will introduce a new engineering program in fall 2011. Learn to launch a rocket into space in an aerospace course or analyze the portrayal of women in Spanish advertising in cultural studies. Classes are taught at the Universidad Complutense de Madrid, the Universidad Francisco de Vitoria, or the Universidad Carlos III in English or Spanish.

Language Schools

As renowned novelist Gustave Flaubert once said, "Language is a cracked kettle on which we beat out tunes for bears to dance to." While we at Let's Go have absolutely no clue what he is talking about, we do know that the following are good resources for learning Spanish.

AIL Madrid Language School

C. de Nuñez de Balboa, 17, 2D

☎91 725 63 50; www.ailmadrid.com

The school, located in Madrid's wealthy *barrio* Salamanca in central Madrid, boasts diverse classes that cater to beginning, intermediate, and advanced speakers. With classes capped at eight students per class and averaging at five, this language school has one of the lowest student-teacher ratios in Madrid.

▶ Ⓢ 2-week courses €320-€640.

Babylon Idiomas

Pl. de Santa Ana, 1

☎91 532 44 80; www.babylon-idiomas.com

Babylon Idiomas is located in Madrid's cultural center, Pl. de Santa Ana, home to boutique shops, trendy bars, restaurants, and theaters. Classes meet 20-30 hours per week, so you should still have plenty of time for shopping.

▶ Ⓢ 2-week courses €280-€520.

Madrid Plus

C. del Arenal, 21-6

☎91 548 11 16; www.madridplus.es

This posh private language school, located in the heart of the city on la C. Arenal, provides courses in grammar, vocabulary, and conversation for beginners and advanced students. A typical class has 6-10 students, and private instruction and evening classes are available.

▶ Ⓢ 2-week courses €215-€295.

Art Classes

Think you have what it takes to be the next Picasso? Do you love reciting stage monologues? Ready to bring sexy back on the dance floor? This cultural and artistic hub of Spain has classes in diverse art forms.

Dance Classes Madrid

C. de Nuñez de Balboa, 17, 2D

☎91 725 41 93; www.dance-classes-madrid.com

Seduce anyone with the sensual, energetic Spanish dance moves you pick up at Dance Classes Madrid. The school is committed to teaching its students the spicy, saucy, and savory dancing styles of salsa, flamenco, and merengue. Group sessions and individual dance lessons are available.

▶ Ⓢ €15 per hr.

El Horno

C. de la Esgrima, 11

☎91 527 57 01; www.centroelhorno.com

This cultural center, whose name translates to "The Oven," has classes in dancing, music, acting, and theater. When selecting a dance class, don't limit yourself to the familiar ballet or tango. Try the flamenco, a genuine Spanish folk art that comes in three forms: *cante* (singing), *baile* (dancing), and *guitarra* (guitar playing).

VOLUNTEERING

If "saving the world" is one of the items on your bucket list, consider checking it off in Madrid. The benefits of volunteering are limitless. Not only will you gain valuable professional and personal experience abroad, but you will also learn about Spanish culture and leave with a sense of accomplishment.

Social Activism and Immigration Issues

Promote well-being of individuals and work toward social equality. Write a letter to the Spanish government, help out at a homeless shelter, or work for immigrant justice.

Associación Comision Catolica Espanola de Migración

☎91 532 74 78; www.accem.es

Work to provide care and shelter to refugees and immigrants in Spain and, in the process, promote social inclusion and equal rights. The group initiates projects that provide care, training, and social inclusion for refugees and immigrants with special attention to the more vulnerable unaccompanied minors, women, and ethnic minorities.

Caritas

C. de Embajadores, 162

☎91 444 10 00; www.caritas.org

Volunteer with this nonprofit organization whose mission is to eradicate poverty through rehabilitation, advocacy, and social support.

Community Outreach

Reach out to local communities and work alongside locals in Madrid by conducting public awareness activities through targeted community interaction.

Beyond Tourism

Fundación Intervida of Spain

C. de Arturo Baldasano, 26

☎92 300 11 01; www.intervida.org

Contribute to sustainable human development by volunteering at Fundacion Intervida, an organization that provides resources for disadvantaged populations and aims to improve their living conditions. Awareness-raising campaigns involve education and advocacy.

Justicia y Paz

C. de Rafael de Riego, 16

☎91 506 18 28; www.madrid.juspax-es.org

This worldwide nonprofit organization uses Catholic social teachings to promote human rights, justice, peace, solidarity, and the preservation of the environment.

Farming

If you are passionate about nature, agriculture, and animals, consider volunteering at farms near Madrid. Not only will you be working toward sustainability, but you'll also learn practical skills like milking a cow. Dairy never tasted so good.

Agrónomos sin Fronteras

www.agronomossinfronteras.org

This nonprofit organization is dedicated to providing a better quality of life for those dependent on farming, cattle raising, or fishing through logistic, technical, and financial help. The group encourages free, fair, and efficient trade.

▶ *i* Though volunteers are not paid, Agronomos sin Fronteras covers all necessary expenses, including insurance.

WWOOF

☎90 201 08 14; www.wwoof.org

WWOOF España facilitates the contact and experience between volunteers—affectionately called the WWOOFers—and rural inhabitants who practice or promote organic and sustainable farming. You will work at organic farms to learn ecological agriculture techniques.

Beyond Tourism

WORKING

Life in Madrid doesn't come cheap—that's where our section on long- and short-term work comes in. Teaching and au pair jobs are one way to go, and native English speakers are especially sought-after. Non-European Union citizens must have a **permiso de trabajo** (work permit) in order to work in Spain; be sure to consult your local Spanish embassy or consular service early in your job hunt.

More Visa Information

Unless you are a citizen of the European Union, you are required by law to obtain a **visa,** a **work permit,** and a **residence card** to work or live in Madrid for more than 90 days. The Spanish Ministry of Foreign Affairs handles all visa processing. You must have a valid passport, a birth certificate, and a clean criminal record to apply.

Long-Term Work

Teaching English

Spaniards tend to prefer British English to American when it comes to learning English. Americans, don't let this dissuade you. The demand for English teachers in general is still pretty high, and, if all else fails, you can usually fake it.

Club de Relaciones Culturales Internacionales

C. de Ferraz, 82

☎91 541 71 03; www.clubrci.es

A 15hr., Monday-through-Friday commitment to teaching English earns you full room and board. This leaves the rest of the week free to pick up cute *madrileños* at local bars.

▶ *i* Ages 18-40. Min. 8 weeks. Formal teaching qualifications recommended but not required.

Global Choices

420 Omega Works, 4 Roach Rd., London, UK

☎+44 208 533 2777; www.globalchoices.co.uk

Miss the feeling of riding in the back seat with your younger brother on the family trip to Toledo? Dad's conspicuous digital camera? Mom's transition lenses? Are we there yet? If that's the case, why not move in with a Spanish family in exchange for teaching them English?

▶ *i* Min. 3 months.

Pueblo Inglés

C. de Rafael Calvo, 18, 4C

☎91 391 34 00; www.puebloingles.com

Sick of hostel life? Each week up to 20 native English speakers are selected by Pueblo Inglés to stay in a four-star resort to mingle with Spanish professionals who want to improve their English. Accommodations, food, and wine are provided in exchange.

▶ *i* How could it be wrong when it feels so right?

Teach English as a Foreign Language (TEFL)

C. de General Yagüe, 70 1A

☎91 572 19 99; www.ttmadrid.com

With a TEFL certification, you can get paid to teach English and live in Madrid. Not a bad way to experience Spanish culture and make some money at the same time.

▶ *i* No prerequisites required to apply for TEFL certification other than native-level English and enthusiasm.

Au Pair Work

Some former babysitters report finding work as au pairs in Madrid. In exchange for caring for Spanish children, au pairs receive room, board, and a small stipend. Preference is usually given to women between 18 and 27.

Geovisions

1124 Olympic Dr., Corona, CA, USA

☎+1-951-549-1234; www.geovisions.org

GeoVisions connects each student with a family in Madrid. Previous childcare or babysitting experience and basic skills in Spanish are a plus.

▶ *i* Applicants must be women ages 18-30 with native English skills. High school diploma required. Full room and board provided by the host family. Stipend €70-90 per week.

Kingsbrook

☎93 209 37 63; www.kingsbrookbcn.com/spanish-school/au-pair-program

Another organization that matches international students with families in Spain.

▶ *i* Stipend provided for 5-6 hr. of work per day. 18+. Basic English required.

Internships

Most internships in Madrid are unpaid, but it might be worth it for some solid international work experience.

CDS International

440 Park Av., 2nd Fl., New York, NY 10016, USA

☎+1-212-497-3500; www.cdsintl.org

Customized internships cater to your previous experience, strengths, and interests. These are unpaid internships, but funding is available through the CDS International Scholarship Fund.

Eurointerns

C. Solano, 11

☎63 754 39 00; www.eurointerns.com

Interested in interning for Spanish firms or non-governmental organizations? Eurointerns was founded by Spanish university professors to provide students with resources to find paid or unpaid internship positions in Madrid. Enhance your resumé with an internship at American Express, Numont School (a bilingual school in Madrid), or Habitat (a multinational furniture store).

Short-Term Work

Sick of asking your parents for money? Consider getting a short-term job in Madrid. These are low-commitment jobs that still pay a decent amount and provide work experience.

Easy Way Association

C. Gran Vía

☎91 542 88 54; www.easywayspain.com

The organization matches students to short-term jobs in Madrid, from waiting tables and washing dishes to making and delivering pizza. Spanish fluency is not a must, but a basic conversational knowledge can help as most jobs in Spain (not to mention the rest of the world) require an interview.

▶ *i* Ages 18-32.

Forenex Summer Camp

Av. de la Victoria

☎91 308 41 99; www.forenex.com

If you miss the good old days of summer camp, apply to become a counselor at Forenex. This residential and day camp combines intensive English classes and sports activities for children aged 4 to 16.

▶ *i* Camp counselors responsible for carrying out English classes 4-5hr. per day and preparing a daily lesson plan.

Tell the World

If your friends are tired of hearing about that time you saved a baby orangutan in Indonesia, there's clearly only one thing to do: get new friends. Find them at our website, www.letsgo.com, where you can post your study-, volunteer-, or work-abroad stories for other, more appreciative community members to read.

Index

Accommodations Index

Restaurants Index

Nightlife Index

Shopping Index

MADRID ACKNOWLEDGMENTS

DOROTHY THANKS: MPMP for being my favorite and doing more than her share of work. All of the RWs for surviving, and being undaunted by the seemingly endless things asked of them. Pod Sinai for being the best "do your f-ing work-themed" pod of all time. All of Masthead for being sweethearts, especially Sarah. Marykate for being calm and wise. Iya for guerrilla compliments. Grooveshark for being free. Tanjore Tuesdays and Bagel Fridays for providing me with essential nutrients. Finally, the best for last: thanks to the Oxford Commas, for being the harvestest; to Maine, for quickly becoming my favorite state; and to my family, for everything.

MARY THANKS: Thank you Dorothy, Graham, Mark, Michal, Patrick, Sarah, and everyone at HQ for all of your hard work.

ABOUT LET'S GO

The Student Travel Guide

Let's Go publishes the world's favorite student travel guides, written entirely by Harvard students. Armed with pens, notebooks, and a few changes of clothes stuffed into their backpacks, our student researchers go across continents, through time zones, and above expectations to seek out invaluable travel experiences for our readers. Because we are a completely student-run company, we have a unique perspective on how students travel, where they want to go, and what they're looking to do when they get there. If your dream is to grab a machete and forge through the jungles of Costa Rica, we can take you there. If you'd rather bask in the Riviera sun at a beachside cafe, we'll set you a table. In short, we write for readers who know that there's more to travel than tour buses. To keep up, visit our website, www.letsgo.com, where you can sign up to blog, post photos from your trips, and connect with the Let's Go community.

Traveling Beyond Tourism

We're on a mission to provide our readers with sharp, fresh coverage packed with socially responsible opportunities to go beyond tourism. Each guide's Beyond Tourism chapter shares ideas about responsible travel, study abroad, and how to give back to the places you visit while on the road. To help you gain a deeper connection with the places you travel, our fearless researchers scour the globe to give you the heads-up on both world-renowned and off-the-beaten-track opportunities. We've also opened our pages to respected writers and scholars to hear their takes on the countries and regions we cover, and asked travelers who have worked, studied, or volunteered abroad to contribute first-person accounts of their experiences.

Fifty-Two Years of Wisdom

Let's Go has been on the road for 52 years and counting. We've grown a lot since publishing our first 20-page pamphlet to Europe in 1960, but five decades and 60 titles later, our witty, candid guides are still researched and written entirely by students on shoestring budgets who know that train strikes, stolen luggage, food poisoning, and marriage proposals are all part of a day's work. Meanwhile, we're still bringing readers fresh new features, such as a student-life section with advice on how and where to meet students from around the world; a revamped, user-friendly layout for our listings; and greater emphasis on the experiences that make travel abroad a rite of passage for readers of all ages. And, of course, this year's 16 titles—including five brand-new guides—are still brimming with editorial honesty, a commitment to students, and our irreverent style.

The Let's Go Community

More than just a travel guide company, Let's Go is a community that reaches from our headquarters in Cambridge, MA, all across the globe. Our small staff of dedicated student editors, writers, and tech nerds comes together because of our shared passion for travel and our desire to help other travelers get the most out of their experience. We love it when our readers become part of the Let's Go community as well—when you travel, drop us a postcard (67 Mt. Auburn St., Cambridge, MA 02138, USA), send us an email (feedback@letsgo.com), or sign up on our website (www. letsgo.com) to tell us about your adventures and discoveries.

For more information, updated travel coverage, and news from our researcher team, visit us online at www.letsgo.com.

HELPING LET'S GO. If you want to share your discoveries, suggestions, or corrections, please drop us a line. We appreciate every piece of correspondence, whether a postcard, a 10-page email, or a coconut. Visit Let's Go at www.letsgo.com or send an email to:

feedback@letsgo.com, subject: "Let's Go Budget Madrid"

Address mail to:

Let's Go Budget Madrid, 67 Mount Auburn St., Cambridge, MA 02138, USA

In addition to the invaluable travel advice our readers share with us, many are kind enough to offer their services as researchers or editors. Unfortunately, our charter enables us to employ only currently enrolled Harvard students.
Maps © Let's Go and Avalon Travel
Interior design by Darren Alessi
Production by Amber Pirker
Photos © Let's Go, Grace Sun and Graham Lazar, photographers

Distributed by Publishers Group West.
Printed in Canada by Friesens Corp.

ISBN-13: 978-1-61237-009-5
ISBN-10: 1-61237-009-8
First edition
10 9 8 7 6 5 4 3 2 1

Let's Go Budget Madrid is written by Let's Go Publications, 67 Mt. Auburn St., Cambridge, MA 02138, USA.

Let's Go® and the LG logo are trademarks of Let's Go, Inc.

LEGAL DISCLAIMER. For 50 years, Let's Go has published the world's favorite budget travel guides, written entirely by students and updated periodically based on the personal anecdotes and travel experiences of our student writers. Although every effort was made to ensure that the information was correct at the time of going to press, the author and publisher do not assume and hereby disclaim any liability to any party for any loss or damage caused by errors, omissions, or any potential travel disruption due to labor or financial difficulty, whether such errors or omissions result from negligence, accident, or any other cause.

ADVERTISING DISCLAIMER. All advertisements appearing in Let's Go publications are sold by an independent agency not affiliated with the editorial production of the guides. Advertisers are never given preferential treatment, and the guides are researched, written, and published independent of advertising. Advertisements do not imply endorsement of products or services by Let's Go, and Let's Go does not vouch for the accuracy of information provided in advertisements.

If you are interested in purchasing advertising space in a Let's Go publication, contact Edman & Company at 1-203-656-1000.

QUICK REFERENCE

YOUR GUIDE TO LET'S GO ICONS

🖎	Let's Go recommends	☎	Phone numbers	🛱	Directions
i	Other hard info	⑤	Prices	◎	Hours

IMPORTANT PHONE NUMBERS

EMERGENCY: ☎112			
Amsterdam	☎911	London	☎999
Barcelona	☎092	Madrid	☎092
Berlin	☎110	Paris	☎17
Florence	☎113	Prague	☎158
Istanbul	☎155	Rome	☎113

USEFUL PHRASES

ENGLISH	FRENCH	GERMAN	ITALIAN	SPANISH
Hello/Hi	Bonjour/Salut	Hallo/Tag	Ciao	Hola
Goodbye/Bye	Au revoir	Auf Wiedersehen/ Tschüss	Arrivederci/Ciao	Adios/Chao
Yes	Oui	Ja	Sì	Sí
No	Non	Nein	No	No
Excuse me!	Pardon!	Entschuldigen Sie!	Scusa!	Perdón!
Thank you	Merci	Danke	Grazie	Gracias
Go away!	Va t'en!	Geh weg!	Vattene via!	Vete!
Help!	Au secours!	Hilfe!	Aiuto!	Ayuda!
Call the police!	Appelez la police!	Ruf die Polizei!	Chiamare la polizia!	Llame a la policía!
Get a doctor!	Cherchez un médecin!	Hol einen Arzt!	Avere un medico!	Llame a un médico!
I don't understand	Je ne comprends pas	Ich verstehe nicht	Non capisco	No comprendo
Do you speak English?	Parlez-vous anglais?	Sprechen Sie Englisch?	Parli inglese?	¿Habla inglés?
Where is...?	Où est...?	Wo ist...?	Dove...?	¿Dónde está...?

TEMPERATURE CONVERSIONS

°CELSIUS	-5	0	5	10	15	20	25	30	35	40
°FAHRENHEIT	23	32	41	50	59	68	77	86	95	104

MEASUREMENT CONVERSIONS

1 inch (in.) = 25.4mm	1 millimeter (mm) = 0.039 in.
1 foot (ft.) = 0.305m	1 meter (m) = 3.28 ft.
1 mile (mi.) = 1.609km	1 kilometer (km) = 0.621 mi.
1 pound (lb.) = 0.454kg	1 kilogram (kg) = 2.205 lb.
1 gallon (gal.) = 3.785L	1 liter (L) = 0.264 gal.